"With raw honesty, deep insight, and a self-deprecating sense of humor, Jon Ward offers an insider's view into the White evangelical world in which he was raised. Rubbing elbows with prominent figures and seemingly destined to take up the mantle of leadership, he instead chose to walk away from it all. Through his eyes we see the inner logic of that world, what draws people in and what drives people away. *Testimony* will be illuminating for those who have walked this path and for those struggling to understand the world of conservative evangelicalism from the outside."

—**Kristin Kobes Du Mez**, *New York Times* bestselling author of *Jesus and John Wayne*

"In *Testimony*, Jon Ward dissects the cultural world of evangelical Christianity from an insider's perspective while employing his skills as a journalist to question its ethos and impact. He narrates an experience that will feel deeply familiar to many evangelicals and then goes on to illuminate the contours and context of the movement as many within it embraced Trumpism. *Testimony* demonstrates the power of truth—no matter who it comes from or where it leads. This book will make you ponder, discuss, and testify about your own journey and beliefs."

—**Jemar Tisby**, *New York Times* bestselling author of *The Color of Compromise* and *How to Fight Racism*; professor, Simmons College of Kentucky

"An illuminating work that shines light into the fissures of spiritual abuses in the church and that documents Jon Ward's journey as a Christian to move forward and find a better way. This honest exposé allows healing in us, and his journalistic insights bring a generative path toward the new."

—**Makoto Fujimura**, artist and author of *Art and Faith: A Theology of Making*

"Jon's meticulous reporting has always brought nuance and life to his writing about politics; his thoughtfulness about faith is the secret weapon he's now sharing with the world. He appreciates the complexity of belief and the deep human desire to connect to something larger than ourselves. Even as he recounts his disillusionment with conservative Christianity, Jon remains a witness: someone who seeks and documents the truth, even when that means turning his sights on himself. This book is honest, vulnerable, scrupulous, and surprising; a must-read for anyone seeking to navigate the fault lines of our polarized moment."

—**Ana Marie Cox**, *New York Magazine* columnist

"Jon Ward's *Testimony* is the book I have been waiting for. I suspect there are millions more like me who will resonate with Jon's powerful witness. And while the book holds important and meaningful content, it also functions in an atypical way; it is an antidote to loneliness and heartbreak. To read it is to participate in a circle of trust where you are not alone, you're not going crazy, and all is *not* well. This is a form of setting things right—a move toward healing. Any words on a page that can achieve this good goal are worthy of our attention and gratitude. I'm listening and grateful."

—**Charlie Peacock**, Grammy Award–winning music producer; founder and director emeritus of Commercial Music Program, Lipscomb University School of MusicTestimony

TESTIMONY

Also by the Author

*Camelot's End: Kennedy vs. Carter and
the Fight That Broke the Democratic Party*

TESTIMONY

INSIDE THE
EVANGELICAL
MOVEMENT
THAT FAILED
A GENERATION

JON WARD

BrazosPress

a division of Baker Publishing Group
Grand Rapids, Michigan

Published by Brazos Press
a division of Baker Publishing Group
Grand Rapids, Michigan
www.brazospress.com

Printed in the United States of America

Library of Congress Cataloging-in-Publication Data
Names: Ward, Jon (writer of politics), author.
Title: Testimony : inside the evangelical movement that failed a generation / Jon Ward.
Description: Grand Rapids, Michigan : Brazos Press, a division of Baker Publishing Group, 2023. | Includes bibliographical references.
Identifiers: LCCN 2022034464 | ISBN 9781587435775 (cloth) | ISBN 9781493440474 (ebook) | ISBN 9781493440481 (pdf)
Subjects: LCSH: Ward, Jon (writer of politics) | Evangelicalism—Social aspects—United States.
Classification: LCC BR1642.U5 W37 2023 | DDC 277.308/3—dc23/eng/20220916
LC record available at https://lccn.loc.gov/2022034464

Unless otherwise indicated, Scripture quotations are from THE HOLY BIBLE, NEW INTERNATIONAL VERSION®, NIV® Copyright © 1973, 1978, 1984, 2011 by Biblica, Inc.® Used by permission. All rights reserved worldwide.

Scripture quotations labeled BSB are from the Berean Bible (www.Berean.Bible), Berean Study Bible (BSB) © 2016–2020 by Bible Hub and Berean.Bible. Used by permission. All rights reserved.

Scripture quotations labeled ESV are from The Holy Bible, English Standard Version® (ESV®), copyright © 2001 by Crossway, a publishing ministry of Good News Publishers. Used by permission. All rights reserved. ESV Text Edition: 2016

Scripture quotations labeled KJV are from the King James Version of the Bible.

Scripture quotations labeled NKJV are from the New King James Version®. Copyright © 1982 by Thomas Nelson. Used by permission. All rights reserved.

Published in association with Aevitas Creative Management.

Baker Publishing Group publications use paper produced from sustainable forestry practices and post-consumer waste whenever possible.

23 24 25 26 27 28 29   7 6 5 4 3 2 1

To Alison,
and to Jethro, Gwen,
Etta, Juniper, and Susie,
who love me into every day.
And to my parents, Chip and Diane,
who loved me into this world.

You never ask questions when God's on your side.
—Bob Dylan, "With God on Our Side"

I believe in you even though I be outnumbered.
—Bob Dylan, "I Believe in You"

Contents

Part 3 Reformation: 2013–2022

Preface

I stepped off the sidewalk and into the dark-marbled lobby of 30 Rockefeller Center on a Thursday morning in October 2016. The presidential election was one month away.

After visiting the security office for a badge, I walked to the large bank of elevators and rode up to the MSNBC studios. I sat for a bit in the green room, which was nothing more than a windowless room, and scrolled absentmindedly on my phone. Then a network producer escorted me to the makeup room, where a makeup artist applied powder to my face to reduce the glare of the TV lights. I asked her to go light.

Moments later, I walked onto the glistening, brightly lit set of *Morning Joe* and sat down next to Willie Geist, the affable sidekick to hosts Joe Scarborough and Mika Brzezinski. Scarborough and Brzezinski were across from me. Congressman Sean Duffy, a Republican from Wisconsin who had endorsed reality-TV celebrity Donald Trump for president, sat to my left. I exchanged small talk with Geist while Scarborough and Duffy—the former and current congressmen—chatted.

After a commercial, they played a brief clip of me talking about evangelical Christians and the upcoming election. It was a promotional tease for a short documentary I had produced for

Yahoo! News.[1] I had traveled across the country to speak with evangelicals about their choices in the 2016 election. Trump, I said, was forcing some Christians "to confront basic questions about their identity and beliefs."

Once the clip was over, I made clear to Scarborough and Brzezinski that this group of believers was not the majority. Most White evangelicals had gone all in for Trump. But a few, I said, did "not feel as if America was the kingdom of God."

I elaborated the point by quoting a rap lyric: "As Chance the Rapper said, 'Don't believe in kings, believe in the Kingdom.'" It was a cheesy line that landed flat. Maybe it was the delivery. But I got the feeling that these well-educated, sophisticated TV personalities had no clue what I was talking about, or that maybe they were embarrassed by the mention of the kingdom of God. It seemed like I was speaking a foreign language.

I had been raised as deeply inside American evangelicalism as you could get and had embraced the Christian faith all the way to the core of my being. I had been loved by sainted parents who devoted their lives to God and showed me how to walk the straight and narrow. The kingdom of God wasn't just words to me. But what I was seeing from the American church in 2016 was at odds with what I had been taught. And when I tried to explain why to people outside the world of regular churchgoers, I got blank stares.

This is a story of a life between worlds.

1. Jon Ward, "Evangelical Exiles: How Trump Is Driving Some Believers Away from the GOP," Yahoo! News, October 6, 2016, https://news.yahoo.com/evangelical-exiles-how-trump-is-driving-some-believers-out-of-the-gop-090055268.html.

Introduction

I t's predawn. Loud music and shouting are coming from the basement. It's 1997, my second year of college.

But it's not a party. I'm in my parents' house in the DC suburbs. I'm alone in my bedroom. I'm singing and dancing and shouting while listening to religious revival music: a live recording of the Stoneleigh International Bible Week conference that year in Britain.

My chest grows warm with emotion. My eyes are closed in prayer. The feelings of euphoria are elusive, but I hunt them like a hound. They're like a holy drug. But I remind myself that even if I don't feel like worshiping God, I should anyway. That's why I am up at this ungodly hour, making such a ruckus that a friend of my brother's who is spending the night is awakened by the noise. He opens his eyes and wonders what the hell is going on.

> This is the time, this is the place
> We're living in a season of amazing grace.[1]

1. Stoneleigh Worship Band, "I Hear the Sound (Distant Thunder)," YouTube video, posted by Brien Doran, October 17, 2016, https://www.youtube.com/watch?v=Rb26qlfYSvk.

That's how I feel: that something special is happening around me and has happened to me. The song proclaims that I and other Christians are at the precipice of some great moment in which we will change the world. I sing my readiness to do whatever God commands.

I never could have imagined those words in the way I read them now, after what I've seen during the past two decades. Certainty disguised as faith, it turns out, can take people to some bizarre places.

What is it, that spark that makes our lives worth living?

Amid the exhaustion and boredom, the frustration and sadness, the grief and heartbreak, there is something that keeps us going. It's a small and quiet sound. I often hear it, or feel it, in the early morning hours. But then it appears in the midst of a lazy summer afternoon, or in an autumn sunset, or in the car on a bleak midwinter Monday morning when I've just dropped the kids off at school and life feels pointless.

It's a sensation in the chest sometimes, a faint burning or warm feeling. Other times it's just a serenity. And sometimes it's a small whisper. It's too quiet for me to make out any words, but that doesn't matter. I listen attentively.

This is an elusive thing. It runs away the moment I try to put it into words. Sometimes I sit down and try anyway. Unless I attempt this right away, the spark is too ineffable to capture later.

The feeling I get from this small flame is that there is a point and a purpose to all this, to my life, to what is happening around me in this big, tragic, beautiful world.

It is the voice of God. I was trained to hear it when I was a child, and this was a great gift.

All my life I have been a *mearcstapa*, or a border-stalker. *Mearcstapa* is an Old English word used in *Beowulf*. Painter and author Makoto Fujimura used this term, and his modern translation of border-stalker, to describe those who "are uncomfortable in homogenous groups" and yet are still present in them, and thus they live "on the edge of their groups, going in and out of them."[2] That's how I existed during my upbringing in a conservative church. I never felt entirely comfortable there. I walked into church one day and a young woman about my age said, "Where's your smile, Jon?" I wanted to scream. I hated the constant pressure to look happy.

My childhood was dominated by talk of demons and angels, speaking in tongues, the return of Jesus, and the end of the world. I was the son of a pastor and the oldest of seven kids. My father led protests outside abortion clinics. I was ambivalent about church until I turned twenty, when I became a radical and was put on the fast track to becoming a pastor. But I could not bear the uniformity of thought in that world. I needed to escape the psychological and emotional distress of trying to meet the exacting standards of our church. This is not a tale of growing up amid corrupt charlatans who used the name of God to amass riches. The leaders in my world were true believers whose intensity of belief blinded them to their errors. It's the same road I am still prone to go down even now in the way I critique the evangelicalism I have left behind.

That world held me tight for many years, and my separation has been a long process. My voyage out into the broader world—this place I had been told was evil and dangerous—came largely via the tradecraft of journalism. I remain a border-stalker who is not fully at home inside the church, but neither am I all that comfortable inside the tribe of journalism and American political elites. I am not fully one of them either. This book will make that clear.

Fujimura's writings have shaped my thinking about how to be a Christian and live in the world. His book *Culture Care* lays out a vision opposed to "culture war," and in this vision, border-stalkers have an important role: "They can become good Samaritans to a divided culture," he writes. They do this through "overcoming caricatures and injecting diversity, nuance, and even paradox into the nature of the conversation, and then moving on to teach society

2. Makoto Fujimura, *Culture Care: Reconnecting with Beauty for Our Common Life* (Downers Grove, IL: InterVarsity, 2017), 58.

a language of empathy and reconciliation."[3] As long as I can remember, I've wanted to do that: reduce confusion, build bridges, tear down lies, slow down the rush to easy answers.

I thought, naively, that this was a straightforward task. It never is. Dishonesty pays—and pays well. These have been especially hard years for the pursuit of truth. The modern world is a violent environment for a border-stalker. It is now the norm to be intolerant of opposing views, to see others as *the other*: to fear them, to hate them. Black-and-white thinking is everywhere. Nuance is vanishing. Complexity is demonized.

The tumult of the last few years has forced me to reassess what I really believe (a process I've gone through a few times in my life now). I've had to pull myself away from the easy anger of opposition and redouble the search to know what I stand *for*, not just what I'm *against*. And, of course, beyond the *what* is the *why*, a set of questions that require even more work to answer. My soul-searching has taken me to the Mississippi Delta and to the Rust Belt, and down the ancient paths of the Christian church. My anger has burned too hot at times and has been cooled by that most precious regulator of dehumanizing passions: face-to-face interactions with others whom I don't understand.

I have thought long about what a more faithful Christian witness would look like. The answers seem more tenuous than ever. So do my blessings, which are many. Maybe as a result, I feel more grateful than I ever have in my life.

This book is more than an essay or an argument. It is my testimony.

The word *testimony* has special meaning for Christians. It is when an individual stands before a congregation and shares what God has done in their life. They talk of working through challenges and struggles, and they share how God reached down and plucked them out of difficulty or helped them through adversity. This was a regular part of church during my childhood. A testimony was always met with hearty amens and ended with applause.

3. Fujimura, *Culture Care*, 61.

But sometimes as I sat listening, I got the feeling that these stories sounded so wonderful that maybe they were too good to be entirely accurate.

This is my account of trying to walk the path Jesus spoke of, despite all the ways I've seen the pursuit of truth sidelined, dismissed, and blocked, often in the name of faith. It has felt bleak at times. This has pushed me deeper into the most essential teachings of my childhood faith. I do still believe that Christianity has much to contribute during this time. But "we need to lay down our weapons based on fear," Fujimura writes. "Weapons of culture war will only lead to a Darwinian victory, if that. Instead, let us become nurturers of lasting beauty, tending to our culture with care, and with tears. Culture is not a territory to be won; it is instead a resource we are called to steward."[4]

I am not expecting a chorus of amens, however. Telling the truth often elicits hostility and anger. As Fujimura says, "Beauty is also sacrifice."[5] Truth is beautiful, but it also exacts a cost—on those who tell it and on those who choose to listen.

From a young age, I latched on to the idea that truth is central to Christian faith. I've always loved the way that Jesus stood for truth. "I am the way and the truth and the life," Christ said (John 14:6). At another point, he promised that his Spirit would "guide you into all the truth" (16:13). When he was about to be executed, Jesus told a Roman official, "The reason I was born and came into the world is to testify to the truth" (18:37). "What is truth?" replied Pontius Pilate, the Roman governor (18:38). It's a haunting question. And yet in some ways, the insularity of my upbringing shielded me from the worldly knowledge about what happens to those who seek truth in the real world. This knowledge can lead to cynicism. History shows that those who seek truth are often

---

4. Makoto Fujimura, "Tears for Fragile Emanations: A Lenten Reflection," March 2, 2014, https://makotofujimura.com/writings/tears-for-fragile-emanations -lenten-reflection-2014/.

5. Makoto Fujimura, "Messiah College Commencement Address, 2013," May 20, 2013, https://makotofujimura.com/writings/messiah-college-commencement -address-2013/.

destroyed by those who will not or cannot face it. Truth is often horrifying in what it reveals about humanity.

But it can also be fuel for adventure. We know truth more fully when we realize it is not easily found. It is elusive and multifaceted. The process by which we find it is maybe the most important thing. It takes work to locate, and often as soon as we think we have grasped it, it slips away. Truth is not a script. It is not a cheat sheet for life. Truth does not come from picking a set of answers and then arranging all the questions so that they line up correctly. Truth starts with the questions. It requires an openness—to other points of view and experiences, to being wrong, to changing one's mind. A commitment to truth involves a passionate embrace of critical thinking.

First and foremost, truth-seekers don't search for battles outside themselves to win. Instead, they examine their own point of view, searching for holes, weaknesses, errors. Truth-seekers don't pretend to understand other points of view. They inhabit them, walk around in them, try to gain perspective. They hold their conclusions with an open hand. And yet, at the end of the day, a truth-seeker doesn't shy away from speaking up.

We can step into the dark night of not knowing, clinging to whatever faith we might be blessed to have, and ask to see and understand. We can walk in gratefulness and the humility of sincere need. Some call this prayer.

Journalism has made me more of a Christian, a better Christian. It has exposed me to the richness and complexity of life and has led me into the kind of adventurous pursuit of truth that has durability, integrity, and honesty. The job of a journalist is to push back against reductionism and dumbing down. It is to stand against self-assured know-it-alls and angry know-nothings and promote the humility of admitting what we cannot know for sure. It is to open one's self toward empathy for the circumstances of others, to develop an appreciation for history, and to acquire deep knowledge in some areas. It is to live a life of curiosity and wonder.

Journalism has taught me to stand in the wash zone of culture and politics. In the ocean, the wash zone is that small area where the waves crash in toward the shore while at the same time water is flowing in the opposite direction, down from the sand and back out to sea. It is hard to stand up amid the tumult: thunderous waves pound your upper body one way, while the undertow tries to pull your legs in the other direction. In real life, this push and pull comes when people in different groups tell a journalist to pick a side. "You are either with us or against us," they say. A journalist's task is to stand firm in that middle ground as the tides of one tribe try to pull them out to sea while the waves of another crash over their head.

Truth has been my North Star over the last two decades as a journalist. I have believed we can know it and that we should strive to do so. Twenty years ago, I thought that the biggest threats to truth were postmodern relativism and godless liberals. Today, to my shock, my own tribe of Christians has taken a battering ram to truth. I think this book will shed some light on why that is.

This world may be hostile to unpleasant truths and complicating narratives. Even so, I offer my story to you.

PART 1

Growing Up Evangelical 1977–2000

1

Revival Child

The women in flowing red dresses danced and twirled on stage as the rock band played on. I was four years old, transfixed by the color and movement. I danced to the beat of the drums and the bass guitar. Around me, adults sang their hearts out—eyes closed, hands raised to the sky, heads tilted back. They were seeking absolution, escape, salvation. I was oblivious. It was 1981.

The band included an electric keyboard, electric guitars, and sometimes a horn section. Music was vital to our church. We did a lot of singing. Services were at least two hours long, and the first hour was always thirty to forty-five minutes of what we called "worship." After that, there were twenty minutes of announcements and miscellanea as a procession of young men strode to the mic to talk about this or that. The second hour was for preaching. The sermon was usually close to an hour. Brevity was not highly valued. We called each sermon a "message." The implication of that word? There was a *messenger*, and preachers were there to deliver a memo direct from the heavens. The adults sat at rapt attention, taking copious notes.

11

If we did more singing after the sermon, things stretched well past two hours. That was when things got most interesting. This was when you could get slain in the Spirit, drunk on the Holy Ghost. The leaders would "release" everyone who wanted to leave to go get lunch, but the band would keep playing. The hardcore folks stuck around to sing, pray, and have others lay hands on them. We believed God's power could be transferred from one person to another this way. Most Sunday mornings I watched all this happen. Whenever I looked to the back of the room, inside the public high school auditorium that we rented, I saw a giant pharaoh head looking down on us. It was a prop from the school's production of *Joseph and the Amazing Technicolor Dreamcoat*.

I spent most of my childhood merely passing time in church, waiting for the service to end so I could go play outside or looking forward to my baseball game later that day. But sometimes the hair stood up on the back of my neck. I would jump up and down, close my eyes, raise my hands, and shed tears.

My parents were leaders in this church when I was a young kid. They entered the world of evangelical Christianity in the early 1970s, and I came along in 1977. I'm the child of a religious revival, a bona fide spiritual phenomenon that swept the nation that decade. My earliest years were saturated by this fixation with euphoric experience that had captured my parents' generation.

When I was twelve, I fell down to the floor and lay prostrate on the ground. I was at a youth retreat, with high schoolers playing guitar and keyboard to set the mood. Parents clustered together with their kids: standing, hugging, praying, singing, trying to save them from hell.

I was raised in the Maryland suburbs outside Washington, DC. We lived among the sprawling federal government workforce, full of middle-class families who commuted into the city each day. But we cocooned ourselves inside our church culture so tightly that we could have been anywhere: the plains of the Midwest or rural Appalachia. My dad was a pastor of this church, which he and his friends started from scratch.

I was the oldest of five kids for most of my childhood, until my parents had two more kids when I was in high school, making me the oldest of seven. My parents named me Jonathan David, after two Old Testament characters. Jonathan means "gift of God," a fact my father often reminded me of. I was a typical oldest child: self-assured to the point of arrogance, with strong perfectionist tendencies. I clashed often with my next youngest brother, Frank, usually when he and our younger brother Lucas were fighting. The three of us shared a room for many years, playing tackle football on our knees and trading baseball cards.

We were taught that anyone not in the church was in "the world." The world was, pretty obviously to us, a bad place. So it was better if we spent the majority of our time with people from church, doing church things, and not thinking too much about non-church things.

I was a pastor's kid until I was ten, but instead of playing the role, I often bristled against it. One time during a church service my dad told me to participate more enthusiastically. I spoke up. "Dad, you're just telling me to do that so you'll look good to other people." To my dad's credit, he admitted I was right and left me alone.

The church meeting location moved around a lot. "Constant change is here to stay," the leaders said with pep every time something had to be switched up. Many years we held our services in public high schools. I walked down the hallway of one of those high schools amid concrete brick walls painted a bright yellow. The hallways were lined with lockers and florescent lighting overhead. Adults were praying out loud, saying something about demons in the building, even in the walls. They believed they were evicting demons out of that physical space by the power of prayer.

My child's brain concluded that we were all living on a knife's edge, with invisible forces at work that could reach out and touch me. I did not suffer night terrors or obsess about these things, but they nonetheless entered my psyche. And, of course, public school was never a place I would want to go for my education, with its filthy demon-infested walls.

I read the Bible constantly. I started as a child with a picture Bible, a sort of comic book version with illustrations and narration. I moved on to the real thing. Most every morning Dad would read us a selection from the Bible at breakfast. Usually it was from Psalms or Proverbs. One of his favorite passages was from the first chapter of the book of James in the New Testament. "Everyone should be quick to listen, slow to speak and slow to become angry," says James, one of Christ's disciples (v. 19). My dad modeled this. I can count on one hand the number of times growing up I saw him lose his temper, and he showed us how to think for ourselves and respect others. Another one of Dad's favorites was this mantra: "Early to bed, early to rise, makes a man healthy, wealthy, and wise." We all rolled our eyes at that one. I don't anymore.

My brothers and I often spent our family devotional times squirming and cracking jokes. A few times, we brought a Nerf ball to Dad's Bible study meetings. One of us would sit on it until we broke wind, then pass it to another for a smell test, and then we'd all fall to pieces. Sometimes even Mom, who had no teaching role and had to sit there with the rest of us, would giggle too. Dad put up with this admirably, forging ahead with his lesson.

We read the book of Proverbs over and over growing up. Dad loved Proverbs. "Get wisdom," the author wrote. "Though it cost all you have, get understanding" (4:7). We spent a lot of time in passages that talked about wisdom and understanding and discernment. This was, in retrospect, the biggest emphasis of my religious instruction growing up, at home anyway. And it had a personal flavor, because the second chapter of Proverbs, for example, begins with the author addressing the reader as "my son."

My father would read these words with feeling, clearly wanting to impart the lessons to us for our well-being. He wanted to train us and protect us. "My son, if you accept my words and store up my commands within you, turning your ear to wisdom and applying your heart to understanding—indeed, if you call out for insight and cry aloud for understanding, and if you look for it as for silver and search for it as for hidden treasure, then you will understand the fear of the LORD and find the knowledge of God" (Prov. 2:1–5).

There is a lot of talk in Proverbs about how wisdom will protect us from "the adulterous woman," and in an evangelical culture that obsessed over sex, this was a particular focus. But in Proverbs 2, just before the warning about the "wayward woman . . . who has left the partner of her youth," whose "house leads down to death" (vv. 16–18), there is another cautionary passage about a different sort of figure: "Wisdom will save you from the ways of wicked men, from men whose words are perverse, who have left the straight paths to walk in dark ways, who delight in doing wrong and rejoice in the perverseness of evil, whose paths are crooked and who are devious in their ways" (vv. 12–15).

As a child, I was limited in my imagination of how this verse applied to real life. I thought of teenagers who smoked and drank and cursed. Little did I know, this warning would have increasing relevance as I grew older.

And I could not have comprehended that the Christian culture I was being raised in—separate from my instruction at home—was actually making me and others around me *more* vulnerable to manipulation by men "whose paths are crooked and who are devious in their ways."

My dad was the great-grandson of Irish-Catholic immigrants from County Galway. His father's father was a police detective in Elizabeth, New Jersey, with five sons and one daughter. My dad's dad, Bob Ward, was a two-time consensus All-American football player at the University of Maryland in the early 1950s. The Terps were a national powerhouse during this time. In 1951, my grandfather's senior year, Maryland won ten games with no losses. They beat the first-ranked Tennessee Volunteers in their final game, the Sugar Bowl, and were designated national champions by several analysts.[1]

1. "Football Bowl Subdivision Records," http://fs.ncaa.org/Docs/stats/football _records/2018/FBS.pdf, 113.

We heard one particular quote about my grandfather a lot growing up. He was the greatest player "pound for pound" that his coach said he had ever seen, my dad would tell us. (That quote was accurate, although his coach had said "ounce for ounce"[2] and a teammate had said the same thing but used "pound for pound."[3]) The main point is that Hardguy, as he wanted us to call him, was not physically imposing at all: about 5′9″ and 185 pounds. And yet he was one of the best football players in the country. Even more extraordinary, he played on the line, where modern players average around 300 pounds. Linemen were smaller in the fifties than they are now, but Hardguy was still quite undersized at the time. He made up for it with an otherworldly tenacity. Everyone who knew our grandfather talked about what an exceptional player he was. He was inducted into the College Football Hall of Fame when I was three, and every time we went to a Maryland football game we saw our last name on the stadium, next to his number 28.

My father's brothers were exceptional athletes as well. One wrestled at Iowa State and became an NCAA national champion. The other brother was a star football and baseball player at West Point. My dad played golf and was very good at it. But he was more interested in intellectual pursuits than his siblings were. He was a gentle soul, soft-spoken, who to this day has rarely uttered a word in anger and has gone through life trying to win people over through kindness and reason rather than charisma or manipulation. I still don't know how much this part of my father was shaped by reacting against his own dad's volatile temper. There was very little emotional support in his household growing up, where it would have been unnatural to verbally express feelings. Words like "I love you" went unspoken, and this left my father emotionally stunted in some respects.

2. "Bob Ward," National Football Foundation, https://footballfoundation.org/hof_search.aspx?hof=1746.

3. "Robert Ward Sr., 77, Football Player, Coach," *Washington Times*, May 2, 2005, https://www.washingtontimes.com/news/2005/may/02/20050502-102907-5201r/.

Both of my father's parents rejected the label of grandparent. My dad's mother insisted we call her Miss Ellen. We didn't see her too often, though she had me over once for a sleepover when I was about ten or twelve after she and my grandfather divorced. We stayed up late watching Clint Eastwood in *Heartbreak Ridge* and eating ice cream. I was shocked and thrilled by all the cussing.

My empathy and emotional intelligence come from my mother. She was the second oldest of four sisters. Her father left the home when she was in high school. He was a World War II veteran, having served on a navy destroyer in the South Pacific. I never knew what he did besides shovel coal into the ship's boiler, and he never really talked about it. His favorite thing to do was to take my little hand in his whenever we came over to visit and to squeeze it until I cried uncle. Usually, we would spend Christmas Eve at his house in the northern Virginia suburbs. We'd show up, and Pop George would be chewing tobacco and spitting into a cup. His hands were as tough and blistered as any I've ever felt. Every inch of the skin on his palms and fingers was hardened by decades of working with those hands—on a navy destroyer, in his garden, and as an electrician. He'd squeeze my hand and test my limits for tolerating that vicelike pressure, and then when I gave in he'd laugh a deep, gravelly mumble. After that he'd take us on tractor rides in his backyard, and later I'd look through his collection of Time Life books on World War II and the Vietnam War.

My mom's mom, Joanne Foster, made a career for herself working as a meeting planner for the National Association of Counties at a time when the workforce was still male dominated. She came from a family of English and Irish descent that had settled in the Maryland suburbs outside Washington, DC. Grandma Jo was always the most involved of our grandparents. She was at every birthday and big life event. She came to many of our baseball games. She always showed up.

Religiously speaking, my father saw the Catholic church of his upbringing as all stoicism and empty rote. He considered it dead ritualism. My dad often told me the story of how he became a born-again Christian. He left the Air Force Academy after marijuana was discovered in his possession. He was hitchhiking back home, where he would have to tell Hardguy and Miss Ellen what had happened. (His mother was actually known as Drac, short for Dracula, among my dad's brothers and their friends because of her imposing and intimidating personality.) In Iowa, he reconnected with a friend who took him to an evangelical church, and my poor, dejected father experienced a kind of church environment where people were friendly and seemed to be excited about Jesus. He heard, for the first time, that Jesus cared about him and wanted to be part of his life. Dad gave his life to Christ. When he got back to DC, dad found that some of his friends were also "high on Jesus." Many young people were getting into this Jesus movement. My mom was part of that scene, and my mom and dad met up going to Bible studies, church meetings, and social outings.

They were swept up in something called the Jesus Movement, which had begun at the end of the 1960s and spread throughout the country in the 1970s. My childhood was dominated by the story of this revival that they and their friends experienced in the years before I was born. It was a national phenomenon, so much so that *Time* ran a cover story on it in 1971.[4] The cover design featured a drawing of a bearded Jesus, his face shaded in purple, in front of a psychedelic background of bright red and yellow and a rainbow. Positioned above him like a halo, the headline read, "The Jesus Revolution." And at the center of that revolution was this same thing I would be chasing in my bedroom two decades later: a personal, profound, emotional experience of God.

My dad's best friend from high school was now "born again." C. J. Mahaney had been an athletic type who came from a rough-and-tumble household and relied on his sharp wit and charisma to draw others into his orbit at Springbrook High School in Silver Spring, Maryland. He was a pot smoker with long, scraggly blond hair, thinning even at a young age. His eyes always seemed to be

---

4. "The Alternative Jesus: Psychedelic Christ," *Time*, June 21, 1971, https://content.time.com/time/subscriber/printout/0,8816,905202,00.html

half-closed, as if he were perpetually squinting. My dad and C. J. were born a few days apart from each other in 1953 and met in ninth grade. Dad became close with C. J.'s family and spent considerable time at their home. C. J. also knew my mom growing up and dated her after high school, before she met my dad.

C. J. found purpose in this new religious movement and turned his life around. He became the leader of a group of young people who were all drawn to whatever it was that was happening. There was something in the air, an excitement, an emotion you can still tap into most easily by listening to some of the music from that era. Find a live recording of the popular musicians of that time—Keith Green or Second Chapter of Acts—and you'll hear the raw power. They were fed up with the conventionalism of their parents' generation, with its emphasis on conformity, duty, stoicism, and bourgeois materialism. And they were unfulfilled with the free-love movement of the 1960s. So they took the hippie culture and merged it with Jesus's teachings on loving their brothers and sisters in the faith and on returning to a communal ethic. They wanted to act out the vision in Acts 4:32–35, where Christians shared their belongings and devoted themselves totally to Christ. One leader told the *Washington Post* in 1981 that their community rejected "American individualism" and wanted to live communally.[5] Melody Green, Keith Green's wife and a leader in her own right, called the revival "a spontaneous combustion of the power of God colliding with a hungry and willing generation."[6]

While there were elements of hippie culture in the Jesus Movement, there was also a rejection of the purely hedonistic, live-and-let-live ethos of the 1960s. The 1960s had ended with assassinations, domestic terrorism, massive social unrest, incredible racial tension, and the peak of the Vietnam War. By the time the 1970s

5. H. Bradford Fish, "Author Waiting for Judgement Day," *Washington Post*, February 12, 1981, https://www.washingtonpost.com/archive/local/1981/02/12/author-waiting-for-judgment-day/a0bc0fa6-4e62-46b3-a975-96f1ca03a53b/.

6. "A Message from Melody Green," Last Days Ministries, September 2013, https://www.lastdaysministries.org/Groups/1000028701/Last_Days_Ministries/LDM/Our_e_letters/Our_e_letters.aspx.

rolled around, America was in a dark, foul mood. My parents were coming of age as the nation wanted stability and reassurance that everything was going to be okay.

The Jesus Movement was a special time. Those teens and twenty-somethings felt close to God and to one another. They came together and sang songs, broke bread, and held each other. They felt drawn into something big. It wasn't just historic. It was eternal. It was life-changing.

The Jesus Movement planted seeds of a radical Christian community. It promised to produce a Christian presence that had a prophetic edge in American life: captive to neither political party, speaking boldly for the poor, the weak, the unborn, the neglected, and the downtrodden. This Christian presence would not be swayed by the appeals to fear used by demagogues over the ages. These Christians questioned the myth of the American dream. They celebrated hard work, individual freedoms, and personal integrity, but they also rejected the consumption, hyper-individualism, and racism that were often part of conservative culture. They were no longer comfortable with the status quo as it related to racial and economic injustice.

C. J. and another leader named Larry Tomczak started leading regular meetings of these young people, and the meetings quickly grew so popular that they moved to a church in DC. The group had begun as a Bible study in the living room of a woman named Lydia Little in 1969 and quickly grew into a large meeting that became known as Take and Give (TAG).

This went on for a few years. Then, in 1977, C. J. and Tomczak started a church and called it Gathering of Believers. I was the first baby dedicated in the church. The end of TAG in the late 1970s was a major shift. This was no longer a loosely organized Bible study. It was an actual church with a budget and membership requirements. It was the end of the honeymoon period and the beginning of a years-long slow-burn conflict between C. J. and others over control and direction. C. J. and Tomczak started to clash, and Tomczak moved to Cleveland—where he'd grown up—to start his own church while still remaining affiliated with the church back in Maryland.

The seeds of harm were planted with good intentions. The men who shaped my childhood, who formed my mental architecture and my inner life, simply wanted something real. There were women around, of course, but they were considered mostly irrelevant when it came to decision-making.

There must have been moments during those formational years when someone said something like this: "We don't really know what we are doing. We need to join a larger group or institution or denomination. We need oversight and accountability and guidance." But that attitude did not prevail. If these young, headstrong men had more fully embraced all that history and tradition had to teach them, they might not have tried to reinvent the wheel. It would have spared many people some of the pain to come.

2

Pro-Life Child

I t was so cold. I sat in the back of a pickup truck that was covered in snow, shivering, wondering if we'd ever get home. The wind and snowflakes whipped around our faces as the blizzard of January 22, 1987, roared on. The storm would end up dumping more than two feet of snow.

Will we be stuck out here and freeze to death?

We were part of an exodus from downtown DC that had turned into a debacle after the Metro trains stopped running, stranding us miles from our house in the suburbs. Unable to get home the way we had come, we had to settle for that frigid ride while exposed to the elements. My father sat beside me and kept his arm around me, trying to keep me warm. By the look on his face, I could tell he was worried about me.

But in reality, nothing could have kept us away from the March for Life. We had gone to join thousands of other Christians who saw themselves as noble crusaders seeking to end a demonic evil: the murder of unborn children. Stopping abortions had become a mission for my father. The year before, my dad had gone to the march even though my mom was due to give birth to their fifth child at any moment. He had to be called on a mobile phone to hurry home because Mom had gone into labor with my sister.

By this time, in the mid-1980s, Dad was still a pastor with the church started by C. J. Mahaney and Larry Tomczak, which by then was under the new name Covenant Life Church. For a time, the church was split into a few separate campuses, and Dad was the head pastor at one in College Park, near the University of Maryland. He also led regular protests in front of area abortion clinics and sometimes brought me along. "We find it very inconsistent for a hospital run by a Christian church to be practicing murder of unborn children," Dad told the *Washington Post* during a protest outside Washington Adventist Hospital in Wheaton, Maryland, in 1985.[1]

At one protest, I was interviewed by the local newspaper. The reporter seemed intrigued by the idea of a young boy speaking out for the cause. At another protest, a woman slapped Dad in his face. According to him, he accepted the abuse without anger, which would have been very much in character for him. He would tell us this story and quote from another verse in the book of Proverbs: "A gentle answer turns away wrath" (15:1). Dad waded into the world of public discourse as well. He appeared on local television a handful of times, at one point debating a spokesperson from the National Organization for Women.

Yet Dad's activism was overshadowed by the increasing violence of some in the antiabortion movement in the 1980s. Between 1977 and 1988 there were 110 cases of arson, firebombing, or bombing carried out by antiabortion activists.[2] A number of these attacks took place in the DC area, and my dad showed up to one of the clinics after hearing about the bombing on the radio. He told a

1. Ruth Marcus, "Abortion Opponents Picket Two Hospitals," *Washington Post*, October 6, 1985, https://www.washingtonpost.com/archive/politics/1985/10/06/abortion-opponents-picket-two-hospitals/8ff8a71d-ac76-4b2d-8402-7e18fc232615/.

2. D. A. Grimes, J. D. Forrest, A. L. Kirkman, and B. Radford, "An Epidemic of Antiabortion Violence in the United States," *American Journal of Obstetrics and Gynecology* 165, no. 5 (November 1991): 1263–68, https://doi10.1016/0002-9378(91)90346-s. PMID: 1957842.

reporter for the *New York Times*, "I'm here to make it clear we have nothing to do with this. I believe abortion is the worst civil rights [violation] in the nation. We repudiate the bombing. That is violence begetting violence. As Christians, we are committed to nonviolence and to peace. We would not lower the nobility of our cause with violence of any kind."[3]

Dad also told *New York Times* reporter Dudley Clendinen that he was familiar with one of the men who had been arrested along with two others for planting bombs at seven abortion clinics in Maryland, Virginia, and Washington, DC: Michael Donald Bray.[4] Bray was thirty-two years old, the same age as my father, and claimed to belong to a self-proclaimed terrorist group called Army of God. He sometimes came to the protests outside clinics that were organized by my father. Over time, Bray hasn't moderated. In 2009, he praised the murder of George Tiller—a doctor who performed late-term abortions—on the Army of God website: "We are anti-abortion without apology and we rejoice in the death of this wicked man without apology and without shame." He lauded the man who shot Tiller in the head, Scott Roeder. "We do not blush in our praise of Mr. Roeder," Bray wrote.[5]

In the late 1980s, a group called Operation Rescue organized massive civil disobedience protests outside abortion clinics. And then in 1993 a gynecologist named David Gunn, who also performed abortions, was shot and killed by an antiabortion activist. Six more murders were committed between 1994 and 1998 by antiabortion extremists. That does not include the 1996 Olympic Park bombing, which killed one person and injured 111 others

3. "Office and Abortion Clinic Damaged," *New York Times*, November 20, 1984, https://www.nytimes.com/1984/11/20/us/office-and-abortion-clinic-dam aged.html.

4. Dudley Clendinen, "Abortion Clinic Bombings Have Caused Disruption for Many," *The New York Times*, February 6, 1985, https://www.nytimes.com /1985/02/06/us/abortion-clinic-bombings-have-caused-disruption-for-many.html. On the bombings, see "3 Men Charged in Bombings of Seven Abortion Facilities," *New York Times*, January 20, 1985, https://www.nytimes.com/1985/01/20 /us/3-men-charged-in-bombings-of-seven-abortion-facilities.html.

5. Michael Bray, "Rejoicing in the Death of the Wicked," June 2, 2009, https:// www.armyofgod.com/MikeBrayRejoicinginTheDeathofTheWicked.html.

and was committed by antiabortion extremist Eric Rudolph. In a statement years later, Rudolph said he planted the Atlanta bomb "to confound, anger and embarrass the Washington government in the eyes of the world for its abominable sanctioning of abortion on demand."[6]

My dad always rejected violence, as did most pro-lifers. But his turn to antiabortion activism in the early 1980s was a transition away from where he'd been a decade before. His parents were conservative, but he had voted for George McGovern for president in 1972, his first presidential election, and then for Jimmy Carter in 1976. He'd been drawn to Carter's faith and his appeals to character and integrity, which were a contrast with the corruption of Richard Nixon and the Watergate scandal. But a massive shift occurred in the late 1970s as the Republican Party began to exploit abortion as a political wedge issue, and my dad was one of the evangelicals who were drawn to the GOP during that time. In 1980 he voted for Republican Ronald Reagan, and he has voted for Republicans ever since.

My father's path mirrors that of millions of White evangelicals in America. The shift wasn't accidental; the Republican Party had identified abortion as a way to consolidate religious conservatives. They were able to merge religious conservatives like my father with cultural conservatives from the South who held on to their White supremacist views. Some scholars have argued that it wasn't abortion that brought evangelicals into the Republican fold during the late 1970s and early 1980s. Instead, they say, it was racism and a reaction against the gains of the civil rights movement.[7] But abortion was truly at the center of my parents' worldview. I was raised in a world of ignorance about the racial disparities in our country. I never heard either of my parents utter anything that was

6. Jennifer Bayot, "A Subdued Rudolph Is Sentenced for Bombings," *New York Times*, August 22, 2005, https://www.nytimes.com/2005/08/22/national /a-subdued-rudolph-is-sentenced-for-bombings.html.

7. Randall Balmer, "The Real Origins of the Religious Right," *Politico Magazine*, May 27, 2014, https://www.politico.com/magazine/story/2014/05/religious -right-real-origins-107133/.

hostile to Blacks or other racial minorities in any way. Our sins, when it came to racial justice, were those of omission and apathy.

There were still remnants of the free-spirited 1960s floating around in the 1980s. My dad was into a heavy rock band called the Rez Band. Rez was short for Resurrection, a reference to the revivification of Christ after the crucifixion. Most Christian music was uninspiring. But the Rez Band actually did rock. There were other exceptions. I loved Mylon LeFevre and Broken Heart's album *Sheep in Wolves Clothing*. LeFevre and his bandmates were all dressed in wild outfits: a rainbow of colors, designer vests cut off at the shoulder, with LeFevre sporting long hair and a red nylon jacket and pants. They were almost like Star Wars characters. They played a few concerts at our church.

For a time, my dad was in charge of pastoring college students and young singles in our church, and so he'd drive a bus of them up to southern Pennsylvania for a Christian music festival called Creation. It was the longest-running Christian music summer festival, basically a Woodstock for Christians and their families, substituting prayer in place of pot. Separate music festivals were part of the separatist mindset that many evangelicals adopted for much of the twentieth century. Non-Christians, the thinking went, carried sin like a virus, and the point of following Jesus was to remain as pure as possible. Christians established their own communities, educational institutions, and music festivals, isolated from the rest of the world.

Creation had a direct line back to the Jesus Movement. In the 1970s, it had been one of several festivals that sprang up to showcase artists like Keith Green, Larry Norman, the Rez Band, Phil Keaggy, Mylon LeFevre, Amy Grant, and many more. There would be preaching during the day and then a bunch of music acts in the afternoon and evening. I loved it. One year I saved my money from my newspaper route and bought a sleeveless camouflage shirt with some Christian design on the front. I was walking on air. But even as a kid, I knew that some of the music was just okay, and much of it was terrible.

My parents didn't expose me to any music or culture unless it was Christian. I wasn't allowed to listen to "secular music" or watch *He-Man* or *Sesame Street*. But so much of Christian pop culture was derivative of mainstream culture: just an attempt to take something everybody liked and make it about Jesus. *South Park* got it right in the episode in which Cartman forms a band and realizes he can make it big by catering to an evangelical audience. "All right, guys, this is going to be so easy. All we have to do to make Christian songs is take regular old songs and add Jesus stuff to them. See? All we have to do is cross out words like 'baby' and 'darling' and replace them with 'Jeeesus.'"[8] John Jeremiah Sullivan captured this in a memorable 2004 *GQ* essay about his own trip to Creation: "Every successful crappy secular group has its Christian off-brand, and that's proper, because culturally speaking, it's supposed to serve as a stand-in for, not an alternative to or an improvement on, those very groups. In this it succeeds wonderfully. If you think it profoundly sucks, that's because your priorities are not its priorities; you want to hear something cool and new, it needs to play something proven to please . . . while praising Jesus Christ. That's Christian rock."[9]

An aesthetically subpar culture gave many of us an inferiority complex. So when a musician had any association with mainstream artists, we clung to that like a lifeline. It also led to pure fabrications, like this story, which I heard more than once. The rumor was that Jimi Hendrix had once praised the Christian guitarist Phil Keaggy, who played with a missing finger on one hand. "Johnny Carson asked [Hendrix] how it felt to be the greatest guitarist ever, and he said, 'I don't know. Ask Phil Keaggy.'" I heard this story more than once, but it never happened.[10]

8. *South Park*, episode 105, "Christian Rock Hard," directed by Trey Parker, written by Trey Parker, Matt Stone, and Brian Graden, aired October 29, 2003, on Comedy Central.

9. John Jeremiah Sullivan, "Upon This Rock," *GQ*, January 24, 2004, http://www.gq.com/entertainment/music/200401/rock-music-jesus.

10. David Mikkelson, "Phil Keaggy Greatest Guitarist?," *Snopes*, June 3, 2000, https://www.snopes.com/fact-check/phil-keaggy/.

Keith Green was another example of this. He had grown up in the music industry in Los Angeles and was on the cusp of becoming a studio-backed pop star at age twelve, when he signed his first record contract. But fame eluded him, and a decade later he was writing songs for CBS when he and his wife, Melody, became born-again Christians. Green became one of the most famous names in Christian music, sometimes referred to as the Bob Dylan of Christian music. In fact, Dylan once played a little harmonica on one of Green's songs. But we inflated these details and told ourselves that Green and Dylan were best buds.

Nonetheless, Green was talented and a huge star. Part of his appeal was his radicalism. He would preach at his audiences, and even reprimand them, as if he were the prophet Jeremiah rebuking the tribes of Judah in the Old Testament. He had a mustache, a big bushy beard, and a round helmet of thick, curly black hair. He seemed a little pissed off. Some of his harshest words were for those who ignored the poor and did nothing to help those in need. His song "Asleep in the Light" asked listeners if they saw those who were in need:

> Don't you care? Don't you care?
> Are you gonna let them drown?[11]

He went on to chastise those in the audience who weren't putting their faith into action. Some would say that all of Green's language was spiritual, that he was simply describing the act of proselytizing, or as Christians describe it, "witnessing." But Green—while he was certainly fanatical about telling people about Jesus—also was talking about people sinking and drowning amid poverty and addiction and illness.

Keith and Melody bought a trio of houses in Los Angeles and used them to shelter people living on the streets. "We have about three houses and 20 young people. And we take people in off the

---

11. Keith Green, "Asleep in the Light," Genius, accessed June 6, 2022, https://genius.com/Keith-green-asleep-in-the-light-lyrics.

streets and we go into prisons and go into ghettos and do different things that I really feel is lacking," he said in a 1982 interview.[12] In that interview, he expressed his disgust for the hypocrisy in much of Christian culture and for the enclosed, self-reinforcing world in which many Christians lived. "All the Christians I knew were so busy getting blessed. They were so busy going to functions and concerts and listening to their Christian albums and going to their fundraising dinners and all these things," he said. He also sang songs that implied God would reject people who claimed to be Christians but did nothing to help those in need.

But there was a tug-of-war inside Green's mind over what it meant to help someone. Green wanted to alleviate suffering, but he also put a high emphasis on spiritual redemption and a profession of faith in a set of beliefs. Many Christians do this, in contrast to other believers who focus on helping people in their circumstances and view salvation as a process that comes from obedience to a few basic instructions from Jesus Christ: love God with all your heart, soul, mind, and strength; love your neighbor as yourself (Mark 12:30–31); and help those in need (Matt. 25:31–46).

Green, however, put a spotlight on getting "saved" in what was often a dramatic conversion experience. This way of viewing faith made a big deal of having a clear demarcation in your life, between your days as a pagan rebelling against God and your moment of decision, when you became a child of God. The need for this clear line—before and after—elevated the importance of a statement of faith in a set of beliefs. This approach nudged aside the kind of faith that is a lifelong journey of growth in which one never truly arrives but is constantly seeking and growing and evolving.

The Greens drifted toward a conservative tradition through other factors as well. Like many Christians at that time, they were drawn into a hyper-literalist reading of the Bible, which accelerated a black-and-white view of the world. They gravitated toward

---

12. "Keith Green 1982 100 Huntley Street TV 01 Keith's Testimony," YouTube video, 15:41, posted by Myke A., https://www.youtube.com/watch?v=oOYQSn 46q08.

the book of Revelation, the notoriously opaque final book in the Christian Bible. For those who read it literally, Revelation can function like a road map, as they try to discern when and where and how the end of the world and the day of judgment will come. Green began publishing a magazine that focused on the end times and formed Last Days Ministries to distribute it.

In 1981, the first year of Ronald Reagan's presidency, Green's Last Day Ministries began to focus explicitly on abortion. Antiabortion advocacy became a particular passion for Melody Green. Then, in the summer of 1982, Keith Green died in an airplane accident. Melody carried on the work of Last Days Ministries, and abortion became a bigger focus. By 1987 she was meeting with President Reagan, along with other antiabortion activists. That one issue became her organization's chief cause.

When Green died, Dad was in the middle of planning a large concert appearance by him at the University of Maryland. And like Green's widow and millions of other evangelicals, my father carried on Green's memory in part by heeding the call to fight for the unborn. Less attention was paid to fighting for the welfare of the born, for those who made it out of the womb and into a world of poverty, suffering, and systemic injustice. And not much thought was given to the women who often ended up caring for these children on their own.

3

The Walls Close In

Our church was growing. In the 1980s, that was part of a larger trend. Mainline Protestant denominations were on the decline, and congregations like ours were on the upswing. It was easy to start a nondenominational church. There was no institutional leadership to report to. There was no accreditation or credentialing needed for those who wanted to serve in positions of leadership, including lead pastor. If you were a good speaker and knew a few good musicians, you could start a church.

Growing families flocked to these more casual and modern congregations. You could wear what you wanted and didn't have to dress up. But the religiosity was far more intense than most mainline settings. The Methodists and Episcopalians and some Presbyterians had been moving in a more liberal direction for some time. There was an appetite for certainty. People wanted to know what was right and what was wrong, what to do and what not to do. Nondenominational churches like ours gave them that.

The rise of nondenominational churches in the 1980s carried an element of consumerism. Some churches encouraged the attitude that you could attend or not, whenever you wanted. This was too casual for our church. C. J. Mahaney and other Covenant Life Church leaders asked attendees to become members if they wanted to keep attending. Once you were a member, you had to submit many of your life choices to church leaders.

We created more new churches in other parts of the country. But as C. J.'s success accelerated, he rose to the top of the leadership structure in our network of churches. Larry Tomczak, the cofounder of the original congregation, was the most high-profile pastor of several who left the church over leadership conflicts. I remember getting the impression that if people left our church and went to another, there was something wrong with them. Only our church had the answers.

Why did my parents stay? Looking back, it seems simple to me: all their relationships were there, and the church had changed their lives. But our world became small. We went to a private school run by the church. Congregation leaders had strapped together enough funds to rent an old school building that shared space with an alternative school for kids with behavioral problems. Only the children of church members could attend. This was another way in which the church created its own tiny world, through which the leaders could eliminate nonconforming thought and behavior.

Our kindergarten teacher was a giant presence in my life. Anytime we misbehaved, he would take us into a supply closet, close the door, and pull out a paddle. Sometimes it was wood. Sometimes it was fiberglass. I was afraid of him, but I didn't think he was mean. He spoke softly and kindly. He had a ventriloquist dummy puppet, a purple *Sesame Street* look-alike. And I just accepted the fact that someone other than my parents was hitting me.

Our parents were told that it was their duty to spank us. Tomczak had become sort of famous, in our world at least, for writing a book about spanking titled *God, the Rod, and Your Child's Bod*. Tomczak taught that if a parent didn't spank their child, they were rebelling against God. "Because some parents don't want to hurt their children, they disobey God, withholding loving correction," he wrote. Then he raised the stakes: if you didn't spank your child, they would probably go to hell and be tortured forever. Those who didn't spank, he wrote, would "allow their children to continue down pathways to inevitable destruction and even eternal damnation."[1]

To make things more extreme, the standard Tomczak laid out for acceptable behavior was impossibly high. We should obey our parents "willingly, completely and immediately."[2] In other words, if we didn't clean our room perfectly, as soon as our parent told us, and make a show of being happy while doing it, then Tomczak said we should be spanked.

Our family spent time with the Tomczak's. One evening, when I was pretty young, we went over to their house for dinner. I did something that displeased my parents. My dad may have felt some pressure to handle it like Tomczak would. He took me to the bathroom and spanked me.

When I was ten, we moved to the suburbs. We had been bouncing around from apartment to rental house in the post–World War II, baby boomer Maryland towns ringing DC. But by the late 1980s, developers were building cookie-cutter homes in what had been until then farmland farther north. My parents bought a house in Gaithersburg, in the Flower Hill subdivision. When we moved in, the houses down the street were unfinished. My friends and I played in the foundations after the work crews left for the day.

My two younger brothers and I spent endless summer days playing modified wiffleball in our cul-de-sac with our older neighbor. The three of us siblings spent many hours together. But there was also something of a distance between us. It may have been the downside of the strong independence each of us possessed, passed down from my dad's family to us in some invisible way. Frank, the second oldest, was always the most distant, in his own world. But we all were distant to some degree. Frank also had the

1. Larry Tomczak, *God, the Rod, and Your Child's Bod: The Art of Loving Correction for Christian Parents* (Old Tappan, NJ: Fleming H. Revell, 1981), 44.
2. Tomczak, *God, the Rod, and Your Child's Bod*, 95.

quickest wit and funniest sense of humor. He was the one who made us all laugh the most.

I made stronger connections with another set of brothers, Steve and Rob, my closest friends growing up. Their father was a Harvard-educated lawyer who did legal work for Covenant Life Church, and they lived a ten-minute walk away. Next door to their house was C. J.'s house. While I was growing up, C. J. and his wife, Carolyn, had three daughters, though later on they had a son. On the rare occasion we saw C. J., it felt like a pope sighting. He came out once or twice and threw the football with us. He was a celebrity in our little world.

I was sports obsessed. For years, I slept with a plastic yellow baseball bat. In junior high, I began sneaking a black-and-white TV into my bedroom during the March Madness college basketball tournament so I could watch the late slate of games, which started at 10 p.m. I'd turn the TV on under my covers with the sound down way low.

My mom said she wasn't going to let me play football. But in the fall of my ninth year, there I was picking up shoulder pads and a helmet at the Summit Hall farm barn, where they stored the gear every winter. I got a headache from trying on multiple helmets and breathing in the scent of shoulder pads that had accumulated several seasons of sweat. My first coach looked like a cross between an accountant and a steel-mill worker. He would yell at us, "I want you to eat that other guy's lunch!" I'd be on one knee, looking up at our coach in awe, my pulse quickening and my heart in an uproar. I was determined to carry on the Ward athletic tradition.

I enjoyed the violence of football. I liked establishing dominance over other boys through my willingness to endure pain. The first time I was thrown into a tackling drill, with pads and helmets, I made a quick mental calculation. Either the kid a few feet away was going to run into me harder than I did into him, or vice versa. I understood I would have to be willing to tolerate more pain than him, and I made up my mind then and there to do so.

Part of the reason I loved football is because I could be dominant in that setting. Off-field, I was a sensitive, sheltered kid who could never think of the right thing to say until ten minutes after the fact. My social awareness was like a wide-open aperture in a camera. The aperture is the hole that lets the light in. Some people have a narrow aperture. They see only what is right in front of them. I saw and felt everything around me. I wanted people to like me a little too much and didn't like conflict. I was scared of fist fights and awkward around girls.

My dad was a fan of the Oxford-trained scholar and apologist C. S. Lewis, whose story of converting from atheism to Christianity is recounted in the best-selling book *Mere Christianity*. Lewis is the patron saint of many evangelical Christians who have experienced some form of adult or teenage conversion to the faith and who also believe that intellectual pursuits and literature are important. Lewis's series The Chronicles of Narnia was also dear to my father's heart. He read the books aloud to us, and I read them numerous times on my own when I was older. My dad would also tell my brothers and me bedtime stories about an imaginary world he created, an imitation of Narnia. He called it the Land Behind the Mirror. The main character's name was Jonathan Sofo.

I don't have a lot of other memories of my father from childhood. Our church explicitly rejected the notion of gender equity. Its leaders taught that the Bible says it is the woman's job to stay home, raise kids, and take care of household duties. My mother did most of the day-in, day-out work of raising us. Dad was a hard worker outside the home, and at Covenant Life Church there were many meetings beyond Sunday services. The expectation was that members would construct their social lives around the church, leaving little time for anyone or anything outside it.

My mom did heroic work taking care of us all. We gave her plenty to worry about. My brothers and I were small-time pyromaniacs. One day I lit a bonfire in the middle of our street by pouring a giant patch of gasoline and lighting it. Another time I made a Molotov cocktail and lit the fuse, waiting for it to explode. I also lit a gasoline fire in our yard that my mom quickly put out before the wind whipped it into something larger.

We sometimes chuckled at my mom's frustration, but she was not to be trifled with. One time when I was fifteen or sixteen, I was standing in the kitchen, mouthing off. The next thing I knew, Mom had somehow flung me to the floor and was sitting on top of me, pinning me down, telling me to shut my mouth. My juvenile laughter could not mask my surprise and embarrassment.

In the suburbs, we kids had more freedom of movement, but we were more isolated. We were cut off from anyone outside the church as well as from any sense of history or tradition. The suburban landscape had no connection to anything that had come before. It was much like our church culture, which had been created from scratch out of nothing, precisely because my parents' generation despised the traditions their parents had raised them in. We were making something new, and what had come before was dead and irrelevant.

But as I grew up, I felt—in my mind and my body—the lack of stability and rootedness that come from traditions and connections to the past. A vague emptiness washed over me as we drove endless loops through the suburbs.

The more insular we became, the more incapable we were of discerning the complexities of major crises happening outside our bubble. We thought HIV/AIDS was a divine punishment for immoral behavior rather than seeing the humanity and tragedy in so many people being caught in the grip of a deadly virus with no cure. We viewed crime as a problem of the cities and were glad we were not there. When we occasionally did enter a city, it was to go into the heart of Baltimore for Orioles games.

We were unaware of the rise of mass incarceration, which began in the late 1970s as a result of policies created by President Nixon and his "war on drugs" but really took off during Ronald Reagan's presidency. The prison population roughly doubled during Reagan's years in office, from 329,000 Americans in jail in 1980 to 627,000 in 1988. This trend accelerated during the Bush and Clinton presidencies. By 2008, there were 1.6 million people in American prisons, with the US leading the world in total prison population and imprisonment rate. And the weight of this increase fell disproportionately on Black men and women.[3] Growing up, I thought we were colorblind, and we were in the sense that we didn't pay attention to the injustices faced by people of color. We didn't pay any attention to politics, except when it came to abortion. Because abortion was the only thing we cared about, our view of politics was reduced to Republicans good, Democrats evil.

This view helped drive the rise of the religious right, led by Jerry Falwell and the Moral Majority in the 1970s and 1980s. This movement signaled that evangelicals knew their retreat from culture was not working out well. America was moving so far away from their view of righteousness that they needed to do something. But instead of becoming participants in culture—stakeholders who worked to represent their interests while contributing to the common good—evangelicals took an antagonistic attitude toward culture. They got involved in politics, but only to condemn those who thought differently and to fight the culture wars: a scorched-earth, winner-take-all battle to secure rights while pushing others' interests aside or down. It was a fear-based strategy.

To be "generative," writes Makoto Fujimura, is to be "fruitful, originating new life or producing offspring (as with plants and animals), or producing new parts (as with stem cells)." It is to "draw on creativity to bring into being something fresh and life giving." This was what I wanted but could not articulate for myself growing up, a "cultural environment" that was "open to questions of meaning, reaching beyond mere survival, inspiring people to meaningful action, and leading toward wholeness and harmony."[4] Imagine if Christians were known for this rather than for what they are against. For as long as I can remember, I have wanted to live toward a positive, proactive vision.

---

3. "Race, Mass Incarceration, and the Disastrous War on Drugs," Brennan Center for Justice, May 10, 2021, https://www.brennancenter.org/our-work/analysis-opinion/race-mass-incarceration-and-disastrous-war-drugs.

4. Makoto Fujimura, *Culture Care: Reconnecting with Beauty for Our Common Life* (Downers Grove, IL: InterVarsity, 2017), 22.

In the late 1980s, my father was asked to resign from his job as a pastor. It would take decades for me to understand why this happened. At the time, I was told that Dad wasn't spending enough time with his family, and the pastors had concerns about whether us kids were "godly" enough. For years, my father was portrayed as being humble for having accepted his firing. It was a big contrast to Larry Tomczak's departure, which was public and messy. Tomczak left the church and went somewhere else. My dad stayed and remained submitted to the leadership of the men who had fired him. But it hurt him.

But the bigger question at that moment was how to make a living. My dad and mom were in their mid-thirties with five kids, and my mother's prospects for work were limited since the church frowned on women working outside the home. For a time, my dad sold mobile phones, which had just become available for sale. Those early cell phones were attached by a cord to a car-battery-size power unit, and if you wanted to take your phone out of your car, you carried it around with the strap on your shoulder. But that didn't last long. Dad met a fast-talking West Pointer who had started a real estate company and who brought Dad under his wing and helped him start selling houses.

All the while, Mom kept doing the laundry, feeding us kids, cleaning the house, driving us all to our many football and baseball games, and a thousand other things. Maybe the hardest thing was trying to be the kind of woman the church kept telling her to be—modest, submissive, gentle, responsive to the needs of her husband—and trying to make us kids into model Christians who followed the church's instructions.

One of the few things I remember Mom doing for herself was playing the piano. She didn't know how to read music, but she had a great ear and could learn how to play songs that way. She worked out her stress sitting on that piano bench in our living room. Gradually, any hopes and dreams she might have had for a life of her own, even a hint of something she could call hers outside of raising us kids, kept getting smaller.

For my middle school years, my parents decided to homeschool me and my younger siblings. The church school didn't extend past sixth grade. We didn't have money for a private education. Public school was out of the question. So for seventh and eighth grade I did all my studies at home, with minimal help from my mom, who had to spend most of her time helping the others. My only exposure to other kids was through playing sports and through a good friend who lived a few houses down. We'd go over to his house when he got home from school and play video games on his Nintendo and watch MTV.

There were some defiant things we did at home. When my parents went out on their weekly date nights, we would turn on *Beverly Hills 90210*—definitely forbidden content. My siblings and I would watch Mom and Dad pull out of the driveway, waving goodbye, then race to the television to watch the adventures of Brenda and Brandon in a world we could barely imagine.

Around this time, I went to South America dressed up as a clown.

4

Apocalypse Pretty Soon

An early morning mist lay low on the ground as I climbed up into a clutch of rocks about six feet high. I sat down, opened my Bible, and began to read in the Psalms: "Keep me safe, my God, for in you I take refuge. I say to the LORD, 'You are my Lord; apart from you I have no good thing'" (16:1–2). I sat silent, pondering these words, praying them silently in my mind. Birdsong echoed in the distance, from the direction of the lake a few hundred yards to my right. Over my left shoulder stood a mountain cloaked in fog and cloud. I was thirteen years old, in a foreign country, with a bunch of strangers, and far from home without any friends or family. As I read the Psalms, I felt a nearness, a realness. Was this God? It must be. I worked the words over in my mind, and I felt comforted, strengthened, reassured.

I walked back to the low-slung buildings in the compound where I was staying, an hour outside Santiago, the capital of Chile. I went to my bunk and began to change into a clown costume, made out of nylon and all the colors of the rainbow. Then I applied white makeup to my face, drawing a red circle around one eye and more

40

colorful makeup around my mouth. I didn't have much time to eat, so I grabbed some bread and scrambled eggs, then hopped on a charter bus filled with teenagers who were dressed up as pirates, sailors, and mimes.

We were here because of a guy named Ron Luce, whose most distinguishing characteristic was his aggressive mullet. Luce was a thirty-year-old hype man who had founded an organization named Teen Mania. He would travel the country, holding events called Acquire the Fire, at which he told teens that they could join the epic battle against evil by traveling to foreign countries to spread the Christian faith. Luce talked a lot about Christians' call to wage war against the enemy. Maybe he meant demons. Maybe he meant real people. It was never quite clear.

"We are ready to take back what the enemy has stolen. I want to know, is there anyone here who is ready to run to the battle?!" Luce once yelled out to thousands of teenagers. He promised "a real encounter with God," which teens would experience with the help of "bands, pyrotechnics, media, and drama."[1]

Luce had a simple growth plan, which explains how I came to be involved. He promoted his conferences to youth pastors at churches in each city where he was traveling, asking them to promote Acquire the Fire to other churches so that their teens would get "fired up" for Christ. Musicians led the audience in loud worship music before Luce came on stage and told us how we were at war with darkness and with demons. We could fight that darkness by winning converts but also by resisting the corruption of popular culture. He encouraged us to go on what Christians call "mission trips"—which was why I was in Chile for a full month. I'd typed up a fundraising letter asking for donations from friends and relatives and had raised a few thousand dollars to pay my way.

In Chile, every weekday morning we would drive somewhere different, get out of the bus, set up some speakers, and do street drama. We had a few smaller skits with one or two characters

1. "Teen Mania History," YouTube video posted May 5, 2009, https://www .youtube.com/watch?v=m6ngJ9rarBA.

designed to build a crowd, and then we'd do our main event. The sailors were the good guys, the pirates were the bad guys. I guess my character the clown was there for comedic filler. And then there were a Jesus character and a Satan character. It was a gospel presentation featuring predictably bad teenage acting, with narration prerecorded in Spanish. After we were done, we were supposed to go out into the audience and pray with any onlookers who hadn't moved on quickly. The goal was to get them to recite a prayer. Then they would be saved from damnation, and we'd be on to the next location.

I can't say I enjoyed proselytizing much. It seemed rather transactional and superficial. But the opportunity to see another part of the world was hard to pass up. When I was getting ready to board the plane for Chile, my dad hugged me and said goodbye, and when I turned to depart, he was tearing up. It was the first time I'd seen him cry. We headed to Miami first to get organized and trained. The vans took us from the airport to the Doral Resort, full of manicured lawns and palm trees. I'm still not sure how Luce justified that kind of expense, but maybe it helps explain why Teen Mania would later go bankrupt.[2] We had revival meetings and met the folks we'd be traveling with. There were teenagers from all over the country. Most of the people leading the groups to each country were quite young themselves, usually couples in their early twenties.

Luce's worldview centered on the idea that America had been a Christian nation and could be once again. We traveled overseas believing that because we lived in the most dominant superpower on earth, we had spiritual resources that people in other countries didn't have. These trips weren't intended for learning about other cultures or for gaining understanding about the world. They were intended to export our particular brand of American Christianity.

2. Morgan Lee, "Teen Mania: Why We're Shutting Down after 30 Years of Acquire the Fire," *Christianity Today*, December 17, 2015, https://www.christianitytoday.com/ct/2015/december-web-only/teen-mania-why-shutting-down-acquire-fire-ron-luce.html.

When we got back from our trips, the "battle" for our own country was still raging. There was nothing that got leaders like Luce more worked up than the idea that America needed to turn back to God. He didn't mean that we needed to renew our commitments to serving the poor and working toward healing and wellness in our neighborhoods and communities. He meant mostly that teens should stop having sex and watching R-rated movies, that abortion should be illegal, and that gay people should not be accepted members of society. Sex was a big deal in this world, and everything was always an emergency. Gay marriage was seen by many as the tip of the spear for those who wanted to destroy Christianity and America.

Several years after my trip, Luce began holding Battle Cry events, which were like Acquire the Fire only more overtly political and apocalyptic. "Christianity may not survive," read his promotional materials. He bought the east Texas compound that had been owned by Keith Green's ministry and started a training school called Honor Academy. In 2008, he got involved in the political battle over Proposition 8 in California, which banned gay marriage in the state and was overturned in court. And his events became more militant. He told the teenagers at the Battle Cry events that they were in a war, he brought members of the military to speak, he incorporated red flags as a major motif, and he mixed that all up with the stuff he'd done in the past: rock music, fireworks, and lots of hype.

Christians were embattled, put upon, even persecuted, and the answer was to "fight" a culture war for a religion based on a God-man who had in his own life on earth taught his followers to turn the other cheek and to be "poor in spirit" (Matt. 5:3). Teens were whipped up into a frenzy. After the culture war rhetoric came the personal appeals for individuals to repent of their own sins and turn back to God themselves. Luce urged teens to stand, one by one, and scream out performatively, "I want the cross!"

One pastor who attended said Luce and his followers "mistake adrenaline for the Holy Spirit" and were "looking for an emotional high."[3] Jeff Sharlet, a journalist who wrote about Luce for *Rolling Stone*, saw something darker: "Ron Luce isn't a fascist, but it is the aesthetic of fascism. It is designed to draw very stark lines and to dehumanize those who are on the other side." He had a different opinion of the kids he'd met at Luce's rallies. "These are some of the gentler and kinder kids I've met. They don't want to be in a war, but that's all they're being offered."[4]

Luce was similar to another leader at Covenant Life Church in its early days: Lou Engle. Engle's voice was perpetually hoarse because whenever he got up in front of people, he would shout himself silly: praying, exhorting, praising, and preaching. He also had the odd and unnerving habit of rocking back and forth when he prayed, front to back, back to front. He didn't sway. There was nothing relaxed about him. He was like a metronome on speed.

Engle and another pastor named Ché Ahn were more aligned with Tomczak in those early days. If C. J. was more about precision and control, these guys just wanted to let it rip. They were big Holy Spirit guys, or charismatics. C. J. over time became more of a theology guy. Maybe the most important contrast between C. J. and Tomczak, Engle, and Ahn was in how they engaged with the world outside the church bubble. C. J. was more of a quietist and a retreatist. He didn't want anything to do with politics. C. J. wanted to talk about the Bible in his sermons, and anything that wasn't explicitly in the Bible he mostly left alone. The only exception was sports, which he did love to talk about. So this was the direction he took Covenant Life Church in, along with the organization he and others founded to oversee all the other churches they were starting around the country. The name of that group changed a

3. Matthai Chakko Kuruvilla, "Faith's Battlefield: SF Event Designed to Get Teens Energized about Evangelical Christianity Divides Believers with Its Combative Language and Emphasis on Culture War," *San Francisco Chronicle*, March 8, 2007, https://www.sfgate.com/news/article/FAITH-S-BATTLEFIELD-S-F-event-designed-to-get-2578496.php.

4. "Hear Their Roar," *On the Media*, April 6, 2007, https://web.archive.org/web/20070527215119/http:/www.onthemedia.org/transcripts/2007/04/06/05.

few times. At first it was People of Destiny International, and that was kind of in line with how Tomczak, Engle, and Ahn thought of themselves.

These leaders wanted a muscular faith that didn't shrink back from a fight. They wanted a dramatic faith too, full of spectacle. They were all big personalities, which they used to compensate for their lack of training, expertise, and experience. Faith, for them, was not the act of extending one's self beyond the realm of what could be known to trust in what one hoped could be true. They had more certainty than anything. Christianity was true, no questions asked.

For them, faith was a belief that they could call down miracles from heaven to heal the sick or predict the future or change world events. Leaders like Tomczak, Engle, and Ahn didn't come across as charlatans. They were very sincere. But early on in their lives, they got locked into a particular type of faith ministry, and they built audiences and followings based on that brand and that kind of faith. At that point, their livelihoods and incomes became dependent on catering to those same types of Christians. Personal evolution or growth became constrained by their business model.

Critical thought, to these charismatic leaders, was an unhealthy questioning of God, and that got in the way of impact. So they sometimes implied that too many questions were a sinful reflex, or Satan's handiwork, which could keep a Christian from claiming their rightful place in God's army. My dad wasn't like that. He didn't emphasize Bible verses about how to overcome any problem with a powerful faith. Instead, Dad's instruction was a lot of wisdom in the Proverbs, pouring out one's soul to God in the Psalms, and a focus on being slow to speak, slow to become angry, and quick to listen—like the apostle James said.

Dad had been working on his master's thesis, an extended meditation on C. S. Lewis, when he took the job as a pastor. He never finished the degree. But that was way more schooling than pretty much anyone else in the leadership ranks had. C. J. was a college dropout. Nobody came in with substantial theological or pastoral training. They were all making things up on the fly. At the time, they thought this was a good thing, because it helped them think creatively and outside the box. By the mid-1980s, Ahn and Engle had left Covenant Life Church to start a church in California. Tomczak had moved to Ohio, and C. J. was firmly in control in Maryland.

None of the charismatic guys—Tomczak, Engle, and Ahn—were as involved in the abortion issue as my dad was. But over time, they would become much more political, while C. J. retreated further into the church bubble.

———

Talk of demons seemed normal to anyone who had read one of the most popular evangelical books of that time. Frank Peretti's *This Present Darkness* came out in 1986, and I read it around the time I went to Chile with Teen Mania. It's the fictional story of a small American town that becomes the battleground for a showdown between angels and demons. The forces of darkness work their wiles in the community through a New Age group called the Universal Consciousness Society.

This Present Darkness, which sold around 2.5 million copies, contains many archetypes that continue to shape the consciousness of many American evangelicals to this day. Millions of Christians came to believe, based almost solely on one guy's imagination, that every action they took was part of a cosmic battle with life-or-death consequences.

In the story, there is a web of conspiracies between the New Age group, a corporation, professors at the local college, and law enforcement. And all of them are being influenced or controlled by demons. Transcendental meditation is portrayed as a gateway to demonic influence, building on the distrust of that practice among many evangelicals, which extended to yoga and psychology. The resistance to this conspiracy is led by the pastor of a tiny church. (If the idea of a satanic cult threatening Christians sounds familiar, that's because the QAnon conspiracy theory contains a similar story line.) Peretti's books riveted me and shaped my view of the spirit world for a long time.

A few years later, in 1995, the first of the Left Behind books was released. Ultimately, there were sixteen, with more for children, all of them set in a postapocalyptic world. Then the movies came out, starting in 2000. All of them told the story of what some believe will happen: faithful Christians will disappear suddenly from the earth in a rapture event, and those "left behind" will have to live through a tribulation period that will culminate in an epic battle between the forces of light and darkness, followed by the return of King Jesus. In theological circles, this is known as premillennialism, premillennial eschatology, or premillennial dispensationalism.

I never read the Left Behind books or watched the movies. I didn't need to because I'd seen older films with similar plotlines. In 1993, my parents sent me to a Baptist-run high school for tenth grade. I spent the next three years at Montrose Christian School in Rockville, Maryland. We had a regular Bible class in which I was treated to the end of the world films *A Thief in the Night* and its follow up, *A Distant Thunder*. The story follows a woman who finds her husband gone, "raptured" into heaven, while she has been left behind. She must survive the tribulation and avoid being given the "mark of the beast," which is a term found in the book of Revelation (16:2). The mark is being distributed by a one-world government set up by the United Nations. Those who resist are killed. Most memorable by far, they are executed by guillotine. I watched tearful Christians being hauled to their deaths by UN soldiers in blue helmets. The production values were low, but the message was clear: follow Jesus now, because if you get left behind, you'll be hunted by the one-world government and the forces of the antichrist.

Revelation is recognized by most Bible scholars to be a book of metaphorical imagery, not a literal description of future events. Nonetheless, millions of Christians have chosen to read it as a road map for the future. Many saw the books and movies as one of the producers did: as a "true story" that "just hasn't happened yet."[5] The books sold as many copies as the Hunger Games series.[6]

5. Dave McNary, "Nicolas Cage's 'Left Behind' Set for Oct. 3 Release," *Variety*, March 28, 2014, https://variety.com/2014/film/news/nicolas-cages-christian -drama-left-behind-set-for-oct-3-release-exclusive-1201149715/.
6. Alissa Wilkinson, "The 'Left Behind' Series Was Just the Latest Way America Prepared for the Rapture," *Washington Post*, July 13, 2016, https://www.wash

My teenage brain was of two minds about all this. I thought much of it was silly, but I also was surrounded by people who believed it and so these ideas were swimming around in my brain when I left for South America. The ideas functioned more as archetypes and myths, shaping the imaginations of many evangelicals like myself. The metanarrative about the evils of a one-world government is a long-standing trope among conspiracy theorists that goes back over a century and overlaps with some of the most dominant strains of anti-Semitism.[7] But this fear of a "New World Order"—to use one particular label that's often bandied about—is seeded through evangelical culture and then makes millions of religious Americans suspicious of any efforts by its government to cooperate with other nations. It is a powerful force for isolationism and antimodernism. It's why such seemingly innocuous labels like "globalist" can be wielded with such potency among many on the political right.

Growing up, I was so ensconced in my church bubble that I didn't see the connections between our private beliefs and the real-world impacts that resulted from them. I was actively, aggressively encouraged to stay in my bubble and not to question anything about it.

---

ingtonpost.com/news/act-four/wp/2016/07/13/the-left-behind-series-was-just-the-latest-way-america-prepared-for-the-rapture/.

7. "A Brief History of Antisemitism," originally published in Grosfeld Family National Youth Leadership Mission Guide (New York: Anti-Defamation League, 2018), https://www.adl.org/sites/default/files/brief-history-of-antisemitism.pdf.

5

Surrender

My dad pulled his car into the parking lot, and the chords to Warren Zevon's "Werewolves of London" came on the radio. But the words were different. Even my zoned-out teenage brain noticed it. The chorus had been changed to "werewolves in Congress." Then the booming voice of Rush Limbaugh came on. It was the early 1990s, and El Rushbo was new to national fame. You could have told me he'd been on the radio for twenty years and I would have believed you. Bill Clinton had been elected president after twelve years of Republicans in the White House. He was the first Democratic president in office since my dad, now forty or so, had started voting Republican in 1980.

Limbaugh regaled us with the hilarity of the Clintons. I was quickly turned off by the unceasing negativity. Sure, he was funny. But it was an acerbic, acidic humor. There was not much joy. I liked people who were for something, not animated by being against something. I wondered what he was excited about and why he didn't talk more on those topics rather than obsessing over someone he hated. It was my first lesson in the power of anger and fear.

I worked for my dad around the office during high school. Every day I was there, the fax machine would get a message from Gary

Bauer's political organization, the Christian Coalition. Bauer was a political operative turned policy wonk who had written a report for Reagan in the late 1980s on the importance of preserving the "traditional family." He was a Southern Baptist who had morphed into a professional culture warrior. In the mid-1990s, he was plotting a 2000 presidential bid, which is why he was sending faxes out all over the country.

The early 1990s combined Bauer's iteration of the Christian right and its methods for reaching people together with two other forces: the newly ascendant Limbaugh and the Republican renegades in Congress led by Newt Gingrich. Gingrich was a congressman from Georgia who revolutionized Republican politics and led the GOP to retake control of the House of Representatives for the first time in forty years. It was a political earthquake, made possible by his new, no-holds-barred tactics that prioritized theater and personal attacks over sober, responsible policymaking. It was justified, many Republican leaders and voters thought, by the increasing liberalism of Democrats, personified by President Clinton and the health-care law he and his wife, Hillary, were trying to pass.

I didn't understand then how few things bring people together like hating and fearing the same enemy. After the fall of the Soviet Union in 1991, Republicans needed a new foe. For decades, communism had been the bogeyman hiding behind every bush, providing cohesion and purpose. When the Iron Curtain fell, the communists were no longer a threat. So the Republican Party turned its enmity en masse toward the Clintons and their supporters.

My dad was trying to spend more time with me in those days because my parents were worried about me. Now that I was at Montrose Christian School for tenth grade, it was the first time I had escaped the highly controlled church environment. I was listening to rap music and growing more distant from my mom and dad. And Montrose seemed like something of a destination for kids who'd been kicked out of other schools. I mostly ended up hanging out with solid kids who didn't get into trouble, kids who listened to Pearl Jam and Nirvana and Live. But I flirted with trouble, and there were a few characters who seemed to find it consistently.

One day at the cafeteria vending machine, Bryan, the most popular kid in school, came up to me and said something nice about my clothes. I walked on air that day. Bryan didn't look athletic, but he had a quick crossover dribble, he could shoot, and he was cunning. I made the varsity basketball team as a sophomore. Bryan was on the team, even if he was often unable to play due to injuries or suspensions for bad behavior. It was thrilling and unnerving to be around Bryan. Every room gravitated around him, and it was intoxicating to get close to that whirling center of power. But if you were unfortunate enough to be the object of his ridicule, it was a memorable experience, and one often had the feeling that such a turn could come at any moment.

I wasn't close to Bryan, but he was good friends with my best friend, Steve, and I was one year behind them both. So Bryan was usually nice to me. At one point, he recruited me into looking through car windows in search of stereo systems or other electronics he could steal. I did it once, but my heart wasn't really in it. I knew I shouldn't be doing it. Another time Bryan, Steve, and I sat outside the house of Steve's ex-girlfriend, talking about beating up some guy who was dating her. But we never saw the guy, and we left. I was a pretend tough guy.

Bryan was not. Twenty years later, his body was found in the trunk of his car.[1] He'd been shot twice in the back of the head by his crime partner in a large-scale drug ring.[2] He left behind a wife and two young kids.

But the main reason my parents should have been concerned about me in high school was because my religious upbringing had given me lots of training in how to feel and what to believe but very little in how to think. Jesus instructed his followers to "love the Lord your God with all your heart and with all your soul and

1. Tim Pratt, "Crofton Man Gets Life-Plus 20 for 2012 Murder," *Capital Gazette*, August 5, 2014, https://www.capitalgazette.com/news/ph-ac-murder -sentencing-20140805-story.html.
2. "Police Tracked Md. Drug Dealer for Weeks before Body Was Found in Truck," *Associated Press*, February 4, 2013, https://baltimore.cbslocal.com/2013/02 /14/police-had-tracked-md-drug-dealer-for-weeks-before-body-found-in-truck/.

with all your mind" (Matt. 22:37). We were quite good at the heart and soul part. But the mind had somehow been neglected.

The roots of evangelical anti-intellectualism run deep. Historian Frances FitzGerald describes evangelicalism as "a distinct form of Protestantism" that "swept back and forth across the English-speaking world and Northern Europe in the eighteenth and nineteenth centuries." It is characterized, FitzGerald writes, by "an effort to recover an authentic spiritual experience: a religion of the heart, as opposed to the head."[3]

In an agrarian age and in the frontier environments of American expansion, these "activistic, populist, pragmatic and utilitarian" impulses did not have too many downsides.[4] But anti-intellectualism became more of a liability as the world industrialized and moved into a global, knowledge-based system of economies and cultures. "The Evangelical Protestant mind has never relished complexity," wrote religion scholar N. K. Clifford in 1973. "Indeed, its crusading genius, whether in religion or politics, has always tended to an over-simplification of issues and the substitution of inspiration and zeal for critical analysis and serious reflection."[5]

In the life of many churches, the habits of anti-intellectualism are planted early. Children are encouraged to open themselves up to the influence of God. And once they do so, they are told—with great specificity—what God's will is. When they are young, they often don't realize that what is represented as God's will is really just the views and preferences of those in charge. Adherents may be encouraged to surrender not just their will but also their independence of thought. They may use their intellect, but only within the narrow strictures set up by the rules and teachings of the leaders.

The notion of surrender and submission to God is a noble one. There is something beautiful, releasing, and cleansing about

3. Frances FitzGerald, *The Evangelicals: The Struggle to Shape America* (New York: Simon & Schuster, 2017), 13.
4. Mark A. Noll, *The Scandal of the Evangelical Mind* (Grand Rapids: Eerdmans, 1994), 12.
5. N. K. Clifford, "His Dominion: A Vision in Crisis," *Studies in Religion/ Sciences Religieuses* 2 (1973): 323.

surrender. And when a person wrestles in a prayer service or during a time of singing with the notion that they are holding something back from God—and all he wants to do is love them, but he must have all of them—it is a deeply personal and moving encounter. But surrender of the will too often becomes surrender of the mind. The call to surrender to God was used to strong-arm me and my peers into accepting, without question, what we were told by adults. Throw in the notion that if you do not surrender you may burn in hell, and that keeps most kids in line.

The scariest message many adults told me growing up was that if I was "lukewarm," God would reject me. This was the most effective talking point to push me and my peers toward an all-or-nothing mindset. I often heard pastors and others quote from Revelation, from a vision that the book's author, John, wrote down. The Lord, John said, told him to write to one church in particular these words: "You are neither cold nor hot. I wish you were either one or the other! So, because you are lukewarm—neither hot nor cold—I am about to spit you out of my mouth" (3:15–16).

The way this vision was taught in my circles promoted absolutism. There was no room for nuance. There was no allowance for complexity or shades of gray. You were either all in with what the leaders said to do, which they said was God's will, or you were out. The heroes and stories we held in high esteem also buttressed this notion. One of my dad's favorite heroes in the faith was a guy named Jim Elliot, an all-American type who went to the jungles of Ecuador to convert indigenous tribes to Christianity and ended up floating in a river with a spear in his back. "He is no fool who gives up what he cannot keep to gain what he cannot lose," Elliot said.[6] Dad repeated that quote all the time with a wistful look in his eye.

One day I had a conversation with a pastor at Covenant Life Church, a kindly man, bookish, a bit impish. He had been at the church since the beginning with my parents. I asked him a question, and he stood askew, as if he were walking somewhere and had

---

6. Tim Chester, "Jim Elliot Was No Fool," *Crossway,* January 18, 2018, https://www.crossway.org/articles/jim-elliot-was-no-fool/.

stopped to speak with me, but only for a moment. As we talked, I mentioned the idea of my subconscious. I remember as clear as day that he arched his eyebrows and asked me what I thought the subconscious was. The implication was clear: he thought there was no such thing, that people who talked like that believed in psychology and diagnosing misbehavior rather than categorizing it into some form of sin. All of that transpired in a few moments as I tried to process this strange form of gaslighting, in which a gentle, middle-aged man told me that, no, there is no such thing as a subconscious. The subconscious was outside our leaders' expertise and thus outside their control. So it was better for them if it did not exist at all.

For church leaders, the idea of surrendering to God is a velvet hammer sitting right there out in the open, for easy use anytime. You don't like my decision? Well, you need to submit to God's will. It was never said that bluntly, of course. We developed elaborate rituals and a pseudospiritual language all our own that could be used to corner and subdue anyone who questioned the accepted beliefs. And it was no doubt easy for the leaders who oversaw my Christian training—in school, at church, at home—to confuse the notion of submission to God with the idea of intellectual surrender. They didn't have much incentive to separate the two.

Here's a typical Friday night youth group meeting. After the songs had been sung and the sermon had been preached and the eyes were closed (by most) and the mood was soft, the pastor would come up on stage and lay it on thick. "How many of you are still holding something back from God? He wants all of you!" The problem is, he would say this to thirteen-year-olds who had no clue who they were yet. So to say, "I give all of myself to God" can easily morph into "I give all of myself to whatever the leaders tell me to do." Talk of surrender is more credible, and a lot more respectful of each child's humanity, if leaders are also giving young people critical thinking skills. Why not teach them Bible basics and the creeds while giving the child space to think for themselves, without emotional manipulation? Well, I can think of a reason. It's harder to control kids that way.

The ironic thing is that many charismatic or Pentecostal Christians think of themselves as free and look down on others who are more restrained as being under a "spirit of control." They fail to see how their focus on expressiveness can be its own form of manipulation, a shortcut to keeping young people in church by engaging their emotions without helping them grapple with the hard questions of life and faith.

In my world, giving all of myself to God meant doing everything those in authority told me to do and thinking everything they told me to think. I resisted in some ways, but there was only so much you could do.

In the early 1990s, Covenant Life Church was caught up in a phenomenon that, at its most extreme, prompted adults to crawl around in church sanctuaries barking like dogs. There was a faddish movement among many evangelical churches toward extreme "manifestations" of the Holy Spirit, and animal noises were one of them. I'm not sure anyone ever barked at our church. The most I ever saw were people lapsing into hysterical laughter and falling over as if having fainted, then lying on the ground for long periods of time. But this became the norm for us on Sundays, for a period of several months. I was not into it. I was more interested in my high school sports career. But I did have my brushes with this bizarre period, which is best known by its association with two places: Toronto and Pensacola, Florida.

The Toronto Blessing began early in 1994, and the Brownsville Revival in Pensacola, Florida, picked up in 1995. They were the epicenters of what some Christians believed was a genuine revival. The hallmarks were outlandish performative expressions. *Toronto Star* reporter Leslie Scrivener described one service of the Airport Vineyard church inside the Regal Constellation Hotel in a dispatch filed October 8, 1995:

> The ballroom carpets were littered with fallen bodies, bodies of seemingly straightlaced men and women who felt themselves moved by the phenomenon they say is the Holy Spirit. So moved, they

howled with joy or the release of some buried pain. They collapsed, some rigid as corpses, some convulsed in hysterical laughter. From room to room come barnyard cries, calls heard only in the wild, grunts so deep women recalled the sounds of childbirth, while some men and women adopted the very position of childbirth. Men did chicken walks. Women jabbed their fingers as if afflicted with nervous disorders. And around these scenes of bedlam, were loving arms to catch the falling, smiling faces, whispered prayers of encouragement, instructions to release, to let go.[7]

At some point in 1994, C. J. Mahaney reportedly preached in Missouri at a church where the congregation began to laugh uncontrollably.[8] When C. J. returned to Gaithersburg, our church followed suit. We began to make it a habit to have extended periods of time after each service when people went to the front of the auditorium to be "slain in the Spirit." Volunteers would watch as people came forward for prayer, catch them when they fell to the ground, and then cover them with white sheets to make them more comfortable, similar to the way Scrivener described it.

At one church conference in 1995, I sat in the bleachers looking down at the stage and watched scores of people going to the front and falling down like dominoes as the speaker walked past them, holding his hand out toward them. It was, in retrospect, either an incredible miracle or a sign of mass psychosis.

Out in California, Lou Engle and Ché Ahn were in their element. This was the revival they had been waiting for. In 1994, they started a church together called Harvest Rock Church on the outskirts of Los Angeles in Pasadena. They held meetings in someone's house, and their attendance grew exponentially, just like in the beginning of Take and Give. After a year, they were hosting gatherings of two thousand people and began doing church services five nights a week, which continued for three years. In 1996,

7. Quoted in Margaret M. Poloma, "The Spirit and the Bride: The 'Toronto Blessing' and Church Structure," *Evangelical Studies Bulletin* 13, no. 4 (Winter 1999), http://hirr.hartsem.edu/research/pentecostalism_polomaart6.html.

8. Dan Bowen, "A Bit of History . . . ," *Life on Wings: A Tribute to Dr. Ern Baxter*, February 10, 2006, https://ern-baxter.blogspot.com/2006/02/bit-of-history.html.

Engle got the idea to start a prayer service that would never stop. It would keep going twenty-four hours a day, seven days a week.[9] This became known as a "burn service."

It is easy to ridicule the people who seek these kinds of religious experiences, but there is great human pathos at play. Charismatic worship offers an outlet for people to express their deepest longings, experience intense catharsis, and receive inner fuel that feeds them for days, weeks, or years. It is also a place where true care is expressed from one person to another, whether in a tearful embrace, in praying for one another, or in sitting with someone as they process trauma they have experienced in their life. It is no wonder, in light of this, that so many humans around the world are drawn to this type of religious experience.

The problem arises when intense experience becomes the point or the main emphasis and pushes other things aside, such as critical thought. And once a group of people experiences these emotional highs, it can become almost like an addiction. I also think it's a mistake to believe that these settings have some kind of special purchase on the presence of God, as if he can be conjured up by skillful music or mood-setting. If God's presence is a thing that can be manifested in unusually powerful ways, then it would most naturally show up in slums and homeless shelters. The presence of God means far more than warm feelings of euphoria or a sense of emotional safety.

I went up to the front of the auditorium during a church service to be prayed for one time during this period. My parents were with me. I don't remember whose idea it was. It somehow turned out that C. J. was the one who prayed for me. I closed my eyes as he prayed for me to experience God's presence, but I didn't feel anything. It's noteworthy, by the way, that this was the benchmark: Was I feeling something? That was our barometer for authentic spirituality. C. J. had been praying for a few minutes, and it was starting to drag on I guess, because all of a sudden he put his fingers

---

9. Harvest Rock Church, "Our Story," accessed April 3, 2022, https://www.harvestrock.church/about.

on my forehead and began to push lightly against my head, as if to signal that it was "time" for me to "fall down."

I didn't want to disappoint. Down I went. But I felt like such a fraud. It didn't even occur to me to consider whether C. J. might be one too.

―――――――

After I graduated high school in 1995, I had no help figuring out how to get into college or where to go. My parents were dealing with being new parents again, adding their sixth and seventh kids in 1991 and 1993, both boys. My high school didn't have a guidance counselor. And my church community didn't want kids going to college unless they could live with their parents and commute, because otherwise we might start conducting satanic rituals and having sex. I don't remember if I ever even talked to my parents about college. I'm sure we discussed it. But a discussion would have been the extent of it. There was no process to figure out where I might go, so by default I did the closest, easiest thing.

My parents said they would pay half the tuition if I stayed local, and honestly, if I was going to pay for half, community college was fine with me. I had no clue what I wanted to study, so I preferred to spend as little money as possible the first year or two. Montgomery College was about fifteen minutes from my parents' house, and I continued to do some work for my dad. Eventually, I got other jobs, but my universe remained quite small.

But in community college, my interests in writing, literature, and history began to emerge. I began to discover that I could have fun without the earth opening up and swallowing me. Molson Ice was the first beer I tasted. Steve and I discovered that a drive-through in Prince George's County would sell thirty-packs of Icehouse to us. We took trips to Ocean City, Maryland, and mixed Absolut vodka into store-bought iced tea bottles. Alcohol was frowned upon in our house. Once, my mother found a shoebox filled with cans of beer hidden under a table in my room. She simply left me a note that said, "This is wrong, and you know it."

I was pretty terrified of girls and also of going to hell if I kissed one. Every year in high school had followed a similar arc: I'd develop a crush and enjoy the thrill of the chase, only to find myself completely nonplussed when it turned out she liked me too. What now? The only girl in high school who I had a moderately normal relationship with was a cheerleader named Dana: beautiful, smart, no-nonsense. We actually did spend time together, like friends. I was attracted to her and enjoyed hanging out. There were at least a handful of times when I stayed at her house late into the night, and we lay on her bed, talking. I never touched her, and years later a mutual friend told me she had assumed I was gay. I was just scared. I was inexperienced and didn't know what to do, but I was also terrified that God would do something terrible to me if I kissed her.

In college, I made clumsy forays into the world of women. One night I met Dana at a bar, and she introduced me to a friend of hers. Dana and I both left, and I drove home on Interstate 270 thinking about how much I'd liked her friend. It felt like a seismic decision to exit the highway, turn around, and drive back to the bar to tell her whatever it was I told her. I'm sure I was incredibly direct and far too honest. We ended up back at her place that night making out.

I was wracked with guilt. After seeing her a few more times, I cut things off entirely, again with a straightforward explanation. In so many words, I told her that I liked her, but it was against my faith to have a girlfriend who wasn't a Christian. I didn't want to get invested to the point where I had to choose her or my faith. It was years before I would even touch another woman.

6

Radicalized

My life changed dramatically in the spring of 1997 on an annual road trip. Every Memorial Day weekend my family packed up the car and drove four hours to Indiana, Pennsylvania: birthplace of Jimmy Stewart and home to Indiana University of Pennsylvania, or IUP. We passed by miles of rural countryside to get there, and I'd look out the window and wonder who in the world lived in those houses in the middle of nowhere.

I can still hear the roar of motorcycles on the highway from those trips too, always going the opposite direction: down to DC as we went north. That's because in 1988, around the same time that we Christians started making pilgrimages to IUP for the Celebration conference, veterans started riding to DC on Memorial Day weekend to hold a remembrance at the Vietnam Memorial for prisoners of war and the brothers they lost overseas. We'd be heading north to pray and sing, and they'd be caravanning south to mourn and take the sacraments of whiskey and gin.

The IUP campus was pretty big, especially to a kid. There was a recreation center with several basketball and volleyball courts. There was a football stadium similar to those at Texas high schools.

And there was a cafeteria with all-you-could-eat meals and unlimited ice cream and soda.

My middle school dramas played out in that little universe. And as I got into high school, the holiday weekend became an endless series of pickup basketball games and watching Michael Jordan take the Chicago Bulls through the Eastern Conference finals. Around the time I hit ten years old or so, my friends and I were given free rein to run around by ourselves. It was heaven. The weekend was a welcome escape, a time when kids like me could cut loose, for once. During the normal routine of my life, everything was constricted and controlled: our behavior, our speech, even our thinking. We were watched—by our parents, our parents' friends, our teachers, our pastors—and corrected for the slightest missteps.

The church services were held in a gymnasium twice a day, with people filling the chairs on the floor and most of the bleachers as well. There were probably between two to three thousand people. It was usually sweltering hot. The meetings followed a pattern. We'd start off with celebratory music and do that for thirty minutes or so, singing and clapping and raising our hands and—if things got really rocking—jumping up and down. Then a preacher would talk for an hour. After this there would be more music and singing while people went forward for prayer.

In 1997 I drove up to the Celebration conference with friends, camping for a day or two beforehand. I had finished two years of community college and was preparing to attend the University of Maryland in the fall. Over the spring, I had been under pressure to get more involved in church. It was gentle and friendly, but it was pressure nonetheless. C. J. Mahaney and the other pastors had decided to hire some new staff to focus specifically on college-age kids. One of these new hires got coffee with me numerous times. We went through a book, and he patiently explained his understanding of Christianity to me. I was still living at home and going to church most Sundays, so the nudges from my family and from pastors who saw me at services—to go to the new meetings organized for students at the community college—were constant.

I began to read my Bible more regularly and to go off by myself to pray and journal. On our camping trip, I sat on a large rock in the woods next to a stream. I told God that as I faced decisions over the next several years that would shape my life, I needed his help in making them. I felt the weight of finding my way and believed that if I tried to do it on my own, I'd get lost or take the wrong path. I prayed for help.

At the conference, C. J. preached about Jesus's death on the cross. I heard it with a new clarity. He rarely preached about anything else, and intentionally so. The church culture he presided over was anti-intellectual in a lot of ways, but C. J. read a lot and encouraged his congregants to do the same. He emphasized the church bookstore and often talked about what he was reading at the time. C. J. believed that most preachers neglected a proper focus on the crucifixion and what it represents: the "propitiation" of God's wrath against sin. He placed the crucifixion in a heavily legal setting. God was the judge. We were the defendants. We faced a death sentence. Jesus volunteered to be punished in our place. But he also gave his status as God's Son to us. So the judge went from being ready to sentence us to a terrible punishment to adopting us as his children.

C. J. cried almost every time he delivered a sermon. It wasn't just a tear or two, or momentary. It was long, extended weepiness. He would take the kind of intensity that many people sought out while music was playing and carry it over to describing the physical and spiritual torture that Christ endured on our behalf.

I still have my notes from May 24, 1997, which I took in a ruled memo book. "I feel as if Jesus died yesterday," C. J. said. He told us that we should be able to identify our face in the crowd calling on Pontius Pilate for Barabbas to be released and for Jesus to be crucified. "Before we can identify that the cross was for us, we must understand that it was by us. . . . Jesus drained the cup of [God's] wrath so that we might not have a drop," he said.

The message of the cross gripped me more than it ever had. As I sat in those bleachers, suddenly I felt as if I had no choice but to throw everything aside that would hinder me from living every moment of my life for God. It was to be total and absolute. From that moment, I was radicalized. I was "on fire." I had a clarity about my purpose in life, and I took extreme measures to pursue it. I stopped hanging out with my best friend, Steve, because he drank alcohol and didn't listen to Christian music all the time and didn't read the Bible every day. I became a fanatic. Part of this fanaticism was trying to match the fervor of those meetings in Pennsylvania. Sustaining the emotional intensity became a marker for whether I was excelling at being a Christian or not. And excelling was important to me. I was competitive, driven, ambitious. Our family mythology encouraged this. But at this point in my life, I'd nearly exhausted the sports route. I'd done pretty well in my two years of playing junior college baseball and thought I might try to walk on at Maryland the coming fall. But it was a long shot. So I poured all my energy into spiritual achievement.

For years I interpreted the events of 1997 through the well-worn grooves of storytelling that are passed down from churchgoing generation to generation. I understood my story as simply miraculous. Now I cannot help but notice the ways in which even before I went to the Celebration conference, the net was closing in around me, pulled by human beings who were being paid to make sure my peers and I got more involved in the church. And I was an easy catch. Pulling me further into the only community I'd ever known wasn't that hard.

I believe miracles can and sometimes do happen. But sometimes we are simply acted on by other people and the worlds they've created, and we call it a miracle. Being open to both is balancing faith and reason. It's not something I was taught growing up.

There wasn't enough money for me to live on or near campus at the University of Maryland, and I had little desire to do so. I was spending all my spare time doing church-related things. I went to endless meetings. Each week we met in someone's house to pray, sing songs, read the Bible, and talk about God.

The only thing that saved me from being entirely lost in this world was going to class in College Park, where one professor in particular had a formative influence on me. Michael Olmert was a Shakespeare scholar who lit my mind on fire with a love of learning. He encouraged my curiosity and my passion for writing with verve and personality, with enthusiasm. He and a few other professors broadened my horizons and showed me that there was a wider world than the small hamlet in which I was cloistered at the moment. Even though there were days I sat in his class drugged out by a combo of Benadryl for my pollen allergies and a huge cup of coffee—I didn't know about nondrowsy medications—there was no escaping the profound excitement of what was happening to me in Olmert's classes.

Olmert taught me about the *Times Literary Supplement*, playwright Alan Bennett, and *The Oxford English Dictionary (OED)*. I wrote an entire three-page paper on the etymology of the word *saucy*, using nothing but the *OED*'s history of the word. Another professor introduced me to the *New Yorker*. I began to see broad pastures outside the confines of church culture and found ways to use my brain and my affinity for writing to explore those avenues. This was a way to love and to be loved, to express wonder and follow curiosity and ask the big questions and communicate the nuance of life. And there was so much beauty in the world that contrasted with the truly soulless aesthetics of nondenominational Christianity.

The Jesus Movement had completely rejected all the trappings of high-church ecclesiology. When Covenant Life Church (CLC) raised millions of dollars and built its own sanctuary in 1993, there was almost nothing to indicate it was a church. The decorating scheme was a flat palette of non-colors. There were few decorations and no paintings or art of any kind that I remember. It had a corporate feel, much like the megachurch model pioneered by Willow Creek Community Church in Illinois.

It would take me many years to make the connection between this aesthetic emptiness and a deeper truth. The CLC church building was just one reflection of a deep and subtle Gnosticism that permeates, still to this day, the White evangelical tradition in which I was raised and formed. Gnosticism is a centuries-old way of thinking about the world that in its purest form is considered by Christian theologians to be a heresy. Essentially, according to this thinking, the physical world is of little value compared to the spiritual realm. Much of this thinking derives from fundamentalists' excessive focus on escaping the world by going to heaven rather than being a good neighbor and working for the common good on earth.

This Gnosticism is fueled by the evangelical obsession with euphoria, because emotional highs are understood as obedience to God, and it is virtually impossible to live in the real world while riding a wave of spiritual ecstasy. Those mornings when I danced and yelled and sang in my parents' basement, I thought this was a way to please God. In fact, I thought if I wasn't in love with God—having these intense emotions about him—I was letting him down. I had been told that God wanted me to praise him all the time. I was a twenty-year-old with little life experience, raised in a religious bubble, who for the first time in his life felt passionate about the teachings that had been drilled into me for my entire young life. I wanted to keep the feelings going. It seemed like I had deep, intense purpose for the first time in my life. And I thought this was how I made God happy, or made him love me, or how I fulfilled my purpose in life.

But because I was so well-versed in the Bible, I also knew that Jesus had prayed that God would keep us Christians "in the world but not of the world." It's a rough translation of a prayer Christ prayed—the night before he was executed in fact—that is recorded in the Gospel of John. He speaks to God about his followers: "My prayer is not that you take them out of the world but that you protect them from the evil one. They are not of the world, even as I am not of it. . . . As you sent me into the world, I have sent them into the world" (17:15–16, 18). This is Christ calling all Christians to be *mearcstapas*, border-stalkers, moving back and forth between and among different groups and tribes.

For much of my childhood, being "in but not of the world" was not a big deal because I wasn't all that serious about my faith.

But when I entered my phase of fanaticism, it became difficult to sustain my spiritual high while going to college and fulfilling my responsibilities. It is hard to live a religious life centered on the demand to feel happy and joyous while at the same time following Christ's example to be fully present in the world, facing reality and actively moving to be an agent of healing, restoration, and peacemaking. How do you keep a happy outlook while staring suffering in the face?

I still fiercely believed that C. S. Lewis was right when he said that the world didn't need more Christian writers. We don't need more books and essays, or music and art for that matter, that merely tell religious people what they want to hear. "What we want is not more little books about Christianity, but more little books by Christians on other subjects—with their Christianity *latent*," Lewis wrote.[1] In other words, the best way to advance the Christian faith was to go out into the world and permeate it with the essence of Christ rather than trying to beat others over the head with a set of instructions or demands.

However, my church was trying to pull me closer into its orbit. Within a few months after my radicalizing experience at the Celebration conference, I was being groomed for leadership by C. J. and others in his circle.

---

1. Quoted in Terry Mattingly, "Beyond the Christian Ghetto: Why C. S. Lewis Has Endured," *Evangelical Press Association*, https://www.evangelicalpress.com/ghetto/.

7

The New Christian Right

I'm very excited to be going on this trip," I wrote on the plane ride to Austin. "There are so many benefits I will receive, none of which I deserve."

C. J. Mahaney invited me on a trip with him and a few others to Texas at the beginning of 1998. We were there to attend the second Passion conference for college students. It was held over the first few days of the New Year and organized by pastor Louie Giglio, a Christian minister who had spent the previous decade working with college students at Baylor University. Giglio had recently moved from Waco to Atlanta to help his ailing father. Over the next two decades, the Passion conferences would become massive, growing to a sixty-five-thousand-person event in 2022 inside Mercedes-Benz Stadium in Atlanta. But in 1998, there were just a few thousand of us.

Joshua Harris was one of the others who went to the conference with C. J. and me. Harris was two years older than I was and had arrived at Covenant Life Church a few months prior as a pastoral intern. But Harris was more than an intern. He'd already written a book, *I Kissed Dating Goodbye*, that would become a massive hit, selling over a million copies.[1] He was a talented speaker who already had years of experience addressing large gatherings. His father was a minor celebrity among homeschool families, and Harris had begun to speak at conferences with his dad. This 1998 trip to Austin inspired Harris to start his own event for college students over the New Year holiday, the New Attitude conference.

Harris hadn't grown up in Covenant Life Church and was not as primed as I was to accept the self-abasement that C. J. promoted. But I had bought in to the self-condemnation hook, line, and sinker. As I sat on the airplane, I wrote in my journal that I was reading a book called *The Holiness of God* by R. C. Sproul. I was learning, I wrote, that "I deserve nothing but justice, which is instant death. I didn't even deserve to even draw my first breath as a newborn." My reverence for C. J. was also apparent. I wanted to "ask him all kinds of questions." I noted exactly which seat he was sitting in: "one row ahead and two seats to my left."

The Passion conference left me wide-eyed. The music was amazing. I heard John Piper speak for the first time. He was a Baptist pastor based in Minneapolis, but he was a strange and rare bird: a bookish, incredibly intense theologian and writer who revered the Puritan pastor Jonathan Edwards. Piper's book *Desiring God* was one of the most formative I read during this time of my life. Piper made the case for "Christian hedonism," which was encapsulated in the phrase "God is most glorified in us when we are most satisfied in him." The basic point was that we shouldn't just obey God dutifully. Rather, we should seek to know and obey God out of self-interest, because in doing so we would find our deepest happiness. Piper in the late 1990s was already a significant figure in American evangelicalism, and he would become even more so over the next decade.

1. Harris would later recant the advice given in the book. See Leah MarieAnn Klett, "Joshua Harris Says 'I Kissed Dating Goodbye' Will Be Discontinued, Apologizes for 'Flaws,'" *The Christian Post*, October 23, 2018, https://www.christian post.com/news/joshua-harris-says-i-kissed-dating-goodbye-will-be-discontinued -apologizes-for-flaws.html.

In Austin, there were hundreds of young people around, staying up late, flirting, playing guitar, and listening to bands play coffee house sessions. I went to the breakout groups, where we sat around in groups of five or six and introduced ourselves and talked about our walks with God and our struggles with sin. All of these college students were there to be around other like-minded young people for a few days right around New Year's Eve to experience amazing worship and to hear powerhouse preaching. Giglio tapped into the idealism of young people and the desire for worship that people like me were experiencing. He oriented the conference around one verse of Scripture, Isaiah 26:8, which says, "Yes, LORD, walking in the way of your laws, we wait for you; your name and renown are the desire of our hearts."

The music was led by guys like Chris Tomlin, who would become one of the biggest names in Christian music over the next several years, along with Matt Redman and David Crowder. We sang songs like "I Could Sing of Your Love Forever," a song written the British band Delirious. Tomlin was an early architect of anthemic soft rock with simple chord structures and melodies that were catchy and could be played by most church bands.

Passion was the first time I'd seen young Christians keep up culturally with non-Christians. It would serve as a model for other, more conservative branches of Christianity, like Hillsong and Bethel. Hillsong and Bethel would each become a powerhouse of Christian worship music over the next twenty years. They produced music that was raw, vulnerable, and compelling. But the melodies masked the fact that the leaders of these two networks followed an apocalyptic theology that led to a reactionary political ideology.

Bill Johnson, the pastor of Bethel's flagship church in Redding, California, which is rooted in the Assemblies of God—the largest Pentecostal denomination in the world—has spent the past few decades leading his congregants in seeking the kind of supernatural experiences he had in Toronto in 1995. Johnson's father had been a pastor at Bethel previously. Johnson's defining paradigm, like that of Lou Engle and Ché Ahn, is fixated on the idea of dramatic revival and spiritual warfare. Johnson's church reported about eleven thousand members in 2018. Over ten thousand young people have spent at least a year in training at Bethel's School of Supernatural Ministry over the past twenty years, being coached in seeking faith healings, casting out demons, and making prophecies in which they proclaim to speak on God's behalf of God.

Giglio—while conservative on issues like abortion and sexuality and LGBTQ rights—was not a culture warrior and didn't view Democrats as evil. However, Bethel leaders viewed the world in Manichean terms, as a war between spiritual forces of good and evil. People were on one side or the other, and this meant their side was noble and righteous and the other side was evil and damned. Much of this war mentality came from their theology. They rejected the idea that the line between good and evil runs through the human heart. Rather, they saw the dividing line as running through an invisible world of angels and demons. So their language of "taking dominion" and "tearing down strongholds" had a deeper meaning. It made their political involvement more aggressive and harmful. Their certainty that they were doing the Lord's work discouraged introspection or nuance.

In 1999 a Kansas City pastor named Mike Bickle, a friend and peer of Engle, launched the International House of Prayer (IHOP), a church service that went twenty-four hours a day, seven days a week, just like Lou Engle's project in California. The idea, basically, was that God's power would be "poured out" in greater measure in response to a more intense effort to sing songs and pray continuously. These Christians—largely Pentecostal in practice and dispensationalist in theology—used the ancient biblical stories in the Old Testament about the Israelite people to give themselves archetypes for action. So they believed in things like the so-called Jehoshaphat principle, that "the worshipers go out ahead of the army to secure its spiritual victory through God's presence in praise," as Adam Perez, a religion scholar, explains.[2]

2. Adam Perez, "There's a Theology Driving Sean Feucht's Worship Music Protests—and It's a Popular One," *Religion News Service*, October 23, 2020,

They also believed they were securing blessings for their nation by singing because they emphasized Scripture passages like Psalm 22:3, which says that God "inhabiteth the praises" (KJV) of his people. Now that's hyper-literalism. It's also bad literary interpretation: reading a poem as if it is an instruction manual. But if people levied this criticism, they were accused of having a spirit of control or of resisting the Holy Spirit or of trying to stifle God's work.

Engle was one of the driving forces behind this new institutionalization of seeking intense religious experiences. Engle's brand of Pentecostalism was married with conservative politics. IHOP began to make two things routine: twenty-four-hour "burn services" that were aimed at ushering young people into the presence of God so they could "burn" with passion for Christ, and lengthy, ongoing prayer services aimed at the American political system. In particular, they would hold weeks-long prayer sessions in a location within a few blocks of the US Supreme Court to pray for the overturning of *Roe v. Wade*, the 1973 ruling that legalized abortion.

In this IHOP movement were the seeds of a new iteration of the Christian right. The kids of the Moral Majority types would not be culturally uncool. They would look the same and sound the same as their peers when it came to fashion or cultural tastes. They had tattoos and maybe drank alcohol. But their parents or pastors still indoctrinated them with their religious and political beliefs. The new Moral Majority would not be a man in a suit and tie taking his freshly scrubbed wife and children to church on Sunday. Instead, it would be a bearded hipster with shoulder-length hair in a slightly more egalitarian marriage whose kids skateboarded and listened to the same music and watched the same movies as their non-church friends. And the bridge between the old Moral Majority and the new one would be a sophisticated network of artistically talented musicians.

---

https://religionnews.com/2020/10/23/theres-a-theology-driving-sean-feuchts-worship-music-protests-and-its-a-popular-one/.

Bethel and Hillsong pumped out artists and albums relentlessly in the decade between 2010 and 2020, churning out songs that supplied devout believers with material for their Sunday services as well as a soundtrack for their lives. These songs were played in homes, in cars, while running, while waking up early to pray and read the Bible. The music tapped into people's yearning for peace and joy and connection to the divine.

This ability to usher people into what is perceived to be a visceral experience of God's presence is probably the most powerful element in evangelical culture. Evangelicals are often very skilled at creating environments in which people feel close to God. I'm deeply grateful that I have the capacity to tap into this openness to divinity from the many years I spent in that world. But over time, it became more and more clear to me that this whole world was part of the problem I was increasingly seeing. The music was central to an overemphasis on emotional experience. I came to believe that this was antithetical to following Christ. It encouraged the Christian to think of their faith as a self-centered, consumeristic, emotion-focused pursuit. The songs were written and promoted by leaders who rejected critical thinking and basic but crucial measures of wisdom like epistemological modesty. These leaders instead pointed their followers toward chasing spectacular spiritual feats that took them further and further away from a faithful Christian presence in the real world.

Back home in Maryland, things were decidedly less glamorous than they had been in Austin. I was placed in a small group with other young adults my age, and a fortysomething realtor was placed in charge. He was awkward but kind and did his best to wrangle us all each week when we met in a friend's basement.

One evening someone decided that a woman who was several years older than the rest of us should speak in tongues. Many Christians believe speaking in tongues is a manifestation of God's presence in someone's life and that it is a form of prayer that comes from so far inside one's soul that it is beyond the ability of language to express. It may have been that she said she wanted to do this. Regardless, we ended up standing in a loose circle around her, with someone playing a guitar, closing our eyes and praying. Some people placed their hands on her shoulders. We started singing a praise song.

Then our group leader decided he'd heard a message from God. He told her he could see her standing in front of a wall or fence, that it was keeping her from experiencing God more fully. "I just feel like God wants you to jump over the wall. Jump over the wall!"

We kept waiting for her to break out into a spasm of gibberish that sounded like Holy Spirit language. The leader kept talking about the wall and how she needed to climb or jump over it. But she couldn't. She stood there as the minutes ticked on, an uncomfortable expression on her face. Eventually, the music died down and we gave up.

Another time I actually broke out into spontaneous singing during a portion of a house meeting when our guitar player was strumming, and we were standing around with eyes closed and "making room for the Holy Spirit." We called what I did a "prophetic song." I kept thinking of one pastor who always said we should "lean forward" into saying yes to any premonition that came into our heads during these times. I don't remember what I sang about, but I do remember it being a very uncomfortable experience. I also remember being mocked about it for years. But I desperately wanted to please God.

8

Suffocation

S o if I got in a car accident, it would be because God planned
it, right?" I asked. I was eager to show off my knowledge.
        The man at the head of the long table shifted in his seat
and looked uncomfortable.

"I think that's taking it too far," he said.

I didn't press the issue that morning, but I was confused. I
was simply applying basic logic to the things we were reading in
the men's discipleship group. We met on Saturdays at 7 a.m. in a
conference room at the church. There were a dozen or so of us,
all guys, all college age or so. A pastor named Kenneth led the
group. He had been the one to ask me to come and who shot down
my theory. He photocopied long chapters out of a book called
Systematic Theology by Wayne Grudem, and this week we were
discussing the chapter on Grudem's view of providence.

Grudem was a Calvinist, believing that God oversees and plans
everything, including who will become a Christian and who will
not. This is how he defined "providence" in the book: "God is
continually involved with all created things in such a way that he
(1) keeps them existing and maintaining the properties with which
he created them; (2) cooperates with created things in every action,

directing their distinctive properties to cause them to act as they do; and (3) directs them to fulfill his purposes."[1]

Calvinism traces its roots back to the French theologian John Calvin, who lived in the first half of the sixteenth century. It is often described in five points, referred to by the acronym TULIP. This stands for total depravity, unconditional election, limited atonement, irresistible grace, and perseverance of the saints. In short, humans are fully and hopelessly corrupt and sinful; God chooses those he will save from eternal punishment; Jesus's death was only for those God chose to save before the beginning of time and not for all; those whom God does choose cannot resist being "regenerated"; and the test of those who are truly saved is whether they stick with the faith or not.

I was thrilled to discover a rigorous and intellectual approach to faith. It seemed to explain so much. I loved going to the discipleship group on Saturday mornings. It fed my need for intellectual stimulation, and I enjoyed the camaraderie. I became good friends with many of the guys in the group. We joked around a lot. Much of our humor was buffoonish. One morning people starting throwing bagels around, and I balled up a piece of bagel into a pretty solid little ball and chucked it at my friend's head. It hit him right between the eyes, and the room exploded into laughter. We were sexually frustrated guys in our early twenties. Most of us were not married or dating.

Grudem's book, released in 1994, helped our church take a hard turn toward Calvinist theology. Grudem was then a professor of theology at one of the biggest evangelical seminaries in the United States, Trinity Evangelical Divinity School. Grudem had gone to Harvard as an undergrad and had a PhD in New Testament studies from the University of Cambridge. He would become one of the most influential conservative theologians in the country over the next thirty years, fighting to spread the view that women are subservient to men (but equal in value!). In 2016, he became a

---

1. Wayne Grudem, *Systematic Theology: An Introduction to Biblical Doctrine* (Grand Rapids: Zondervan Academic, 1994), 315.

prominent defender of Donald Trump's presidential candidacy. But in the mid-1990s, Grudem's book helped ignite the next significant movement within White conservative evangelicalism: the New Calvinism. I had a front-row seat to how this movement took off and was a part of it early on.

Our church's turn toward Calvinism took us away from the charismatic expressionism that had been a hallmark since I was a child. Even when Covenant Life and many other churches in C. J.'s movement were caught up in the Pentecostal movement of laughing and falling down, C. J. was already gravitating toward Calvinism.

It was called the New Calvinism because it had been out of favor for a while but was catching on among younger men like myself.[2] But it turned me and everyone else in on ourselves in an endless search for imperfections. If we were totally depraved, there was no end to the work we could do to search out the ways in which we were actively offending God and to be in constant repentance. We called this the "doctrine of indwelling sin." The church organized daylong seminars where speakers would help people diagram the ways their own hearts and minds were rotted through with evil. Even I thought these trainings were a bit much. But I was still drawn to the dense writings of Puritan theologians like Jonathan Edwards and John Owen. No one ever mentioned that Edwards enslaved Black people.

The Calvinist theology was an even more effective instrument for controlling people than the teaching of surrender to God's will. Any time someone said or did something that a person in power above them didn't like, there was always an easy way to stop them: thank them for their loving-kindness in speaking up, and then raise the question of whether some sinful impulse was behind their words. And if they didn't listen, they were being proud and unteachable. The pastors also kept up a steady drumbeat of how important it was to have "unity" and would often cast criticism or even questions as gossip and slander.

2. Collin Hansen, "Young, Restless, Reformed," *Christianity Today*, September 22, 2006, https://www.christianitytoday.com/ct/2006/september/42.32.html.

My notes from a December 1997 sermon by C. J. record him talking about "self-appointed critics" who have a "love of finding fault." He preached that day from 1 Timothy 5:19, which says, "Do not entertain an accusation against an elder unless it is brought by two or three witnesses." The common interpretation of this passage is that evidence from multiple witnesses is required to find someone guilty, but in our context it was used to prevent criticism from even entering one's mind, much less being discussed. So if you couldn't entertain a thought that was critical of your pastor until at least two other witnesses brought it to you privately, then that stopped any two individuals from discussing complaints about C. J. or other pastors. To even talk about criticisms with another person could be sin.

The New Calvinism also wreaked havoc among young people like me who were unattached but at the peak of our sex drives. In my early twenties, for a few years I went regularly to meetings to talk with other guys about how often we had looked at porn or masturbated. It was awful. The point was to feel shame in the hopes that this would help us stop. But if I had to point to anything that made my years of intense religiosity a psychologically painful time, it was this. It wasted so much of my mental and emotional energy. It took my sense of self and my masculinity and stomped on them. It warped my view of sex and sexuality. I walked around most of these years battling a crushing shame. This led to depression. And the only way out of this, really, was to battle my way to an emotional high through religious services, or through prayer and devotion. It was this obsession with the doctrine of indwelling sin that created a culture of self-hatred. There were those within this group who confessed that they had actually considered self-harm in order to fend off unwanted thoughts and actions.

The Starbucks meetings were the worst. Someone thought it would be a good idea to meet in groups of three or four or five, often on a Sunday morning before church, to have "accountability." These often turned into nightmarish sessions of opening the floor to see who wanted to share about their struggles. I always tried to get my chair as close to the others as possible so that the people sitting a few feet away wouldn't hear us. "Who wants to go first?" someone would ask. Other times the question was just there, hanging in the air like an unexploded grenade. In those situations, my approach was to jump in, because if I didn't, I was giving in to what we called "fear of man."

"Yeah. It's been a tough week. I stumbled a few times," I'd say. Sometimes a group leader would ask for specifics. "How many times? What are you doing to change?"

Why were we talking about this? Well, we were holy rollers, spiritual strivers, caught up in a moment, ensnared in a nightmare of devotion. The term *stumbled* was a gussied-up euphemism, one of the many ways in which we cloaked normal human experience in spiritual language. Often I'd go on to say exactly which days and where and when I looked at porn, because, again, I wanted to be the best Christian I could be, and these were the rules I was playing by. We weren't supposed to have sex or ever even have an orgasm, until the inevitable wet dream, which we never discussed but was (I think) morally permissible.

We were American Shiites. We may have been sitting in a Starbucks in suburbia trying not to be overheard. But in our own way, we were essentially doing the same thing—metaphorically, emotionally, psychologically—as Shiite Muslims did when they marched through the streets of a holy city like Najaf each year, whipping themselves during the observation of Ashura.

"Thanks for being humble and confessing," the leader would say. The other guys shifted in their seats, dreading their turn. *Why do we do this in a Starbucks?* I often thought. *Why are we sitting in public talking about this?* Maybe I wondered why we did it at all. But I lived in a hermetically sealed world. We did it because we were pursuing holiness. God is holy. We are worms. We must abase ourselves to become more like him and to know how far away we are from holiness and will always be. One guy made a big deal of how he would walk around a college campus looking at the cracks in the sidewalk so he didn't look at any women. This guy was on the fast track. He had figured out, I think, that the whole thing was a sham. He was simply playing the game. When he wanted to play humble, he'd sit with his elbows on his knees, hands clasped, close his eyes, and suck on his teeth while he talked about how big a sinner he was.

We used to sing a song in church in which the chorus was literally "all of us deserve to die." So imagine about two thousand people standing in an auditorium, many of them raising their arms and closing their eyes, singing those words to a dirge-like melody. In fact, the word *die* kind of landed with a thud of emphasis at the end of the sentence. *All of us deserve to DIE.* It took strong powers of self-delusion to sing those words over and over without having a sneaking suspicion that something was off.

Because of the way that a cult of imitation had built up around C. J., many people would also act out feelings of grief and self-abasement as they sang. They would hang their heads, slump their shoulders, and shift their weight back and forth, from foot to foot, working themselves up into a frenzy. This was the kind of thing C. J. often did: head down, eyes closed and frequently tearing up, shifting back and forth while singing. C. J. would often raise his arms while doing this, and his imitators added this as well.

There was never an end to the spiritual hamster wheel we were taught to stay on, always measuring our intensity of feeling and spiritual vigor. Some days I was up. "I want so much to be filled with passion for Jesus every day, yet my flesh is so weak," I wrote on May 30, 1997. "I must continually be renewed by dwelling in God's presence and on his word." On days I was down, I told myself that my unhappiness was a sin, that I needed to repent to get back into a state of mind where I was rejoicing in God's goodness and glory.

I was a virgin and hadn't kissed a girl in years. It was a testament to the incredible power of the cultural system that raised me, the force of the dogma with which we were indoctrinated, and the degree to which I and many others took it seriously. I would spend most of my early twenties consumed with self-loathing and hatred of my sexuality. Leaving aside the ways that church culture made relations between young men and women awkward, I was being taught, day after day, week after week, month after month, to detest and be embarrassed by my basic nature.

A few months after I traveled to Austin with C. J. and Josh Harris and the others, I wrote a poem about my dad for Father's Day in June. I obsequiously emailed it to C. J. He invited me to read it during the church service that week. On Sunday morning, with C. J. standing behind me, I stood in front of two thousand or so people and mythologized a false version of history, one in which C. J. was right to fire my dad and my dad was right to accept it. The reality was far different. It wasn't until years later that my parents would share the ways that the church community had mistreated my mom in the process, the details of which I will keep private.

But on Father's Day, with my father and mother in the audience, C. J. introduced me to the congregation. He began by saying something completely inaccurate, stating that I would soon be attending the year-long Pastors' College that the church had begun a year or two prior. I had not applied, had not been accepted, and had no plans to attend. I had never even discussed any of this with C. J. Again, like the moment when he had nudged my forehead when praying for me, something in the back of my head told me something was awry, but I brushed it away. And then I read a nineteen-stanza poem that included these lines:

> The Father was going under
> In no direction could he see
> He humbled himself and did not fight
> Trusting God he said, "I know these men care for me."

It was a version of the story that allowed my dad to save face. There was no trace of my mom in this retelling. At this time, I didn't know any of the details I'd come to know years later about the real reasons for my dad's ousting. But C. J. allowed me to stand there in public and give a testimony built on false pretenses. It was a textbook case of the way that power was often used and abused in this insular world and then sanctified with pseudo-spiritual language and concepts.

At least I was earning our family some status points in the tiny world of Covenant Life Church, which was our entire universe. During this time, the oldest of my younger brothers, Frank, was on the outs with the church community, largely because he was insufficiently robotic. By this point, he'd separated himself from our family emotionally and psychologically and would spend the next several years around a group of friends outside the church. I barely ever saw Frank or spoke to him. To the extent that I did, it would have been to try to self-righteously coach him back into the fold.

A year later, I graduated from the University of Maryland with a bachelor's degree in English literature and spent the summer working for a few guys from the church who had made money in business consulting and had started their own firm. We played golf, went to lunches, and had numerous brainstorming sessions. But there wasn't much work going on, and I was bored. When a job teaching literature at the church's high school opened up, I figured it would be worth doing at least temporarily and took the position, which paid about $21,000 a year. I was also by this time leading a small group, called a "care group." The people in the group were about my age, with most of us unmarried but feeling the pressure to pair off. Trying to be a leader, in all its awkwardness and forced religiosity, was painful and uncomfortable.

My position inside the pecking order of the church was unsteady, because I was not sufficiently certain. Probably somewhat like my father, I wasn't quite enough of a yes man or a manipulator to climb the ladder. I questioned things, even as I sought to make it all make sense. Josh Harris brought me along on two trips to speak at the Creation festival. But he and I were never close.

In my job at the church school, I taught my tenth graders about the sexual themes in *Lord of the Flies* that I had learned about at university, which I'm sure had never been done before at the church school. There wasn't really a curriculum for me to follow, so I created one from scratch without seeking input from the principal. I was troubled by the intellectually lazy mindset of so many students.

To read through my journals during these years is to wade through mountains of BS cloaked in religious language. It was like being stuck in one of those foam ball pits, trying to walk forward but unable to move. My journals really are a monument to how I was like so many religious people who are trained to chase their tails endlessly for years—talking and thinking about faith and writing Scripture verses and ethereal thoughts—all the while avoiding reality and failing to be of much use in the world.

But occasionally I had moments of clarity when I wrote directly. After returning from an educators' conference, I noted that the high school was teaching its students not *how* to think but *what* to think. "Plato himself said that true learning can only be found through inquiry and dialogue, and that is truly what is missing from the students we are producing at [Covenant Life School]: a spirit of inquiry," I wrote on June 24, 2000. "I believe that certain people's preferences and convictions (even if they are pastors) have been elevated too highly. This has led to a black/white, legalistic approach to such ever-touchy areas as relationships, music and drinking.

"It is not an exaggeration for me to say that the high school largely consists of semi-mindless drones who chafe and rage against regulations that don't make sense to them and ARE NOT explicitly prescribed in Scripture," I wrote. "The fruit of this is that we then have teenagers who have as much ambition in them as a housefly, who have been so conditioned to not only do as they're told but THINK as they're told, which I believe makes them feel they have absolutely nothing to offer, to the church, to the school, to the body of Christ, and most importantly (if we are thinking evangelically) to the world.

"It appears to me we are largely breeding hypocrites at CLS," I concluded.

I preached in the high school chapel once or twice. I still have my sermon notes from April 25, 2001. I titled my sermon "Christ Will Cost You." I quoted extensively from John Stott's *Basic Chris-*

tianity. In fact, most of my sermon notes are just quotes. But I did tell the students that "you did not inherit faith in Christ" and "you must choose it for yourself." I quoted Stott as describing Christ's call on the life of the Christian: "to deny ourselves, to crucify ourselves, to lose ourselves. . . . He does not call us to a sloppy half-heartedness, but to make a vigorous, absolute commitment."[3] But my imagination of what that call looked like in real life was so small, limited to renouncing personal sin rather than applying it to all of life and to the broader world. This narrowness extended to the way I closed the sermon: "If there are things in your life which you do not want to give up right now, you are probably not saved. You need to recognize the perilous situation your soul is in." I shudder to think I said those words out loud to those poor kids, weighing them down further than they already were. I had become the youth leader urging teenagers to surrender all and submit to God and the adults in their lives.

I was suffocating. I could feel how small my existence had become, so lacking in a diversity of perspectives and sealed off from the rest of the world. The 2000 election came and went, and I paid scant attention to the recount in Florida. A close friend and pastor told me during this time that the main job of the church was to keep itself pure from corruption from the outside world and wait for Christ's return. Another friend seemed shocked when I mentioned that Jesus had taught us to pray that his kingdom might come on earth as it is in heaven. He said he'd missed the application for earthly life and thought it had to do only with heaven.

I yearned for a way to connect my youthful strength and my faith with tangible needs, to do something more than talk or pray or discuss. I wanted something real. I wanted to be in the mess of life, bringing light and aid. The most I ever saw Covenant Life Church's ministry for young adults do is hand out water and soda at an intersection. The whole point of that was to invite people to our church. Others would have to come to us. Not only was I going to church meetings all the time, but I was also working

3. John Stott, *Basic Christianity* (Downers Grove, IL: InterVarsity, 1958), 112.

at the church. All my friendships were there. I was drowning in introspective self-loathing.

"I am tired, weary, and I have no understanding of what is going on around me, inside me, or what to do about it," I wrote on February 13, 2000. Early in 2001, I took a selfie in my room, printed it out on a piece of paper, and wrote a melodramatic poem: "And so I sank / Into a mire of hopelessness / And hatred of a life I hated / In my twenty third year."

I needed to get out.

PART 2

Separation
2001–2012

9

Escape

After two years of teaching, I was done. I had wanted to quit after one year but needed to prove to myself that I could handle the job. And my second year of teaching did, in fact, go much better than the first. I learned how to take control of the classroom. I had created a curriculum on my own and so did not have to come up with lesson plans from scratch every day for four or five classes. I coached the varsity baseball team. And after finishing my second year, I started trying to figure out what to do with the rest of my life.

I knew I wanted to be a writer. But that was about it. As the school year wound down, I spent a few months seeking advice from people I knew and from others I didn't, and a number of them said they thought working at a newspaper would be a good place to start for any kind of writing. In college, the news had bored me. It was too ephemeral and transitory. Everything changed from day to day. I wanted to contemplate the mysteries of the universe. It had never crossed my mind to try writing for the college newspaper. So obviously I had no experience and no clips of articles I'd written that I could send to potential employers. I sent an application to the *Washington Post* that went nowhere. Even the small local paper, the *Gaithersburg Gazette*, rejected me. I had few prospects.

In the summer of 2001 I was still living at home, so I could indulge my desire to write creatively. I went to Barnes & Noble and tried to summon inspiration. I wrote some poetry and fiction, but I realized I had very little life experience to draw from.

> I look inside myself
> to see what's there
> to mine everything out
> and pour it out
> I'm not finding anything
> of interest or substance
> But still I keep digging
> scraping at nothing
> It's like trying to dig up metal:
> the shovel gets bent out of shape
> from hitting a substance
> that won't render up a thing

Journalism continued to come up in my conversations with people who were kind enough to meet with me or take my phone calls asking for advice. It was clearly a way to get out into the wider world. But it scared me. I felt more suited by temperament to writing alone, with a minimum of human interaction. And my upbringing had made it normal to stay isolated and comfortable. The world outside was foreign and frightening.

The logjam began to break early that fall when I came across a small item in the *Gazette* about a high school football coach. I had a jolt of inspiration. That coach might be a good subject for a long-form magazine article. Bob Milloy had already been around for many years and had won eight state championships in Maryland over thirty years. But he was moving to a private Catholic school. I knew he'd be able to build a powerhouse there, since he could now recruit more easily.

I was unemployed and had no agreement from anyone to publish whatever I was going to write, but I was getting desperate. I called Milloy and left a message. A few days later, he called me back. He asked me what I wanted to write. I rattled off how I'd read newspaper articles in which his players talked about his ability to inspire them. I wanted to understand what made such a difference in a group of players who had lost more games than they'd won the previous year. What makes a coach able to inspire greatness?

When I was done, he paused and with genuine warmth said, "Sure, Jon, I'd love to help you out." I put on my running shoes and sprinted out the door, jogging down the road for miles, exhaling excitement and relief.

Four days later, I was awakened by the sound of my mom yelling at the TV. For the next forty-eight hours, I watched coverage of the 9/11 attacks mostly by myself, trying to absorb what had happened and wishing I had some meaningful way to respond. For the next few years, I'd question whether I should join the military but always felt like I was meant—called—to write more than fight. Two days after the attacks, I escaped to a large field on a sunny day to attend my first practice with Milloy's football team. He got out of a blue Jeep Cherokee, shook my hand, and asked me right away, "So this is going to be more than just a one-day thing, right?" He was talking about my article, but since it was also my first day as a journalist—albeit one without an actual job who had never published anything in his life—the comment also applied to what would end up becoming my profession for the next two decades.

My time with Milloy became the first of many instances when journalism served as a magic carpet, a wonderful gift. It escorted me into places I'd never seen and upended my assumptions about the world. It repaired my cloistered imagination with the balm of reality.

I was expecting Milloy to be someone like Gene Hackman's character from *Hoosiers*—an authoritarian who yelled and screamed. But Milloy was not an imposing presence: short, stout, a bit hunched, with a weather-beaten face and squinty eyes. He did not put much stock in words. His practices were big on repetition. Things were calm, workmanlike, and relaxed. There was not much yelling at all.

"They're gonna forget those locker room words and all that crap," Milloy told me. "And I've done some crazy stuff over the years: paint the school and s—t like that. . . . We still got our a— kicked." I laughed and he paused, thinking for a moment. "What is it?" he asked himself. "The five Ps: Proper Preparation Prevents Poor Performance, and I believe in that, you know, just working hard and being prepared." Milloy and his assistants spent hours each weekday night watching game tapes of their opponents, drawing up game plans.

Milloy also told me how much he enjoyed being around the young men on his team. "I tell them the first day, 'Guys, I have so much respect for you . . . , all the hard work and lifting weights, and the running, and the heat, and the summer, and the contact.' And they're beat up," he said. "Sure, I get disappointed when we don't do what we're supposed to do, but as far as people are concerned, I just love 'em. I just enjoy seeing them every day."

Tim Kurkjian, the former *Sports Illustrated* writer who was at ESPN and became a fixture on *Baseball Tonight*, had grown up in the area and had once worked at a small paper called the *Montgomery Journal*. Incredibly, he agreed to grab coffee with me and then connected me with the sports editor at the *Journal*, who published a long-form series that I wrote about Milloy's first season at Our Lady of Good Counsel High School.

My instincts that he would build a powerhouse were correct: Milloy coached fifteen more years, and for four consecutive years, starting in 2009, his teams won the Washington Catholic Athletic Conference championship and were the top team in the *Washington Post*'s rankings of all schools in Maryland, Virginia, and DC. He coached several future NFL stars. He retired in 2016 at age seventy-three as the winningest high school football coach in Maryland's history.[1]

1. Jacob Bogage and Jesse Dougherty, "Longtime Good Counsel Football Coach Bob Milloy Retires after 47 Years, 405 Wins," *Washington Post*, February 15, 2017, https://www.washingtonpost.com/sports/highschools/longtime-good -counsel-football-coach-bob-milloy-retires-after-47-years-405-wins/2017/02/15 /647dda30-f3be-11e6-8d72-263470bf0401_story.html.

I learned an important lesson from Milloy: an effective leader does not have to motivate through fear, guilt, shame, and anger. He was one of the first people to show me how leadership is less about personal charisma or giving a good speech. It is much more about preparation, hard work, being a good and dependable person, and taking care of the people under you. It's funny that it took a football coach to teach me that, after I'd spent so many years around Christian ministers.

I scratched together some money that fall waiting tables at Macaroni Grill, where I spilled soup on one of the guests, at my first table, on my first day. I spent many a late night after closing next door at Joe's Crab Shack with some of the other waiters, drinking beer and talking about nothing. It felt vaguely sinful and transgressive, but I decided I didn't care.

At some point, I got a call from a teacher at Covenant Life High School who said she would be taking over the yearbook and wanted my advice. As we talked, it came up that I was looking for a job working for a newspaper. Her husband was an assistant managing editor at the *Washington Times*. I called him five consecutive days before getting a call back, and then I got a meeting in his office at 3600 New York Avenue Northeast. I would spend the next eight years of my career working out of that grungy, gritty building.

The *Washington Times* was owned by Korean cult leader Sun Myung Moon and run by Wesley Pruden, a neo-confederate whose father had led the charge to stop the Little Rock Nine from integrating an Arkansas public high school in 1957.[2] But some serious journalists had come through the *Times* before me, including Peter Baker and David Brooks of the *New York Times*, and Major Garrett of *CBS News*. I didn't know any of that at the time. All I knew was that I had a job writing.

2. Heidi Beirichh and Bob Moser, "The Washington Times Pushes Extremist, Neo-Confederate Ideas," Southern Poverty Law Center, August 15, 2003, https://www.splcenter.org/fighting-hate/intelligence-report/2003/washington-times-pushes-extremist-neo-confederate-ideas.

They gave me a choice to be an unpaid intern on the sports desk or the local metro desk. I chose the latter. I walked into the dimly lit newsroom, with twenty-foot windows that looked out onto the National Arboretum but were often covered with blinds. The deputy metro editor—a short, balding man with glasses—greeted me gruffly, then grabbed a stack of press releases off the fax machine and shuffled through them. He singled one out, handed it to me, and said, "Go cover this. See if there's a story." This editor, David Eldridge, would become a beloved friend and mentor, but on that day this was the extent of his guidance. And I didn't mind a bit.

The fax had information about an anti-gang press event the next day in the Columbia Heights neighborhood. I drove over to a nonprofit in the neighborhood and interviewed the director. The next day at the event I spoke with a high school senior named Enrique Morales, who told me he was trying to escape gang life but was still being hunted by a rival gang. He didn't tell me that he was a gang leader who just three months earlier had shot at members of a rival gang, according to a police indictment filed a few years later.[3]

I wrote an article. It went through an editor, then a copy editor. The next day I drove to a convenience store to pick up a copy of the *Times*. I turned to page A9 and saw my name in the paper. I almost couldn't believe it. Two days earlier I had been a nobody. Now I was a published journalist.

My first appearance on the front page of the newspaper, weeks later, was an earth-shaking exclusive about how the local soft-rock radio station would begin playing Christmas music before Thanksgiving. I wrote about pothole repairs and winter storms, shootings and red-light cameras, and other miscellanea. Every day was different. I still preferred to sit at my desk and read and write rather than make phone calls. But I was being forced out into the

3. David A. Fahrenthold and Henri E. Cauvin, "Alleged Leaders of Latino Gang Indicted in D.C.," *Washington Post*, May 30, 2003, https://www.washingtonpost.com/archive/politics/2003/05/30/alleged-leaders-of-latino-gang-indicted-in-dc/77ac3ef3-a0a1-4e62-be35-60febc087293/.

real world. After six months of hustling, I got hired in the spring of 2002 and gave my notice at Macaroni Grill.

I visited my brother Frank in New York City in early 2002. He had joined up with Youth with a Mission, a Christian missionary group, and was supposed to head to Tibet for a lengthy spell. But the 9/11 attacks changed all that, and instead he was sent for several weeks to help the Salvation Army distribute meals to emergency workers who were combing through the wreckage at Ground Zero. I had never been to New York, so I went to visit him. "As the bus approached NYC and rounded a curve, preparing to enter the Lincoln Tunnel, I sat in my seat erect, an awe-filled spectator," I wrote in my journal. "Frank was right there at the door [of the bus station] to whisk me to the subway, so we could scurry over to the Salvation Army and get me a pass to work at Ground Zero. It was good to see him, but also awkward, our patchwork relationship obvious to me at least."

Frank handed me a Walkman so I could listen to a song he'd written. "I felt again the pressure of his expectations and tried to be honest about what I thought. It was actually very good, and I told him that, though I added that I thought it short on content." After a few days, I headed back to DC. "I have ceased to hound him about things he will not discuss," I journaled. "And though there is much unsaid between us, we are learning to love each other as brothers should. We walked into the Port Authority and down the escalators to the line waiting to board. As I put my bags down, I felt a sadness creep over me that made me glad. I realized there was goodwill and love between Frank and me, and I was sad to say goodbye. I hugged him, he grunted and walked off, and I turned away, a melancholic smile on my face."

In 2002, I got a small taste of danger when the DC sniper started picking people off at gas stations and Home Depots. Each time there was a shooting, I raced to the scene. The hunt for the killer was grotesquely thrilling. A year later, I lived for two months in Virginia Beach and covered the trial of the sniper John Allen Muhammad, who had committed the killing spree with Lee Boyd Malvo, a teen boy whom Muhammad had brainwashed into becoming his disciple. I sat in the courtroom every day over several weeks, staying at a rundown Days Inn a block from the ocean during the late fall and early winter of 2003. Outside my window navy SEALs sang as they ran past in formation while I prepared for the upcoming day in the early morning hours.

By the time I left for Virginia Beach, I had extricated myself from the church bubble. I stepped down from leading the care group, telling my direct report pastor that I couldn't stop looking at pornography so I wasn't fit to be a role model. I attended a humiliating, teary-eyed meeting with the entire care group that I can't remember very much about. I just wanted to be done with it all. I would have suffered almost any humiliation by then to get out of the role.

I got an apartment in a rundown complex in Beltsville, Maryland. I shared the apartment with a student at the University of Maryland who attended the church, but I stopped going on Sundays. I was a burned-out case. Yet I didn't sever all connections. Eventually, I started going to a small Bible study at the house of a friend I'd grown up with. Rob and his wife, Mary, showed me kindness and treated my spiritual scars with gentleness.

It was at their house that I met a woman who was not like most of the others I'd met at church. She did not seem to care what other people thought of her. She had somehow been raised in an environment similar to mine but had turned out quite differently. Alison had once been kicked out of an REM concert at age sixteen for repeatedly ignoring a security guard's warning to stop puffing on her joint. When Rob asked us one night to break off into groups and pray for one another, she put her hand on my arm. An electric charge went through my body.

I had known for years that when it came to men and women, the church culture was terrible. "The state of male/female relationships in the 18–25 ministry is at an all-time high level of weirdness," I wrote in 2000. By 2004, I'd gone through a series of failed relationships that I'd ended before they ever got anywhere. There was no room to flirt, be human, and explore. We were not allowed to date. There were only two categories for men and women: friends and courtship. And courtship, a concept introduced largely by *I Kissed Dating Goodbye*, was intended to happen only with someone you were serious about marrying. There was some room for ending a courtship, but there was immense pressure not to do so.

In January 2000, I'd written down some questions for myself before asking a girl I liked out. We had been friends through church. I wrote: "Count the cost right now. Am I ready to pursue this relationship with the goal in mind that if it follows through, I'm prepared to be a husband, a father, and am prepared to love this woman as Christ loved the church and give my life for her?" I also asked myself if I was attracted to her enough that I could spend my life with her. The very night I asked her to "court," I was consumed with regret and anxiety. I ended things a month later, and we barely spoke after that.

Alison was different. I was quickly infatuated with her. I found it natural to spend time with her. She was extraordinary: beautiful, stylish, regal, wild, honest, and true. She had an integrity and a strength that I had rarely encountered. Ali had grown up the daughter of a pastor in a fundamentalist evangelical church, just as I had, but she had resisted most notions of female inferiority. She gave as good as she got, and then plenty more. And she tested me, keeping me at arm's length for six months. I first told her I was interested in her at RFK Stadium just as Jay-Z was about to come on stage at a music festival during Memorial Day weekend. She looked at me weird and said, "I barely know you." We were both relieved when Jay-Z came out, the music started, and deafening noise made further conversation impossible.

I wrote long email letters to her and penned many poems about the agony of my unrequited desire. I showed up any time a group of mutual friends was hanging out. I told her again over the summer that I wanted to be with her, and again got the stiff arm. I prayed a lot. I was miserable. By fall, I was thinking about giving up and started to create some distance. This was apparently intriguing enough for Ali to go out with me a few times. She asked me to accompany her to her best friend's wedding, and we swayed cheek to cheek to Elton John's "Tiny Dancer." It felt like a surreal dream.

Many years later, as I reflected on this part of my life, Ali asked me why I put up with the bizarre and harmful environment inside the church. Her question stopped me short. But I guess the answer is that if you're told that thinking and behaving in a certain way is the only path to pleasing God, that carries a lot of weight. The power of that logic to crush people's will and their critical thinking is hard to resist.

I was at Ali's parents' house watching the presidential election returns roll in on November 3, 2004. The day after, the school board in Montgomery County, Maryland—where I'd grown up— approved a sex education curriculum that provoked a backlash from conservative parents. I spent much of the next several months writing about this dispute. The parents who supported the new curriculum, which encouraged acceptance of gay and lesbian students, thought I was biased against them. It was true that my background predisposed me to be uncomfortable with their point of view. But I worked hard to understand and get to know them and learned another important lesson of journalism: how to be a fair-minded person. It involves taking time to sit for extended periods with another person's point of view, especially on topics that are emotionally charged and dear to one's heart.

The sex ed story was my first real engagement with modern culture war. I saw where the debate over gay rights was heading, and I sensed then, twelve years before it happened, that the legalization of gay marriage was inevitable. I witnessed the way that local activists could harness the power of the internet to raise awareness and fight political battles. I began filming a documentary, which I tried unsuccessfully to get funded. I wrote in my proposal that I thought both sides were driven by fear. "Parents opposed to the course were haunted by images of their children learning that they could be gay," I wrote then. "Parents in favor feared a religious takeover of schools. . . . [They] have told me in extended interviews that they fear . . . a theocracy." George W. Bush's reelection had set off a robust debate over whether the Christian right had become so powerful that it could impose its will on the rest of the country. I wanted to do work that demystified and explained each side of the sex ed debate to the other in an effort to reduce tensions.

Around this time, I started to feel existential despair, as if nothing in my upbringing had prepared me for the world in which I now moved. It seemed like there were no answers in the religious beliefs I'd been taught for the questions I faced about modern life. I couldn't see any connections between Christianity and the world outside the four walls of the church.

In the summer of 2004, a friend told me he'd applied to be part of something called the Centurion Course, which was starting that year and being run by Chuck Colson. Colson was a former hatchet man for President Nixon who had served seven months in federal prison for his part in the Watergate scandal. After leaving prison, Colson had written a book about his conversion to Christianity and started an organization called Prison Fellowship. In 1991, he had launched another organization focused on "Christian worldview" and in 1999 cowrote a book with Nancy Pearcey called *How Now Shall We Live?* That book was a response to what Colson and others saw as the growing influence of postmodern thought, in which truth was relative and Christian beliefs were viewed with increasing skepticism. Much of this was driven by a sense that efforts by the religious right to influence the political process were becoming less successful. Bush may have won the presidency in 2004 by using gay marriage to energize the evangelical base, but Colson sensed that hostility for Christians was growing.

For me, the Centurion Course sounded like a good way to figure some things out, even if the name's martial tone struck me as tone-deaf. The goal of the course was to "equip" Christians with arguments to defend the Christian faith in the public square. I found the approach too propositional. I believed that authenticity, relationship, and narrative would do more to win people over. But I enjoyed the experience of meeting Colson and others who attended the course. Most of the hundred or so attendees were much older than I was, but a few of us were in our twenties. Gabe Lyons went on to start his own Christian conferences called Q (not related to the conspiracy theory), and Michael Lindsay became president of Taylor University, a private evangelical college in Indiana.

My year in the Centurion Course reassured me that there could be intellectual rigor in the Christian faith. I was shedding most of the extraneous cultural baggage that I'd acquired at Covenant Life Church. I stripped down my faith to essentials and resolved to build my identity around Jesus Christ, his sacrifice for me, and nothing else. I didn't want to find ultimate meaning in my work, possessions, accomplishments, friends, interests, or even family. I thought often of the passage in the second chapter of Galatians, where the apostle Paul writes, "I have been crucified with Christ and I no longer live, but Christ lives in me" (v. 20).

To many people, this might seem like a doubling down on the very things I'd been taught as a young person. But because I was choosing to leave Covenant Life Church and the influence of its leaders behind, it felt like a radical act, almost akin to apostasy. That's how deeply the leaders had insinuated their authority into the narrative of what it meant to be a faithful Christian.

It was at one of the three Centurion gatherings in 2004 that I experienced the first meaningful celebration of Communion I'd ever seen. Communion was rarely celebrated at Covenant Life Church and was completely informal. This time it was more solemn and followed a liturgical script that resonated with deep meaning.

I also grew that year in my conviction that our church had ill-served the majority of its members by teaching them that only pastors and those who worked at the church or in explicitly Christian jobs were doing meaningful work. I had renewed purpose that my profession in journalism was a noble calling. I believed truth existed, and I believed it could be found out, pursued, preserved, and promoted. I still believe that.

10

A Strong Man

Dad," I said, "do you see life as a struggle or as a war?"
We were driving down the road, just the two of us, in
the fall of 2005. The top on Dad's convertible was down.
We were cruising the flat, single-lane highways of Maryland's
eastern shore, part of a father-son trip before I got married. I'd
grown up traveling these roads back and forth to family vacations
in Bethany Beach. I did not yet appreciate the region's rich history
as the place where Harriet Tubman and Frederick Douglass grew
up as slaves before becoming some of America's greatest patriots
and freedom fighters. Nobody I knew talked about that.

I asked my dad about life as we headed down to Ocean City for
the night. And this question—Is life a struggle or a war?—was one
that I'd been thinking about. I looked at my father and saw him,
having turned fifty a few years prior, as kind of beaten down and
tired. He said he thought of life as a struggle. I wasn't surprised. I
was twenty-eight and wanted my life to have a clear purpose. I was
viewing life as a war because it gave me energy. I was about to get
married and was awakening to the responsibilities of adulthood.
The nation was at war in Iraq, and the 9/11 attacks still lingered in
my psyche. I was grappling with how to think about abortion and

sexuality now that I understood more of the political complexity. The Montgomery County sex ed story was fresh in my mind. My time in the Centurion Course had trained me how to argue against postmodernism and relativism. In addition, the broader evangelical culture was full of martial rhetoric. The Christian publishing industry was pumping out books on the need for Christian men to be warriors. I read one of them around that time: *Wild at Heart* by John Eldredge.

I had spent considerable time over the previous few years trying to figure out what I thought about masculinity, strength and weakness, power, and violence. Partly this was because Covenant Life Church was an odd environment for men. In our church, men were trained to be docile and submissive to the men who were leaders, and the leaders exercised influence by bending over backward to appear the most humble. There was little overt aggression. In fact, such displays were considered bad form, even sinful. Covenant Life was a bit of an outlier in this way. Many evangelical churches encouraged men to be assertive and dominant. We kept those without power—especially women—in places of subservience, but we did it nicely, with big smiles and lots of gentle Christian words. I enjoyed Eldredge's book because it was a corrective to Covenant Life's emasculating culture.

Wild at Heart was part of a larger reaction against a "feminization" of evangelical men around the turn of the century. The Promise Keepers gatherings in the 1990s were seen as part of the problem by some, encouraging men to sing and pray expressively, to weep over their shortcomings, and to hug at outdoor rallies inside football stadiums. Racial reconciliation was emphasized at Promise Keepers events. But more egalitarian attitudes toward women were taking shape. One of the institutions that formed to push back against notions of gender equality was the Council on Biblical Manhood and Womanhood (CBMW). This group defended "biblical" gender roles, something they called "complementarianism." Men were to lead and direct, and women were to submit and support. The reality of power was spiritualized away. Men and women had different roles but equal value. The CBMW was formed expressly to fight against what leaders perceived as the growing influence of feminism on the church, and later to push back against LGBTQ acceptance.

C. J. Mahaney was becoming a national figure and was recruited to join the CBMW, where he came into closer orbit with some of the most influential men in conservative evangelicalism. Wayne Grudem had helped start the organization, and three of the most powerful leaders from the Southern Baptist Convention (SBC)—the largest Protestant denomination in America—were involved as well. This trio included Paige Patterson, who led a "conservative resurgence" in the SBC during the 1980s; Richard Land, who oversaw the SBC's public policy arm; and Al Mohler, the head of the SBC's biggest training ground for young pastors, Southern Baptist Theological Seminary.

C. J.'s relationship with Mohler would become the most significant. Patterson had led the takeover of the denomination's institutions and grassroots leadership. Mohler had picked up Patterson's campaign and extended it into the seminary. He got rid of professors deemed too liberal. But Mohler projected an image of an urbane and learned form of conservative Christianity. He gave regular TV interviews and produced a steady stream of writing and multimedia content through podcast episodes and his daily radio show.

I ran into C. J. one day and briefly discussed another nationally known evangelical name: Mark Driscoll. It was a short interaction on the sidelines of a high school soccer game. I hadn't seen C. J. much since a few years earlier, when he'd incorrectly told the church that I was going to the pastors' training school. I never attended the Pastors' College and wasn't even going to Covenant Life Church by this point. But as we chatted, I told him I'd been listening to sermons by Driscoll, a pastor in Seattle.

I'd discovered Driscoll through a book by Donald Miller called *Blue Like Jazz*. Driscoll was confrontational in a way most Christian leaders would have never dreamed of. Miller described him as "Mark the cussing pastor," and that was enough to intrigue me. I discovered a bracing form of Sunday preaching in Driscoll's online sermons. I hadn't been getting that at Covenant Life Church. When C. J. began to focus more nationally, he installed Josh Harris as senior pastor, and Harris began to preach most Sundays. Harris's sermons were like Hallmark Channel movies. I felt like he was tucking me into bed rather than equipping me for battle.

C. J. wasn't impressed with Driscoll, though. It was obvious that my mention of the Seattle pastor bothered C. J. He made a dismissive comment and ended the conversation. A few years later, I heard that C. J. had flown out to Seattle specifically to meet with Driscoll and offer him support and guidance, and I wondered what had led to his change of heart.

C. J.'s networking was paying off elsewhere, beyond the CBMW. In 2006, he and Mohler joined with two other pastors—Mark Dever of Capitol Hill Baptist in Washington, DC, and Ligon Duncan, a leading Presbyterian pastor from Jackson, Mississippi—to start a conference called Together for the Gospel (T4G). It became an annual gathering for conservative, predominantly White, evangelical pastors who belonged to the New Calvinism. John Piper was a regular speaker. The attendees were mostly pastors who read a lot of theology and history and wanted to understand and debate the finer points of doctrine. Politics and local affairs were not a big focus. They often said that all they wanted to do was "preach the gospel" and leave the rest to God.

C. J. stood out from the three other leaders of T4G because they wore suits and ties and had a high-church, restrained style. C. J. wore blue jeans, told jokes, and spoke in a demonstrative, emotionally charged way. His style was a big draw for the new conference.

Lou Engle could not have been more different from the New Calvinists. He was consumed by a passion to overturn *Roe v. Wade*. He was a wild-eyed radical who was willing to live his life with a single-minded focus. By the late 1990s, he was building toward something he dubbed "The Call." He rallied thousands of people on the National Mall in Washington, DC, most of them teenagers from youth groups, much like Ron Luce had mobilized them in the 1980s and 1990s.

I ran into Engle one day in 2005. I hadn't seen him since my childhood, and then one day I saw him leading a demonstration outside the US Supreme Court. A group of young people led by Engle had placed duct tape over their mouths and written the word *life* on the tape. They stood silently while others prayed. I met Engle's son and was struck by how different he was from his dad: quiet and soft-spoken. Engle came over and chatted with me for a moment. He remembered my dad from their time at Covenant Life Church.

I had always thought Engle was well-meaning—if a bit strange. Even if I wouldn't serve God the way he did, I thought I shouldn't criticize him. I did have concerns about the real-world consequences of his political activism, but mostly because I thought it was too one-dimensional and ineffective.

For Engle, it was simple. Abortion was murder. There was no point in asking him questions that would complicate this view, such as: When does life begin? How do you know that? What about cases in which the life of the mother is in danger? What about rape and incest? What should we do about the systemic causes of teen pregnancy? Should the government make laws about what its citizens can and cannot do inside their own bodies?

Engle never discussed political strategies beyond electing presidents who would appoint pro-life conservatives to the Supreme Court. He didn't tell his followers the political reality that if *Roe* was overturned, abortion would remain legal in much of the country under state laws. He never mentioned that there were Democrats seeking to reduce the number of abortions through greater access to health care, sex education in schools, contraception, and a social safety net that would reduce the number of women who couldn't afford to have a child. In fact, the number of abortions did go down under Democratic presidents, just as it did under Republicans, in part because of efforts like these.[1]

1. Rachel K. Jones, Elizabeth Witwer, and Jenna Jerman, "Abortion Incidence and Service Availability in the United States, 2017," *The Guttmacher Institute*,

Even as Engle became increasingly political, he claimed to be nonpolitical. I saw this attitude among many Christians we knew. They thought of politics as dirty, messy, unseemly. So they focused on doing things they knew were obviously Christian, like going to church, praying, singing, tithing, listening to sermons, and helping others in their church. Engle offered an outlet for these types of Christians who were isolated from most things outside their church lives. Many people in C. J.'s movement of churches fit this description too. But whereas C. J. was someone who designed and organized the internal life of the church, Engle was a leader who went out and waged battle against the outsiders: the Democrats, abortionists, atheists, homosexuals, liberals, and the mainstream media.

Because Engle did not think of himself as operating in political action but rather in supernatural warfare, there was no distinction in his mind between his spirituality and his politics.[2] So his politics became defined by a vision of violent combat. He would say that Christians should wage battle on their knees, so he did not advocate for physical violence. But he viewed his political action as righteous, and those who opposed him were influenced by demons and forces of evil. The task then was to defeat them. He would do the praying. But he and his followers would support those who would do the more complicated work of actually fighting in the political arena. The stakes were high and simple: vote Republican and vote to save the lives of millions of babies, or vote Democrat and vote to support the murder of millions of unborn, innocent lives.

Despite the fact that I viewed life as a war in my late twenties, I did not ever think that the Christian attitude toward politics should be one of conquest. John Piper had a lot to do with this. I had never been a fan of a triumphalistic Christianity that I encoun-

September 2019, https://www.guttmacher.org/report/abortion-incidence-service-availability-us-2017.

2. "Lou Engle's Dream of Donald Trump—Interview with @Lou Engle," YouTube, September 4, 2020, https://www.youtube.com/watch?v=qY4HbiCAXPM.

tered in the church. The idea that Christianity should in any way lead to domination or coercion of others had always struck me as antithetical to the Christian message. So too did the notion that following Christ should lead to an easier life or to getting things I wanted out of life.

Piper has been rightly criticized for his comments about gender roles and his egregious advice to women that in situations of domestic abuse they should put up with "perhaps being smacked one night" before asking for help from church leaders.[3] But in one sermon from 2005, he indelibly marked the way I thought about how the Christian faith applies to politics, because it resonated so deeply with what I saw Jesus talking about in the Gospels. Piper talked forcefully about how the greatest strength of true Christianity is that it gives people the courage to endure defeat and even suffering without bitterness and that this is the way that the faith will advance, not through vanquishing enemies.

When he said this, Islamic terrorism was top of mind for Americans. "We do not advance the kingdom of Christ by fighting. We never, ever, ever undertake with the sword to advance the gospel, ever!" Piper shouted. "We will advance the kingdom by preaching, by suffering, by dying." He extended this principle to the way Christians should think about the public square, advocating for a pluralism that allows religious freedom for all faiths. "A coerced conversion is no conversion. Therefore I will not undertake to advance conversion by the sword or any other manipulative, coercive means. And in wanting that for myself I will defend it for everyone," Piper said.[4]

And he went even further than that, saying that self-sacrifice is the true superpower of the Christian faith, not political strength or military strength or physical strength or any other thing that

3. Libby Anne, "John Piper on Domestic Abuse and Group Sex (Yes, That Combination Is Weird)," *Patheos*, May 9, 2018, https://www.patheos.com/blogs/lovejoyfeminism/2018/05/john-piper-on-domestic-abuse-and-group-sex-yes-that-combination-is-weird.html.

4. John Piper, "Submission to Civil Authority," *Desiring God*, July 17, 2005, https://www.desiringgod.org/messages/submission-to-civil-authority.

could be used to overpower or dominate. Piper's rhetoric might have been a tad dramatic, but the principle was sound. It was a vision I found compelling and consistent with the message of Christ, who himself overcame evil by giving up his very life as a sacrifice. Self-sacrifice was at the core of this vision: for love, for service, for others.

Piper was also well known for a sermon he gave two years after I saw him speak at Passion 1998. In May 2000, he spoke at an outdoor Passion event called OneDay to a massive crowd. He did not mince words. "With all my heart I plead with you, don't buy that dream, the American Dream: a nice house, a nice car, a nice job, a nice family, a nice retirement," Piper said.[5] He called on young people to live their lives for God's glory, not their own, and to aggressively reject materialism, greed, and selfishness. The central focus, like with C. J., was the death of Jesus Christ on the cross. He was our example: this King who laid aside his glory and strength to die for those he loved, this Lord of all who taught us to turn the other cheek, whose anger was reserved primarily for hypocritical religious leaders.

I embraced the idea that Christians are not to put their ultimate hope in this life, that we are—to some extent—pilgrims in this life. This is what Chance the Rapper meant when he said to "believe in the Kingdom," not in "kings." "My kingdom is not of this world," Jesus said to Pontius Pilate (John 18:36), who ruled over the Roman province of Judea for roughly a decade. I sought to live in between these two worlds: the kingdom of man and the kingdom of God. I did not want to put my head in the sand and live as if this world did not matter. I wanted to be fully present, invested in my community, loving my neighbor, and letting God's light and life shine through me to others. But I wanted my "treasure" to be in God's kingdom, the one that would last forever. That meant that no matter what happened in this life, even in suffering or in grief, I could still hang on to hope and meaning.

5. John Piper, "Boasting Only in the Cross," *Desiring God*, May 20, 2000, https://www.desiringgod.org/messages/boasting-only-in-the-cross.

Over the years, I saw the Christian right again and again do the opposite of what Piper spoke about. Its leaders talked about bringing America "back to God" and married this rhetoric with a Republican agenda that put the wealthy and powerful ahead of the poor and marginalized. Tax cuts and deregulation were the priority rather than making sure that the poor were given a lift. A healthy economy was the best thing for the poor, we were told. But we were also often told that if people were poor or vulnerable, it was their own fault.

Of course, Democrats have had their own major failings in protecting the weak. They have been too influenced at times by corporations and Wall Street donors, just like Republicans. And the party's drift toward an uncompromising position on abortion rights has been a huge failure in this regard as well. On the other hand, they do consider the less-well-off to be a key part of their constituency, and so they legislate and communicate with them in mind.

As for setting a high standard of conduct in the political realm, I saw many conservative Christians seeking to dominate in the political sphere rather than to serve or work toward the common good. They justified it by pointing to a basic confusion about the nature of America. I saw many people acting like if things didn't go their way politically—as in, if America didn't become more like what they imagined God wanted—they would lose hope. Abortion played a large role in this, but so did a belief that America was chosen by God to be a Christian nation. They acted as if America and the kingdom of God were the same thing. To me, faith was the thing that spurred me to act for good and to work hard for what I believed was right, but it also anchored me in a hope beyond this world. America was not the kingdom of God. That meant that no matter how bad things got, I did not need to despair. But it wasn't an excuse to check out either.

Again, that Gnostic, overspiritualized view led many Christians to believe that the highest form of love was converting others to save them from hell. Never mind their immediate needs. Get them saved and that would all work itself out, many thought. But this dominant mindset added up to something pretty repellent when you could look at it straight: a group of people who talked about God and their own goodness a lot but measured that goodness by how many people they could get to think and believe like them.

———

Ali and I were married in the fall of 2005, and we moved to Washington, DC. My upbringing had trained me to believe that I needed a divine reason for where we were going to live. The city felt like a place of purpose to me, more so than the suburbs. If I was to live out my faith, I wanted to do it in a place upstream of culture, where there were many competing points of view, and where there was real material need. At that time—an era in which many White people were moving back into city centers—the suburbs seemed like a place where everyone had more than enough. That wasn't true, but it was the way I thought of it. Ali and I bought a one-bedroom condo near Catholic University, the same year we got married, and fixed it up. We started attending a Presbyterian church that met in Chinatown. We took a three-week trip to Thailand in 2007 and then had our first child, a son, in October. We also continued to attend a small group from Covenant Life Church with other married couples who were good friends.

The spiritual world was more real to me than ever. One night in our tiny condo, I had a feeling that there was a presence in the hallway. I became convinced that it was an evil spirit, a demon. I was scared and searching for answers about how to think and act, so I went back to Grudem's *Systematic Theology*. I wondered if it said anything about demons. In fact, it did. It explained things in a matter-of-fact tone. The detail that stood out to me the most is that demons cannot know what we are thinking. That made me less afraid. It's hard for me to understand why, years later, but it did. When I sensed the same presence the next night, I spoke to it and told it to leave in Jesus's name. I never felt bothered again after that.

My view of the world and others was still hyper-spiritualized. I was also self-absorbed. On the night before our first child was born, Ali was having contractions. Somehow, as my wife prepared to give birth, this experience was all about me. I wrote a day later in my journal that "at this moment . . . the Lord really gave me grace to switch completely out of selfishness to serving Ali." I wanted to read a book, but "I heard the still small voice of the Holy Spirit whispering that I should do whatever I could to make Ali more comfortable—to be wholly devoted to serving her and helping her." The saints in heaven must have been in awe as they looked on.

I wrote that as I massaged her feet, "I began to feel a joy that I have not experienced whenever my mind has been primarily on what interests me or is of importance to me—such as my job or what I want to read or the latest email I've gotten and may want to respond to." Reading these words years later almost made me physically ill. I was one of those "poor driven creatures" described by novelist Thomas Flanagan who were "so blinded by the light of faith that they can see only the light itself and not the world which faith reveals."[6]

At work, I had an array of experiences that deepened my understanding of the world—of politics and government, of how power works, and of culture and communication. I spent months on a project about the size of government that gave me an up-close look at conservative dogma. I didn't know enough history to understand that White Southerners had often objected to federal government interference as a cover for racist opposition to desegregation and civil rights. And over the years, small government conservatism had morphed into an attitude that held almost all government in contempt, which became the seedbed for a growing nihilism on the political right among those who don't want politics to solve any problems at all.

In 2006, I spent the year covering state government in Maryland. I began to understand how a legislature works. I also covered my first political campaign, a fascinating contest for the US Senate between a young, Black, charismatic Republican named Michael

6. Thomas Flanagan, *The Year of the French* (New York: New York Review of Books, 1979), 305.

Steele and an older, White Democrat named Ben Cardin. I began to grasp the ways that Maryland was split into political power centers. I got to know several Steele staffers well and saw firsthand how campaigns are germinators for talent and relationships. Reporters and staff cut their teeth and learn on the fly in an environment without the same structure or restraint as a legislative setting like Congress. Even at the level of presidential politics, there's no better way for a journalist to develop relationships with key advisers to a politician than by covering the primary. You're in small settings together over a long period of time, often staying in the same hotels as the candidate and his staff, eating at the same restaurants and drinking at the same bars.

I came to understand the vastness of my ignorance. I had seen government budgets as tiresome and irrelevant but came to recognize that there was little else that mattered more. My schooling had given me little in the way of civics education, and I did not have a natural interest in politics, so I had to struggle to grasp even the most basic elements of how things worked.

Through experience and hard work, I was becoming less ignorant and gaining a basic level of knowledge and competence at my craft, year after year and day after day. Most days I would write eight hundred or so words that required research, phone calls, face-to-face interviews, and fact-checking. In 2007, the *Washington Times* assigned me to cover President Bush and to start working at the White House. It wasn't all that much of a promotion. All the newspaper's best reporters were covering the presidential election campaigns, and the *Times* simply needed a warm body at 1600 Pennsylvania. Nonetheless, that circumstance led to a three-year run of covering George W. Bush and then Barack Obama.

Being a White House reporter was the opportunity of a lifetime. I traveled the world with Bush and Obama, flying on Air Force One more than a dozen times. I learned to stomach the pressure of questioning a president, which I did on national television on a few occasions. I interviewed Vice President Dick Cheney. I traveled to the United Nations multiple times. I saw Africa and Asia with Bush, and Europe with Obama.

I studied how power works, up close and in person. I grew familiar with the nuances of our political system that the average person does not have the opportunity to see. And in the years after I covered the White House, I also traversed this country, able to talk to countless Americans face-to-face. I sought to understand their thinking, their choices, their worldviews. It was the long path of acquiring experience and a little bit of expertise.

I have always found the notion of apprenticeship to be in line with one of the basic principles my father taught me, repeating the words of Christ: "Whoever is faithful with very little will also be faithful with much, and whoever is dishonest with very little will also be dishonest with much" (Luke 16:10 BSB). I have seen in recent years how valuable experience and expertise are, and I have been shocked at how widely so many in our society do not share this view. But I've also seen how I was trained in church to despise these crucial qualities.

11

A Dark Turn

The day the Republican Party took one of its sharper turns away from conservatism I didn't notice it at first. It was August 29, 2008. I was with my parents in Bethany Beach, Delaware. It was a hot, sunny day—another scorcher—and before we walked up to the ocean to spend the day swimming and reading and talking, we heard that John McCain was going to announce his running mate that morning. We crowded around the television to watch Sarah Palin make her national debut at a rally in Dayton, Ohio. I was intrigued and generally favorable about McCain's choice. My dad was very excited, as my sister and I both remember.

Five days later, I was twelve hundred miles away inside XCel Energy Center in St. Paul, Minnesota, watching Palin give her speech at the convention. My bosses had assigned me to cover the four-day event, and it was the first national party convention I'd ever attended. I lapped up the spectacle for the first few days, and on the convention's third and penultimate night, I watched from a great seat off to the side in the massive hall as Palin strutted to center stage and blew the roof off the place. It was hard not to be impressed with her raw charisma. The packed arena was electric. But I watched her with an eye that was in the process of being trained in objective critical thinking. The *Washington Times* was conservative and severely biased on a few issues, but it took journalism seriously. I was still getting an education in how to view politics prophetically. And when I use the term *prophetic*, I don't mean I was being taught how to tell the future. I was being taught how to tell the truth. Because of this tutelage, I had earned more discernment. I had a lot more to acquire, and still do. But I was a different person that night in 2008 than I had been just a few years before.

Because of these experiences, when I crowded around the TV with my family in Bethany Beach, I was on a different path than my parents and siblings. Growing up, I had never been taught to think much about politics. *Politics* was a dirty word, beneath us Christians. I did not vote in 1996, the first presidential election in which I was eligible. I paid little attention to the 2000 election. In 2004, I cared a little and voted for George W. Bush. In 2008, I didn't vote, but that was because I had come to believe that journalists shouldn't vote in elections they covered. It's likely I would have voted for McCain.

Like Lou Engle, I didn't think of myself as all that political. But because of my background, I was actually quite political, in that I was a knee-jerk Republican. I was still under the spell of my upbringing, which had taught me there was *nothing to think about*. Just vote GOP. This dismissal of thinking carefully was based on the notion that because Democrats support abortion, voting for any Democrat was unthinkable.

By 2008, I had come to believe that American Christians who despised politics were making a grave mistake. But I still retained a fairly black-and-white view of Democrats, though that was becoming harder as I met more actual Democrats who were real people and who were doing good in the world. I had not yet come to believe, as I do now, that dismissing politics was, in fact, an un-Christian thing. The attitude that Christians shouldn't put too much thought or time or passion into "worldly" things like politics ignored one of the core teachings of Christianity: to fight for the marginalized, the oppressed, the weak, and the subjugated.

Ignoring politics is possible for those who are comfortable, have enough to eat, do not worry about where they will sleep or what they will wear, and are not victims of injustice. It is a luxury to check out.

However, politics has high stakes for those who are on the margins or being abused, because often they need the government to step in, and they need advocates to help them get the assistance they need. We had taken Christ's message—"whatever you did for one of the least of these brothers and sisters of mine, you did for me" (Matt. 25:40)—and limited the application to only one group of the weak and defenseless, the unborn. My church culture then made excuses for why the other groups—the poor, racial minorities, drug addicts, prisoners, refugees, and immigrants—were to blame for their own misfortune. We ignored the ways in which many people fell into suffering and hardship because they lacked the safety nets that others were given at birth, often related to family support in various forms.

Palin's emergence marked a more aggressive rejection of humility, nuance, and the prophetic edge that put Christian principles and self-sacrifice before power and political tribe. It was a doubling down on an us-against-them view. She appealed to the most populist, anti-intellectual, and nativist instincts on the right. She had little in the way of qualifications for the job of vice president, and even less for the presidency. But she could give a good speech.

Republicans countered that Obama was no different. It was true that he was less experienced than most American presidents. It was also true that much of his popularity was due to his identity and image. But Obama and Palin thought about the world in very different ways. Palin's approach was to oversimplify everything and to lean hard into scapegoating the other side. She insinuated that her opponents were foreign, dangerous, and immoral. In contrast, Obama saw the world as a complicated place. He seemed to be introspective and self-critical. I wasn't that impressed with his speeches, and I thought he put too much faith in his own point of view and could be annoying self-righteous. But there was far more self-doubt in him than in Palin. He emphasized the common good. Palin preached tribalism.

For someone like Palin, truth was something we already knew. It was settled and beyond questioning, and the job was to fight against the godless heathens who refused to acknowledge it. For someone like Obama, the fight was not so much against people as it was to strive toward a clarity that was elusive. He was sure of his proposals but less dogmatic about ultimate things, knowing our limitations, understanding that we each see through a glass dimly. He didn't always live up to the standards for political combat that I held, especially in 2012, when his campaign cut Mitt Romney to pieces with a series of caricatures that I thought were unfair.

But Palin's rise took a party already imbalanced against the weak and made it more hostile to those on the margins. It also intensified an antiestablishment attitude. Palin's lack of knowledge and experience prompted her, when called out by the press, to double down on her inexperience and to claim it was an asset. Many conservative Christians already thought that expertise was bad and that insiders were inherently corrupt simply because they were insiders. Palin encouraged that thinking.

Both the ignorance and the combativeness came from the same Gnostic scorn that most Christians held for anything that was not explicitly Christian. White conservative Christians viewed most of the political world as tainted and beyond redemption, so why would anyone want to know anything about it anyway? And there was a sizable number of Christians who, while lamenting the decline of America into a growing godlessness, would also interpret decline and even catastrophe as good, because those things hastened the return of Christ, the rapture that would usher us out of this world and into the next. This was a confused and dark nihilism mixed with a Darwinian "survival of the fittest" individualism.

Our second child was born in 2009. We moved to Capitol Hill, a few minutes' walk from the Capitol. We settled into a period in which I was fulfilled at work and busy at home—having success and being promoted—but Ali was increasingly isolated. I thought we were egalitarian in our marriage, but that was within the limits of my own male-dominated point of view. As work pressures grew greater, I became less attuned to the toll my absences were taking on my wife.

Ali's background was similar to mine. Her father had been a pastor in a small nondenominational church. But she had not spent years enveloped in the same cultish environment I had. Her parents had encouraged her to go to college. Nonetheless, she had still absorbed and internalized messages from church culture that said it was better for women to stay home with their children than go to work and put children in day care. So as our family grew, it wasn't just Ali's ambitions that began to be sidelined. Her whole identity began to recede from view.

We had a few conversations about whether we should do things differently than our parents and put the kids in day care before they were school age, but we never seriously considered it. Ali insisted she wanted to stay home. I did not do much to challenge that thinking.

C. J. Mahaney's church now comprised congregations all over the country and was beginning to spread into other nations and continents, with at least twenty-eight thousand members.[1] He was speaking around the country and publishing books.

C. J. and the other church leaders called themselves the apostolic team. The original apostles were the dozen chosen disciples who lived and traveled with Jesus. After his death, other apostles were chosen to continue the work of the faith. But it was always a select, small group. Becoming an apostle, or thinking of oneself as one, carried with it massive implications for the infallibility of one's judgment. This imbued these self-proclaimed modern "apostles" with a sense of righteousness and bestowed on them incredible authority over others. When this culture was paired

1. Tiffany Stanley, "The Sex-Abuse Scandal That Devastated a Suburban Megachurch," *Washingtonian*, February 14, 2016, https://www.washingtonian .com/2016/02/14/the-sex-abuse-scandal-that-devastated-a-suburban-megachurch -sovereign-grace-ministries/.

with a governance structure that placed decision-making authority within a small group of men, the result started to resemble a cult.

C. J. had installed Josh Harris as senior pastor of Covenant Life Church in 2004. Harris was thirty by that time, having worked at the church for seven years. Harris was someone who wouldn't push very hard against anything C. J. wanted. But the leadership around C. J. was fraying. One "apostle" in particular, Brent Detwiler, was increasingly agitating for C. J. to be more accountable to other leaders. Detwiler was not concerned about sexual or financial impropriety but rather about arrogance. C. J. and Sovereign Grace Ministries had retreated from political or public engagement years before, but he could not escape the politics within his own leadership structure. He was being caught in a trap of his own making. The culture of hypersensitivity to any possible sins—in oneself and others—was being turned against him.

Meanwhile, on the other side of the country, Lou Engle and Ché Ahn continued to move in a more political direction, even though they were much farther away from the nation's capital than C. J. was. Engle's antiabortion rhetoric became more violent and threatening. "The Bible says that no atonement can be made for . . . innocent blood that is shed except the blood of the one who shed it," Engle wrote in his book, *The Call of the Elijah Revolution*. "Does the blood of Christ release us as a nation from the bloodguilt of 44 million unborn babies?" He wrote that America could not "turn back to God" unless it ended all abortions, and he sounded ominous notes: "Make no mistake: God will deal with [abortion], either with a mercy, compassion, and prayer movement, or with a justice and judgment movement." He concluded, "The Lord is mounting his holy war horse, and He is releasing a call. Will you ride with him?"[2] He did not call for violence. In fact, he called for a peaceful movement of prayer and fasting. But the implication of his statements was that a violent judgment was coming if America did not repent.

2. James W. Goll and Lou Engle, *The Call of the Elijah Revolution: The Passion for Radical Change* (Shippensburg, PA: Treasure House, 2008), 78.

Engle's focus was also increasingly on fighting against gay rights. Engle threw himself into the debate over Proposition 8, the ballot question in California intended to ban same-sex marriage that passed in 2008 and was later overturned by a federal judge. Engle's appeal, for some, was in his radicalism. He called on young people to give up everything to serve God single-mindedly, and he portrayed the fight to end abortion as a way to do that. He also offered his followers a chance to be part of something historic. He referred to his first gathering of young people on the National Mall as "a spiritual watershed in America's history."[3] Those self-aggrandizing statements are easier to make for those who believe that God speaks directly and uniquely to them through their intuitions and dreams.

Engle was building up a national network of relationships with other religious figures and politicians. In August 2008, he appeared at a press conference with former Arkansas governor Mike Huckabee, who had been a leading contender for the Republican presidential nomination, and Tony Perkins, president of the Family Research Council, a DC-based right-wing advocacy group.[4] Engle sought to build a movement that was diverse—racially and denominationally. He saw the power of having a coalition of Whites, Blacks, Latinos, and Asians that cut across Protestant and Catholic lines.

Engle was lukewarm about McCain at the press conference appearance, but his tone changed when McCain nominated Palin. Just before Palin debated Joe Biden in the vice presidential debate on October 2, 2008, Engle sent an email to Palin. "Sarah, I could be wrong, but I've been praying for five years for an Esther, with dreams of being a Mordecai to that Esther. I believe you're the one," he said.[5]

3. Goll and Engle, *Call of the Elijah Revolution*, 40.

4. Sarah Posner, "'The Call' Warns of Antichrist Legislation in California and Beyond," *Religion Dispatches*, June 15, 2009, https://religiondispatches.org/the-call-warns-of-antichrist-legislation-in-california-and-beyond/.

5. Michael Joseph Gross, "Is Palin's Rise Part of God's Plan?," *Vanity Fair*, September 17, 2010, https://www.vanityfair.com/news/2010/10/sarah-palin-as-queen-esther-201010.

Esther, whose story is told in the Old Testament book bearing her name, was a Jewish woman who rose to become queen of Persia when the king chose her as his wife, based in large part on her beauty. But then Esther foiled a plot to kill the Jewish people hatched by the king's adviser and helped the Jewish people living in exile in Persia avoid genocide. She won them permission to fight back as well and to kill those who intended to attack them. Esther was helped through these challenges by her cousin Mordecai. Engle's grafting of an American political figure into the biblical mythology was his way of convincing himself, his followers, and Palin herself that she was on a divine mission from God and had God's blessing. But the particulars of the story reflect a violent struggle against other groups. And his comparison of himself to Mordecai was clear as well: he saw himself as an adviser to those with political power.

This use of biblical stories as allegory for current events was a way to place certain political figures on a pedestal, where they could not be questioned or criticized. It was part of a trend, foreshadowing the way that other politicians would be deified using Old Testament stories several years later.

As Engle involved himself with mainstream partisan politics, he also associated with some of the most right-wing figures in American politics, men like Mike Bickle and Rick Joyner. Bickle, the founder of the International House of Prayer in Kansas City, was apoplectic after Obama was elected president. He urged young people to come to his end-of-the-year conference Onething, calling it the most important gathering in his lifetime. "We are living in crisis right now," Bickle said in one video, with Engle standing next to him.[6] In another video, Bickle said that the "prayer movement," which he and Engle were leaders of, was missing out on God's will, or God's mission.[7]

And what God wanted to happen, Bickle said, was super bloody.

6. "IHOP TV Podcast," YouTube video, 6:38, posted by onething TV, November 24, 2008, https://www.youtube.com/watch?v=rVwMmLxBOWY.

7. "IHOP TV Podcast 3," YouTube video, 10:59, posted by onething TV, December 3, 2008, https://www.youtube.com/watch?v=K5FMsDrNyn4.

"Jesus wants the prayer movement to be at the point of the arrow to shift history to the age to come. . . . I'm not just talking about praying and the guys over there changing the laws," Bickle said. "I'm talking about the stuff Moses did. Moses prayed and the heavenly arsenal from heaven struck the military bases of Pharaoh. I'm talking about physical destruction of evil systems and evil resource-bases, coming from heaven. We don't strike them with our hands. We pray, but the military strikes come from heaven."[8]

To be clear, Bickle said that Christians should be praying for God to send missiles from heaven to destroy entire cities. "I'm talking about the prayer faith that heals, and I'm talking about the prayer faith that kills," Bickle continued. "Yes, I said kills. The book of Revelation, you read it. Revelation 11, verse 5, the two prophets at the end, they pray and fire comes down from heaven and kills people. We're talking about a heavenly arsenal, from heaven, striking people and resources. . . . I'm talking about cities, whole resource centers will be destroyed."[9]

This is a Christian leader, a peer of Engle's, exhorting Christians to pray that God carry out mass genocide against those whom Bickle deems to be evil. Think about the implications: If God were to kill thousands, it couldn't be wrong, right? It would be somehow righteous. If God can kill thousands, maybe his followers can too.

While Bickle told his followers to pray that there would be "places in the earth where there's utter destruction," he also warned against other less conservative Christians. Bickle said he wanted to "confront" the "deception in the Emergent church," a group of Christians who were questioning much of the dogma that had come out of the religious right's marriage with the Republican Party. At his conference at the end of 2008, Bickle would teach that there was "a counterfeit justice movement" claiming to represent Christianity, which he said was actually satanic. The hallmarks, he

8. "IHOP TV Podcast 3."
9. "IHOP TV Podcast 3."

said, would be "a religion of affirmation and toleration without absolutes."[10]

Bickle said Satan would trick people into doing terrible things. They would "feed the poor and be deeply involved in humanitarian projects," Bickle said. "[Satan] will inspire acts of compassion but for all the wrong reasons. The goal will be the dignity and happiness of man."[11] Feeding the poor. Humanitarian projects. Acts of compassion. Working toward the dignity and happiness of man. These could all be bad things, Bickle said, because they could somehow lead to Satan worship once people became less politically conservative.

10. Mike Bickle, Onething 2008 Teaching Notes, https://www.mikebickle.org /pdfs/onething2008_Complete_Teaching_Notes_Booklet.pdf.

11. Bickle, Onething 2008 Teaching Notes.

12

Revelation

In 2009 and 2010 I worked for Tucker Carlson, helping him launch *The Daily Caller* website. During this time, I was gaining stature in Washington as an up-and-coming reporter. After eight years at the *Times*, I was now awash in the buzz of working for a media celebrity who could attract real attention and knew how to leverage it. Carlson in 2009 was not yet a right-wing demagogue. Months before hiring me, he'd given a speech in which he had made a compelling case for how conservatives could reform the news media.

"If you create a news organization whose primary objective is not to deliver accurate news, you will fail. You will fail," Carlson told the Conservative Political Action Conference (CPAC), an annual super bowl of sorts for conservative activists and college Republicans. "*The New York Times* is a liberal paper, but it's also—and it is to its core a liberal paper—but it is also a paper that cares about whether they spell people's names right, by and large. It's a paper that actually cares about accuracy."[1] The crowd booed him.

1. Conor Friedorsdorf, "Tucker Carlson Is Hurting America Again," *The Atlantic*, June 20, 2018, https://www.theatlantic.com/ideas/archive/2018/06/tucker-carlson-is-hurting-america-again/563138/. A clip of Carlson saying this is avail-

When *The Daily Caller* launched, Carlson was a dynamo, sitting for profiles with big newspapers and websites, hosting dinners at his home, and making us all laugh every day. Our office was like a Silicon Valley knockoff: Ping-Pong table, beer keg, and bean bags. Conservative voters, meanwhile, were in a different kind of partying mood. The Tea Party was the name for the angry Republican voters who had not been paying attention to politics until two things happened: the 2008 economic crash and the election of Barack Obama. Many of them lost a lot of money in the crash, and they were angry that Wall Street got bailouts. I heard some version of the same story everywhere I went over the next few years as I talked to Republican voters, and I talked to a lot of them. "We were all up on our cloud nines. Had our flat screens. God bless America. Support the troops. We didn't know nothing. We didn't read our Constitution," said a guy named Tom Jones, a small business owner from Lancaster, Pennsylvania, who I met in August 2010 at a rally on the National Mall in DC.[2] The rally was organized by Glenn Beck, a *Fox News* host who specialized in wild-eyed exaggeration and conspiracies. Most conservatives who worked in professional politics inside Washington, DC, saw him as a fringe character. They didn't see that the energy among right-wing voters was increasingly fanatical and antiestablishment. I saw it, but I hoped for the best. I knew these people. They couldn't be that bad.

Many of the voters I met that year were talking about the Constitution and invoking the nation's founders. I was reading many new books about that era too: David McCullough's book on John Adams, Ron Chernow's book on Alexander Hamilton, and Joseph Ellis's books on Thomas Jefferson and George Washington. I was

---

able at "CPAC: Tucker Carlson Tries to Defend the New York Times, Gets Booed [RightWingWatch.org]," YouTube, February 26, 2009, https://www.youtube.com /watch?v=6tD2H6AX1fE&t=1s.

2. Jon Ward, "In Front of Historic Crowd on the Mall, Beck Makes Plea for Spiritual Renewal and Self-Government," *The Daily Caller*, August 28, 2010, https:// dailycaller.com/2010/08/28/in-front-of-historic-crowd-on-the-mall-beck-makes -plea-for-spiritual-renewal-and-self-government/.

drawn to the debate between Hamilton and Jefferson over the size of the government and the role it should play in public life.

At the time, the deification of the founders and the Revolutionary era didn't seem like anything more than sincere patriotism mixed with a bit of jingoism. I did not think that talk of revolution, which occasionally popped up in covering the Tea Party, was literal. I understood concerns about government debt, but I did not agree with the assessment that the country was in a terrible place. Yes, the government was far bigger than it had been at the nation's founding. But the nation was bigger. The population was exponentially larger. The world was more complex. Hamilton had foreseen the need for an evolving government that met the needs of its moment, and he understood the need for a strong central government. Many Tea Party devotees had not considered that our government had at first been built for a rural economy and a small population, and that our country no longer fit that description.

I went down to the National Mall the night before the Beck rally. People were camping out overnight to get seats close to the stage. I talked to a few guys under the trees near the Lincoln Memorial. It was a Friday night. They were planning to sleep in camping chairs under the stars, so we had plenty of time to chat. As I chatted up the Glenn Beck superfans, I started talking about the things I was learning in my reading. I brought up the disagreements between Hamilton and Jefferson over the need for a central bank. I might as well have been speaking Russian. All I got were blank stares.

As I talked to more people around the country over the next few years, I realized that most lacked a rudimentary understanding of the founding figures and ideals they were supposedly fans of. Many of these voters had been able to coast along for a long time during the prosperous 1990s into the new millennium. But the world was changing, and they didn't like it. Economic inequality was growing. Their retirements weren't looking so great. Health care was more expensive. And America was changing. It was more sexually permissive and more racially diverse.

Some people liked to call the backlash to all this an awakening. Another word for awakening is revival. The Great Awakening of the mid-eighteenth century was the first of several religious revivals in America and was followed by a Second Great Awakening early in the nineteenth century. Several other periods of religious fervor had followed in our nation's history, including the Jesus Movement of the 1970s. Beck himself predicted another Great Awakening of personal morality and faith in the summer and fall of 2010. "Something huge is happening in America. I believe it's the third Great Awakening," he said.[3] But this use of the term *awakening* confused a political point of view with a spiritual movement.

Lou Engle, and people like him, had been talking about revival for decades. Friends of my wife's family talked the same way. When we saw them, they'd tell us that they believed revival was just around the corner. Even in my most fanatical period, I was never as obsessed with revival as they were. However, revival was still a part of my own mental framework. I still saw politics as a lost cause for the most part. Government could not change people's hearts. The only thing that could "turn the nation back to God" was a revival in which large numbers of people were converted to Christianity. That's why at many church events, and Republican gatherings, someone will quote from the Old Testament book of 2 Chronicles: "If my people, who are called by my name, will humble themselves and pray and seek my face and turn from their wicked ways, then I will hear from heaven, and I will forgive their sin and will heal their land" (7:14).

It wasn't new for the religious right to cloak its quest for power in the flag and in religious language, claiming that God was on their side. But the Tea Party era created a resurgence in this merger of the ideas of religious and political revival, deepening the conviction of many on the right that they were on the right side of a cosmic contest between good and evil.

----

3. Glenn Beck, "America's Third Great Awakening," transcript of September 3, 2010, radio show, *Fox News*, January 14, 2015, https://www.foxnews.com/story /americas-third-great-awakening.

About six months into working for Carlson, it was clear that he was not serious about "finding the facts and bringing them to people," as he had claimed at CPAC. I left in early 2011 and went to work at an ill-fated project started by Rupert Murdoch's Newscorp called *The Daily*, which poured tons of money into a beautifully designed news product with a fatal flaw: it wasn't updated more than twice a day. It was a static digital product trying to compete with the always-up-to-date internet. Two weeks into this job, I got a call from a top editor at the *Huffington Post* who was close to Arianna Huffington. He met me on Capitol Hill and offered me a job to cover the Republican presidential primary. I knew many Republicans in Washington because I'd worked for conservative news outlets, and I understood the conservative point of view. It wasn't a hard call to say yes.

In my new job, I traveled the country talking to voters. I acquired new levels of insight into the ways our political system worked and into the ways that many Americans thought. Mostly these were Republican voters, since I was writing about the 2012 primary. As a result, I spent countless hours talking with people in Iowa, New Hampshire, South Carolina, and other states like Ohio and Nevada. Most of these people had a right-leaning point of view. I asked them questions, wrote down what they said, then tried to write about it in a way that respected their perspective.

I've always thought of this in recent years when arguing with friends and family over the direction of the country when they make comments about how I don't understand their point of view or, worse, that I can't or don't want to. It has been my job to enter into the perspectives of those I write about, and it has been my privilege to spend much of the last decade writing about American conservatives and Republican voters.

In the summer of 2011, C. J. Mahaney's world exploded. Brent Detwiler posted several hundred pages of documents online.[4] They

---

4. Brent Detwiler, "The Documents," BrentDetwiler.com, http://www.brent detwiler.com/the-documents/.

included email exchanges and notes of meetings. Most of the hundreds of pages of documents went to great lengths to allege that C. J. was prideful. This might sound relatively harmless. We tell our loved ones we are proud of them. We take pride in a job well done. But in the alternative universe I grew up in, to be proud in any way was the ultimate sin. C. J. wrote an entire book about this called *Humility: True Greatness*. And as was often the case with C. J., there were some good things in his book. But the world C. J. created and exercised control over remained self-contained and isolated from the broader world. Only those who were non-threatening were allowed in. Anyone who posed an obstacle to C. J.'s power and influence was removed or marginalized. Another key element of this toxic mix: anyone not in the church or not praised by C. J. and his top pastors was outside the circle of trust and had nothing to offer. In fact, they were suspect.

When Detwiler published the documents online, showing examples of C. J. ignoring or dismissing "observations" from other pastors that he was arrogant, this was a scandal in their world. Detwiler noted that the other apostles had "a very limited view of what is going on in [C. J.'s] life, a narrow window to look through, and limited opportunity for observation of C. J."[5] C. J.'s brother-in-law was quoted as saying that he hadn't "heard C. J. confess sin, like lust."[6] In one 2005 meeting, Josh Harris was quoted as saying, "Maybe C. J. doesn't sin as much as we do."[7] Another top leader, Dave Harvey, stated in a meeting in which others were challenging C. J. that "it is an honor and a blast to serve C. J. regardless of whether he agrees or makes any changes."[8]

On and on it went for hundreds of pages. Ultimately, the documents were an indictment of the leaders themselves. It was like

---

5. Brent Detwiler, "Brent Detwiler Documents: Parts 1–7," part 2, p. 111. Available at http://static1.1.sqspcdn.com/static/f/970485/14056602/1315502713813/Brent%27s+Documents+Parts+1-7.pdf?token=uZ%2BvAIjLIXooG8iFuSeIC3r%2F0Fs%3D.

6. Detwiler, "Brent Detwiler Documents," part 1, p. 24.

7. Detwiler, "Brent Detwiler Documents," part 1, p. 23.

8. Detwiler, "Brent Detwiler Documents," part 1, p. 10.

reading internal memos detailing infighting among Soviet Union bureaucrats. Many of them tried to outdo the others with their flattery and self-effacement. They had become consumed with a weird witch hunt for the slightest imperfections in each other. They were being eaten alive by the very thought and control mechanisms they had used to dominate those below them. And C. J. had helped make it possible.

The documents exposed one of the greatest tragedies of this church movement. For people who claimed to have a message of life and hope that they wanted to share with the world, and who believed in a God who commanded them to care for those in need, the leaders seemed to spend a lot of their time in an endless procession of meetings in which they scrutinized each other to try to identify the most insignificant peccadilloes.

But there was one bombshell. Buried in the documents that Detwiler published online was the transcript of a phone call from 1997 in which C. J. had threatened to blackmail Larry Tomczak.[9] C. J. had wanted Tomczak to leave the church under the pretense that he was morally deficient. Most likely, C. J. thought this would marginalize Tomczak in the eyes of church members and reduce the threat that he would pose to C. J.'s position of leadership. Tomczak said he was leaving over theological differences. C. J. became so angry at this that he told Tomczak that he would share details with the church of a sexual incident involving Tomczak's teenage son. Detwiler's documents showed that C. J. had convinced the boy to talk to him about what had happened by promising confidentiality and then had used that information against the boy's father. We know all this because Tomczak and his wife tape-recorded a phone call in which Tomczak baited C. J. into repeating his threat. "[My son's] name has been floated out there when there's statements like 'revealing more details about my sin.' What are you getting at?" Tomczak said, setting the trap.[10]

9. Detwiler, "Brent Detwiler Documents," part 3, beginning at p. 131.
10. Detwiler, "Brent Detwiler Documents," part 3, p. 139.

"[The son's] name isn't just 'floated out there'—I'm stating it!" C. J. said.

"C. J., how can you do that after you encouraged [my son] to confess everything; get it all out. Then when he did, you reassured him—'You have my word, it will never leave this room,'" Tomczak exclaimed.

C. J.'s response was no different from that of a corrupt politician or a duplicitous lawyer: "My statement was made in the context of that evening. If I knew then what you were going to do, I would have re-evaluated what I communicated," C. J. said. His word was not his word. It was contingent, fungible, flexible, breakable.

Tomczak's wife spoke up at this point in the conversation. "C. J., are you aware that you are blackmailing Larry?" Doris said. "Shame on you, C. J.! As a man of God and a father, shame on you!"[11]

I was shocked. It was only then that I realized how deep a spell C. J. had cast over so many of us. It was the kind of raw power play that I had not conceived was part of C. J.'s DNA. I had been out of his circle of influence for many years, but when I read the transcript of that call, it was like scales fell off my eyes, and I saw that—whatever his good qualities—he was a calculating leader intent on consolidating power. The fact that it took me so long to see this is testament to how deeply I had been bewitched.

The whole episode reminded me of the scene in C. S. Lewis's *The Silver Chair*. A queen of the underworld puts the protagonist and his friends under a spell with the help of an entrancing fragrance being released from a fire around which they are gathered, a magical instrument, and by singing a captivating song. But then Puddleglum, a pessimistic and odd character, rouses himself, walks over to the fire, and stomps it out with his webbed feet.

Puddleglum's solution—like Detwiler's decision to publish those documents—was messy, but it broke the spell.

---

11. Detwiler, "Brent Detwiler Documents," part 3, p. 139.

13

Theocrats on the March

By the summer of 2011 I had been gone from Covenant Life Church for several years, but when I heard that C. J. Mahaney was going to address the church about Brent Detwiler's documents, I made sure to show up. I walked into the auditorium at the church, turned on my recorder to capture the moment, and watched as C. J. came to the stage. He spoke for about twenty-five minutes. He began by dismissing much of Detwiler's report but then portrayed himself as a humble sinner. "I don't agree with a number of Brent's charges and conclusions, nor with the manner with which he has presented his offenses," C. J. said. "However, here's my purpose this evening, here's why I'm here, here's why I wanted to be here, here's what I want to do this evening. My purpose this evening is not to criticize Brent or to defend myself. My purpose this evening is to inform you about various ways I have sinned. That's my purpose. Various ways I have sinned, various ways I have failed. That's primarily what this evening is about."

But C. J. then wove a tale of how much he had done to atone for his shortcomings and how he had been wronged by Detwiler.

He portrayed Detwiler as a vengeful and punitive critic who was obsessed with C. J.'s shortcomings and refused to forgive him. C. J. said he had drafted an apology but that "Brent wrote back and informed me that my confession was not specific enough. . . . I then drafted a second confession about ten pages or so. It saddens me to report to you that Brent did not find this confession adequate."

Near the end of his presentation, C. J. broached the elephant in the room: his attempt to blackmail Larry Tomczak. He had a surprise for the congregation. Tomczak had, a few months earlier, written him a letter "appealing that we meet and that we be reconciled." C. J. said he had held "a series of meetings" with Tomczak. "And I am humbled and I am delighted to report to you that when we met and I confessed my sins to Larry and [another pastor], they freely and immediately and graciously and with tears of joy forgave me." The timing of this revelation was certainly questionable. C. J. was only telling the church about his rapprochement with Tomczak now that his past behavior had been exposed. But he sought to convince the congregation that it was all water under the bridge, the problem had been solved, and he had invited Tomczak to speak at an upcoming pastors' conference. "We will once again stand side by side," C. J. said. He would be taking a "leave of absence" from his position as president of Sovereign Grace Ministries, but his comment about leading an upcoming conference with Tomczak made clear he wasn't going anywhere.

I didn't spend much time thinking about C. J. and Covenant Life Church after that. I had a growing family I loved to be with and an exciting career covering the 2012 presidential campaign. A little over a year after C. J. was exposed, I was in Denver watching rapper will.i.am try to rouse a lethargic crowd of Democrats at Sloan Lake Park on a very cold weekday morning. Temperatures were in the low forties on that October day. But there were a few hundred people at a rally for Barack Obama the day after he had laid a massive egg in the first debate of the presidential election against Mitt Romney. I'd watched it from the media room at the

University of Denver and then quizzed Obama's campaign advisers afterward in a scrum of other reporters. Obama was clearly peeved about having to answer to some Mormon management consultant, and he pouted and glowered all night while Romney offered vigorous and upbeat plans for the future.

But that next morning, after will.i.am left the stage, I stood and watched as Obama unleashed a new wave of attacks against Romney, portraying him as an enemy of women and even of Big Bird, the *Sesame Street* character. I thought the attacks were unfair and dishonest, but they worked. It was a lesson in hardball politics, and the attacks paid off with the many millions of American voters—of both parties—who don't know much about politics and vote based on personality and image. It was the first presidential election I'd covered full-time, and I spent each day that year digging into the truthfulness of what each candidate was saying, studying their plans for governance, talking to their advisers, and speaking with voters at rallies across the country. It was startling to uncover how little most people knew about any of this.

Granted, I knew that most people didn't have the time or the patience to put into the effort to understand the politics at play in the election. But that was why journalists and media outlets are a resource for regular people: to help them make sense of it all. Yet increasingly, it seemed like so much of public opinion was moved by the superficial or simplistic. People love to complain about media bias, but most often it's news consumers who create the demand for frivolous outrage-bait in televised news reports because they watch it in large numbers. Most also change the channel when programming is less entertaining. This conditions media executives to give the audience more of what they want, to reap the financial reward of better ratings and higher ad rates. To me, superficiality is a far greater problem than point-of-view bias because it drives the political debate away from solving real problems, deepens polarization, and erodes trust in government.

And then there were the charismatic Christians like Lou Engle, who was agonizing over whether to support Romney. Engle said Romney was the "lesser of two evils" because even though he opposed abortion and had supported overturning *Roe v. Wade*, Romney made exceptions for rape, incest, and the life of the mother. In a *Charisma* magazine column, Engle said, "My position has been to reject the compromise of simply voting for the lesser of two evils, believing that my allegiance is given to a higher King and a higher kingdom." He concluded, "Therefore my no-vote actually becomes a prophetic act, a vote of conscience, not abdication."[1]

Then Engle raised a hypothetical scenario that showed how "the wrong application of right principles" could cloud the judgment of "the righteous," which he clearly considered himself to be. "If I had been a Christian conservative in pre-Nazi Germany, as the nation floundered in moral and economic woes, and there I heard the rousing moral clarity of a leader promising a strong economy, who was also pro-family, pro-marriage, anti-debauchery and drunkenness, etc., could I have actually made the mistake of voting as a matter of conviction for Hitler (who in fact adopted those many good positions)? Could principles in fact blind me to the moment, such that I would support the raising of a king whom Christ Himself would want torn down?" Engle wrote. "Whoa! This is a deeply troubling thought."[2]

Indeed. This kind of self-examination would be absent in a few short years with a different Republican candidate for president.

Engle ended up supporting Romney because his friend James Goll, with whom he coauthored a book, remembered a dream he'd had four years prior in which God showed him a vision of a baseball game and told him that "when the nation has been thrown a curve ball, I will have a man prepared who comes from the state of Michigan and he will have a big mitt capable of catching whatever is thrown his way."[3] Engle said that "these prophetic experiences

1. Lou Engle, "Lou Engle Ponders Prophetic Implications of Romney Vote," *Charisma News*, October 30, 2012, https://www.charismanews.com/opinion/34408-lou-engle-ponders-prophetic-implications-of-romney-vote.

2. Engle, "Lou Engle Ponders Prophetic Implications."

3. James Goll, "Liberalism Will Give Way to True Conservatism," *Charisma*, November 1, 2012, https://www.charismamag.com/spirit/prophecy/15742-james-goll-liberalism-will-give-way-to-true-conservatism.

seemed to indicate that Romney was a sort of window of mercy to America on several fronts."[4]

Engle played an active role in the 2012 election. In 2011, his Call events were said to be the inspiration for a rally in Houston with thirty thousand people where Texas governor Rick Perry spoke and prayed. Engle and others like him began getting more attention in the press, often in reference to something called the New Apostolic Reformation (NAR). This was a term used by missionary and writer C. Peter Wagner, who had deemed the twenty-first century to be a "Second Apostolic Age," according to journalist Sarah Posner.[5] Just as Covenant Life Church leaders had called themselves apostles, Wagner believed there were men who could hear directly from God in a way ordinary people couldn't.

Wagner and other leaders in the New Apostolic Reformation—or the neocharismatic movement, as scholar Dale M. Coulter called it—focused a lot on demons. "Wagner suggested that there was a hierarchy of governance among evil spirits with some being over nations while others were over neighborhoods," Coulter wrote. "Spiritual warfare took on a strategic dimension. A congregation that wished to evangelize an area could map out the strongholds and then begin to pray specifically against them, or even go on a prayer walk around those areas."[6] This was the imaginary world of Frank Peretti essentially catechized into the religious practice of millions of Americans.

"Books began to be written about seeing angels and even activating angels who were also over geographical regions as the counter to demonic forces," Coulter wrote. "Moreover, prayer and worship became weapons to actualize the presence of the

4. Engle, "Lou Engle Ponders Prophetic Implications."

5. Sarah Posner, "Rick Perry and the New Apostolic Reformation," *Religion Dispatches*, July 19, 2011, https://religiondispatches.org/rick-perry-and-the-new-apostolic-reformation/.

6. Dale M. Coulter, "Neocharismatic Christianity and the Rise of the New Apostolic Reformation," *Firebrand*, January 18, 2021, https://firebrandmag.com/articles/neocharismatic-christianity-and-the-rise-of-the-new-apostolic-reformation.

kingdom."[7] In other words, some of the people jumping up and down and singing at Christian worship services thought they were summoning angels and playing an active part in defeating evil spirits by doing so. It all brought to mind the words of C. S. Lewis: "There are two equal and opposite errors into which our race can fall about the devils. One is to disbelieve in their existence. The other is to believe, and to feel an excessive and unhealthy interest in them."[8]

Another key belief of the NAR movement was that Christians should not withdraw from or avoid involvement in culture and politics. In fact, Christians should "take dominion" and bring the "seven mountains of culture" (arts and entertainment, business, family, government, media, religion, and education) under God's control—through their leadership, of course.[9] The seven mountains terminology was in some ways just fresh paint on old ideas. Some of it even had roots in the Calvinist theology that Covenant Life Church had embraced, which charismatics like Engle had rejected at the time. But now they were embracing some of these Calvinist-tainted beliefs. In 2013, Bill Johnson, the powerful head of Bethel Churches, published a book called *Invading Babylon: The 7 Mountain Mandate* with Lance Wallnau, a Pentecostal author and business consultant.

This was also a shift away from the political and cultural withdrawal of traditional Pentecostalism. My own upbringing had been more traditionally Pentecostal in the sense of staying in church and away from "the world." Margaret Poloma, a sociologist at the University of Akron who closely studied Pentecostalism and charismatics, made the following observation: "Whereas their spiritual forefathers in the Pentecostal movement would have eschewed involvement in politics, the New Apostles believe they have a divine

7. Coulter, "Neocharismatic Christianity."

8. C. S. Lewis, preface to *The Screwtape Letters* (1942; repr., New York: Harper-Collins, 2001), ix.

9. "The Evangelicals Engaged In Spiritual Warfare," August 19, 2011, heard on *Fresh Air*, NPR, https://www.npr.org/2011/08/24/139781021/the-evangelicals-engaged-in-spiritual-warfare.

mandate to rescue a decaying American society. Their apostolic vision is to usher in the 'Kingdom of God.' Where does God stop and they begin? I don't think they know the difference."[10]

It was also a shift away from a theology that believed in the rapture. "Taking dominion" was a stance held by those who believed that Christ's return would come only after his followers had reformed the world sufficiently for him to come back. Apparently, the rapture had been called off, but none of these leaders were telling their many followers. It was easier to let these enormous changes in theology go unnoticed.

<hr/>

Meanwhile, after the revelations in the documents published online by Brent Detwiler, C. J. took a brief leave of absence, but he was soon back at the job of running Sovereign Grace Ministries. At Covenant Life Church, however, Josh Harris and other pastors decided to withdraw the congregation from Sovereign Grace.[11]

C. J., in response, moved to Louisville and in 2012 started a new church with two of his sons-in-law as pastors and a few loyal advisers and fellow pastors. His proximity to Al Mohler and Southern Baptist Theology Seminary gave him access to a steady stream of young graduates who emerged from the seminary ready to assume pastoral positions in his wounded movement.

But in the fall of 2012, two more dominoes fell. A civil lawsuit was filed in October alleging that C. J. and other pastors had taken part in "an ongoing conspiracy" to "permit sexual deviants to have unfettered access to children for issues of predation, and to obstruct justice by covering up ongoing and past predation."[12] And in December, a county prosecutor indicted a former youth group leader at Covenant Life Church, Nate Morales, for mo-

10. Quoted in Forrest Wilder, "Rick Perry's Army of God," *Texas Observer*, August 3, 2011, https://www.texasobserver.org/rick-perrys-army-of-god/.

11. Brent Detwiler, "Joshua Harris Asks Covenant Life Church to Leave Sovereign Grace Ministries over Ungodly Leadership Culture," BrentDetwiler.com, November 28, 2012, http://www.brentdetwiler.com/brentdetwilercom/joshua -harris-asks-covenant-life-church-to-leave-sovereign-g.html.

12. Case No. 369721, Montgomery County Circuit Court, Maryland Civil Division, filed October 12, 2012, http://www.brentdetwiler.com/class-action-lawsuit/.

lesting several boys in the church during the 1980s and into the 1990s.[13]

The lawsuit from 2012 was a dizzying document. It included allegations that were credible alongside others that were clearly less so. Morales was convicted in state court of molesting at least four boys over several years in the 1980s and early 1990s, when I was a young boy myself. Morales was allowed to lead youth meetings and attend sleepovers with younger boys, and his crimes were never reported by pastors to police, despite pleas from the victims that they do so. Morales was sentenced to forty years in prison in 2014.[14]

The civil lawsuit against the church for other abuse cases eventually had five named plaintiffs and six other anonymous plaintiffs but was dismissed in 2013 because of the statute of limitations, and an appeal was dismissed by the Maryland Court of Special Appeals.[15] Nonetheless, there have been "four other sex offenders [who] were convicted of sexually abusing children as young as 2 years old," and "police files confirm pastors knew of the abuse but, as the victim's [*sic*] families note, the pastors were not involved in reporting," according to Rachael Denhollander, a lawyer and victims' advocate.[16]

Amid all the controversy, one pattern emerged: pastors had encouraged church members not to involve the police in sex abuse cases because they wanted to resolve all issues within the church, in an environment that they controlled. They believed

13. Eric Tucker, "Md. Church Member Accused of Molestation in 1980s," *Associated Press*, February 4, 2013, https://www.culteducation.com/group/1146 -sovereign-grace-ministries/19233-md-church-member-accused-of-molestation -in-1980s.html.

14. Brianne Carter and Kevin Lewis, "Judge Calls Former Church Youth Group Leader Nathaniel Morales a 'Cowardly Pervert' before Sentencing Him to 40 Years in Prison," WJLA News, August 14, 2014, https://wjla.com/news/crime/na thaniel-morales-former-covenant-life-church-leader-convicted-of-sexual-abuse -to-be-sentenced-thurs.

15. Morgan Lee, "Sovereign Grace Sex Abuse Case Appeal Dismissed by Maryland's Court of Special Appeals," *Christian Post*, July 1, 2014, https://www.christian post.com/news/sovereign-grace-sex-abuse-case-appeal-dismissed-by-marylands -court-of-special-appeals.html.

16. Rachel Denhollander, "Response to Sovereign Grace Churches," Facebook, last edited May 5, 2021, https://www.facebook.com/notes/1625049014354463/.

they had superior discernment and morality and higher values than the world outside the church. When I was inside Covenant Life Church, we thought that we were holy and that those who were not on the same path as us were lost souls, pagans, sad cases.

So the idea of allowing civil authorities inside the tent to adjudicate or control what happened was anathema to these leaders. Here's one summary of the claims:

> According to a former member of a Sovereign Grace church, victims' families were compelled or misled into not pursuing legal action. If charges were brought, church leaders wrote letters requesting leniency, or urged victims' families to do so. Families were pressured to forgive perpetrators, and "even children as young as three were forced to meet their abusers for 'reconciliation.'" One woman was informed by church leaders that her husband's urge to molest their ten-year-old daughter could be attributed to her own failure to meet his sexual needs; she was told to take her husband back, lock her daughter's bedroom, and have sex with him regularly.[17]

There was also a cultural allergy to looking life square in the eye. Our churches always wanted to keep life from being too complicated or messy. We wanted to keep breathing the same purified air we thought we were breathing all the time. Keep the mess out. Keep the complications away. Keep smiling. Keep praying. Keep singing praise songs. Keep raising your hands and closing your eyes. Keep feeling the Holy Spirit. Keep feeling joyful. Keep your soul in hope and faith. Keep your eyes on Jesus.

I'll never forget knocking on the Mahaneys' door one time. Somebody opened the door; I don't remember who. I just remember that I could hear a worship album playing loudly from one of the rooms. The house looked spotless. The impression I had then was that there was some holy smoke rolling around in there. It was the holy of holies. But it was also like the homes of many

17. Kristin Kobes du Mez, "Far-Right Evangelicals Excused Sexual Abuse Long before Donald Trump," *Flux*, June 5, 2021, https://flux.community/kristin-kobes-du-mez/2021/06/evangelical-sexual-abuse-russell-moore-trump.

Christians I knew. It was like my own home at times. We played that religious music almost as an incantation to ward off the spirits: the spirits of complicated thoughts, of hard-to-answer questions, of problems that required more than a Bible verse. We were trying to ward off the many questions that can be answered with only silence or the words "I don't know."

Finally, there was the chauvinism. The pastors' belief that men and fathers were vital, more valued than almost anything in life, led them to essentially erase and run roughshod over the dignity and worth of women. Whenever pastors counseled couples in conflict or got involved with cases of physical or sexual abuse, women and children were treated as collateral damage.

The example of David Adams is instructive. He confessed to molesting his stepdaughter until she was fourteen and was eventually sentenced to five years in state prison as part of a plea deal. But the pastors made decisions and statements that treated women as little more than accessories. According to the lawsuit, pastor Gary Ricucci told Adams's wife, Peggy, that Dave wasn't a pedophile but was attracted to the woman his stepdaughter "was becoming."[18] And the priority for Ricucci and other leaders, always, was that Adams be allowed to "reconcile" with his family and take his place back inside the family unit. For our pastors, the idea of a family without a father and a husband was the ultimate evil. Protecting a young girl from further abuse and seeking justice were less of a priority than this. The lawsuit alleged that women were "threatened and ostracized if they resisted efforts to 'restore' their abusive husbands and fathers to a position of 'leadership' in the family."[19]

These cultural attitudes are a big part of the reason why Ali and I had not thought about her career when planning our family. We believed children were a blessing. But as our family grew, we did not spend enough time thinking about Ali's personhood. We

18. Tiffany Stanley, "The Sex-Abuse Scandal That Devastated a Suburban Megachurch," *Washingtonian*, February 14, 2016, https://www.washingtonian.com/2016/02/14/the-sex-abuse-scandal-that-devastated-a-suburban-megachurch-sovereign-grace-ministries/.
19. Kobes du Mez, "Far-Right Evangelicals."

sought to have a home where I shared the duties of domesticity. We recoiled at the lack of involvement in home duties that we had seen in the men of our parents' generation. But both of us had been taught to think of her ambitions as a second-tier concern. So her work in landscape design was cut down after we had our second child, and she stopped working entirely after we had our third.

Our marriage was looking more conventional than we had planned. We talked about how we didn't want her identity and purpose to be wrapped up in motherhood but, for the time being, they were. My career was going well, but Alison felt as if her identity was increasingly not only being consumed by child-rearing but to a large extent erased. She might not have been able to put it into words yet, but I was too busy with work—caught up in the drama of the election and a sense of self-importance—to be all that curious about it.

The abuse cases were damaging to C. J.'s status, but he remained in good standing with Al Mohler and other religious leaders in the evangelical world. In addition, the lawsuit's use of the word *conspiracy* gave him something to fight. "I have never conspired to protect a child predator," he said.[20] He and the other pastors didn't think they had been hiding anything. But the focus on a legal term seemed to prevent him and others in his orbit from grappling with the deeper issues of the toxic culture they had created. Sovereign Grace went into a defensive posture, and so there was little chance its leaders would examine the more subtle and pervasive systems of thought and behavior they had created that had done damage to so many. Not all the suffering was debilitating or traumatic. As usual, those who were most vulnerable or weak already were most affected. I didn't think of myself as a victim, and still don't, yet the scars of the intense self-scrutiny and self-loathing would last for years.

20. C. J. Mahaney, "A Statement from C. J. Mahaney," Sovereign Grace Church of Louisville, May 22, 2014, https://www.sgclouisville.org/blog/post/a-statement-from-c-j-mahaney.

Around this time, Alison and I severed the last of our connections to Sovereign Grace and Covenant Life Church. We'd been attending a church launched by friends of mine from Covenant Life. I'd known from the beginning there was too much old residue—too many mental habits and cultural norms that were suffocating and counterproductive.

After we left, we didn't go to church much for a year or two. But when we started sending our kids to public school, we felt the kids should have some religious instruction. So we started going to church at a congregation a few blocks away from the row house we were renting on Capitol Hill. I didn't think I'd ever be back in a church with a rock band, but the services were short, the childcare was great, the sermons were sensible and well done, and we could walk there. The church was also racially diverse and involved in community work. Ali and I both felt like we were able to reconnect, slowly, with our faith in a positive way that gave us space to sort through things. And they gave out donuts afterward.

PART 3

Reformation
2013–2022

14

Reckoning

The phrase "Black Lives Matter" made me feel defensive and fearful when I started hearing it regularly in 2013 and 2014. All kinds of questions went through my head. *Why just Black lives? Are they saying White lives don't matter? Is this going to lead to people like me being targeted?* I thought the slogan was divisive and off-putting.

When Michael Brown was killed in Ferguson, Missouri, in the summer of 2014, I didn't understand the outrage about it. I focused on the things he had done to provoke the officer. I couldn't hear the larger outrage about systemic injustice in policing and criminal justice. I had a lot of wax in my ears and many obstacles blocking my view.

But I saw that people of color reacted differently to Brown's death, and I wanted to understand why. So I decided to put into practice my father's mantra from the Bible: "Be quick to listen, slow to speak and slow to become angry" (James 1:19). I started seeking out conversations with Black people about race and, most important, resisted the instinct to become fearful and defensive whenever conversations about race made me uncomfortable.

My own experience in journalism had proven that talking to people from different backgrounds—with a focus on listening and not trying to get some point across—could be transformative. Encountering different points of view, with a learner's posture and without defensiveness based in ego and identity, is a gift. For years, I had practiced this in conversations with conservatives all over the country. Now I tried to apply the discipline to the issue of race.

One of the people I spoke with at this time was Benjamin Dixon, a Black Bostonian who had started a talk show online and writes a popular blog. I was surprised that he was a Christian. I had been programmed from a young age to equate conservative political positions with authentic faith. Dixon was quite liberal. He was a Bernie Sanders supporter. My presumption about his background betrayed my ignorance. I approached him as a reporter, and I said things like "Help me understand this." I didn't hide where I didn't understand his point of view, and I asked critical questions. I was worried he would attack me for doing so, but instead he was more than happy to graciously talk with me.

Those conversations with Dixon and others, face-to-face and over the phone, drew me out of my narrow point of view. Ever so slowly I began to see that I had been raised to think about racism as a matter between individuals, with no connection to a larger context. I began to grasp that police shootings in some cases were just one way in which systemic injustice against Black people had deep roots in American history and culture. I began to see that almost everything about American evangelical religion primes a person to resist thinking about the way racism can have a systemic effect. The emphasis, all the time, is on the individual's relationship with God. Sin is individualistic, never systemic. Actions are viewed in isolation. The outside world is shunned. History is deprioritized. The poor are blamed for their suffering because of their own moral shortcomings. Very slowly this onion was being unpeeled in my mind.

Videos of police brutality kept emerging. The footage of Walter Scott being shot in the back in Charleston, South Carolina, by a White officer[1] and then of Eric Garner being choked by police

1. Alan Blinder, "Michael Slager, Officer in Walter Scott Shooting, Gets 20-Year Sentence," *New York Times*, December 7, 2017, https://www.nytimes.com /2017/12/07/us/michael-slager-sentence-walter-scott.html.

officers in New York[2] was horrifying and galvanizing. The implication was clear: How many killings of people of color by police weren't caught on cell phone video? I thought about the fact that I knew my own safety was valued differently than that of others. If I, a White, educated, professional male living on Capitol Hill was killed or robbed by criminals, the response from police, politicians, and the press would be significant. My death would get attention in places of power that impacted policy and led to action. By contrast, the murders of Black people went regularly unnoticed by those outside their community. This was one way that White lives mattered more than Black lives. This was one reason why people said Black Lives Matter.

My conversations with others reduced my defensiveness and gave me room to think about things like Black Lives Matter and terms like *White supremacy* from a more objective, less emotional point of view. *I was engaged rather than simply defensive.* That was a crucial development. I was still troubled by much that was said. But I was listening. I had started down a path that I think is the one Jesus calls all his followers to walk. Jesus, I have come to see over and over, calls his followers to self-sacrificial love, to vulnerability in a quest for reconciliation, healing, and justice. This process is often uncomfortable. I came to see that by emphasizing reconciliation without justice, I often wanted to skip to the feel-good part without the necessary hard work of repair.

My education continued as I worked on a book about Ted Kennedy and Jimmy Carter. My research took me on a journey into Georgia's past. Tunneling back into Georgia history was eye-opening. In some ways, it was like taking a shovel to the foundation of a house and unearthing a massive sinkhole underneath it. There was so much American history I didn't know, and so little

2. Al Baker, J. David Goodman, and Benjamin Mueller, "Beyond the Chokehold: The Path to Eric Garner's Death," *New York Times*, June 13, 2015, https://www.nytimes.com/2015/06/14/nyregion/eric-garner-police-chokehold-staten-island.html.

about the history of race I had been taught. Carter was born in 1924, and so I spent a lot of time reading old newspaper articles and conducting historical research about that period of time in Georgia. I had never known that Georgia was central to the history of the Ku Klux Klan (KKK). More importantly, I had never known that the KKK had been born and had died three different times, surging back to life each time in response to civil rights advances.

Georgia was the birthplace of the Klan's second iteration, which came as the country was experiencing massive levels of immigration. It was the lynching of a Jewish man named Leo Frank in 1915 that sparked the KKK to rise again. This was an alarming discovery. If the KKK had died out and come back three times already in our history since the Civil War, it was conceivable that something similar could happen again. This would have been pretty much unthinkable to me growing up as a White child coming of age in the 1990s in the suburbs.

My understanding of America's story was woefully impoverished. I knew virtually nothing about the Jim Crow era and the decades of state-sponsored terrorism that were inflicted on African Americans after the Civil War and Reconstruction. I began to see that the pattern of American history was not a straight line of progress on race but rather an uneven and often painful process of progress followed by backlash. We hadn't moved as a country from the Emancipation Proclamation to Martin Luther King Jr. to Barack Obama. Rather, the rights of Blacks to vote and hold office and own property were steadily eroded and erased after the end of Reconstruction, the bodies of Black men and women stayed effectively enslaved through convict leasing, and this apartheid system was upheld and enforced through terrorism, mob torture, and vigilante justice.[3] Slavery had effectively continued in many parts of the country, under other names, even as America was liberating Europe during World War II.

3. "Reconstruction in America: Racial Violence after the Civil War," Equal Justice Initiative, 2020, https://eji.org/report/reconstruction-in-america/.

One of the things that sickened me most was learning the stories of vicious lynchings of Black men and women in the Deep South.[4] To my horror, many took place at the hands of White Southerners who claimed to be devout Christians. This is one of the dark legacies of American Christianity. The example of Mary Turner is sickeningly illustrative.

Turner was a thirty-three-year-old Black woman, a mother of two who was eight months pregnant in 1918 and lived in southern Georgia. That year, White mobs erupted in a spasm of violence in Lowndes and Brooks counties when a Black farmworker murdered an abusive White plantation owner. Rather than allow the matter to be adjudicated in the courts, Whites decided to send a message. They killed at least thirteen people over a two-week period, lynching most of them. One of them was Hayes Turner, Mary Turner's husband. He was lynched by the mob, and his body was left hanging from a tree. Many onlookers came to gawk at the spectacle after attending church services.

Mary Turner reportedly was heard by others denouncing the mob and stating she would swear out a warrant if she found out the names of those responsible for her husband's murder. In response, a mob seized her, hung her upside down, and burned her alive. And then someone in that mob took a knife, sliced open her stomach, pulled her unborn child out, and stomped on it. The mob then riddled her body with bullets.[5]

In 2010, a marker was erected at the spot where Turner is believed to have been killed. In the years since then, the plaque—made of a heavy metal material—has been filled with a dozen bullet holes and pocked by several other bullets that didn't go all the way through. I know because I visited that plaque in 2018 on a trip to Georgia to write about a case in which local Black citizens were being terrorized by law enforcement—just one decade

4. "Lynching in America: Confronting the Legacy of Racial Terror," Equal Justice Initiative, 2017, https://lynchinginamerica.eji.org/report/.

5. "Mary Turner, Pregnant, Lynched in Georgia for Publicly Criticizing Husband's Lynching," Equal Justice Initiative, https://calendar.eji.org/racial-injustice/may/19.

ago—because they successfully organized to win school board seats in an election.

There is story after story like Turner's. To begin down this path of discovery is to stare into a deep, deep darkness. This racial terrorism occurred across the South in the early twentieth century, sparking the Great Migration of millions of African Americans to northern states. They were refugees, fleeing an epidemic of ethnic cleansing. They were escaping a vast swath of America where Christianity dominated but where power stayed in the hands of White majorities, reinforced by the always looming threat of violence, murder, and torture. And much of this barbarism was committed by people who believed they were acting justly, righteously, on behalf of the Christian faith. The soul of America is not clean and bright. It is diseased by a long and sordid past of brutal oppression levied against those who get in the way of prosperity and power and control for those in charge.

Historical research for my book intersected with the journalism I was doing on modern-day politics. I was a witness to the confrontations between Stacey Abrams and Brian Kemp in modern-day Georgia, starting with my reporting in 2014 on Abrams. I approached accusations of voter suppression with an open but skeptical mind. But as I learned more about the history of politics in Georgia, one thing was clear: the entire South had a long history of making it very difficult for Black people to vote, even after lynching became more rare. Sometimes this voter suppression had been brutally violent. And sometimes it had also been embedded in laws, bureaucracy, and complex legalese.

Georgia's county unit system was a perfect example of the kind of scheme that was complex enough to keep Black people from gaining political power while giving the White-dominated power structure a means to explain it away.[6] Under this system, statewide and congressional elections were decided not by popular vote but

---

6. Scott E. Buchanan, "County Unit System," *New Georgia Encyclopedia*, April 15, 2005, https://www.georgiaencyclopedia.org/articles/counties-cities-neighborhoods/county-unit-system/.

by adding up points given to each county. And White politicians could say that the eight urban counties got more points than the rural counties, with six points per urban county to just two for each rural county. But this was fatuous to anyone who understood what was actually going on. There were 121 rural counties to just eight urban counties, and so even though only 32 percent of the population in 1960 lived in the urban counties, those majority White counties controlled 59 percent of the vote, more than enough to decide elections in their favor. The system was ended in 1962, and things improved in the state for people of color. But history has shown that race-based voter suppression usually adapts to fit new circumstances.

I found within myself a rising determination to look this history in the face, to be honest, to follow the teachings of Christ to live in truth. Bryan Stevenson provides a model worthy of respect. He is the author of *Just Mercy* and founder of the National Memorial for Peace and Justice in Montgomery, Alabama, which commemorates the victims of lynching. He is gentle in soul but fierce in spirit, seeking healing and justice. He understands, or at least has a vision of, how these two things can go together. He is not out for revenge. But he is insistent that America must stop suppressing the truth about its past. "I don't think we can get free until we are willing to tell the truth about our history. I do believe in truth and reconciliation. I just think that truth and reconciliation are sequential: That you can't have reconciliation without the truth." People do not want to admit wrongdoing in America, Stevenson said, because they expect only punishment. "I'm not interested in talking about America's history because I want to punish America," Stevenson said. "I want to liberate America."[7]

The growing tribalism in the country deeply concerned me. In 2015, I began to plan a project for Yahoo! News—where I was

---

7. Campbell Robertson, "A Lynching Memorial Is Opening. The Country Has Never Seen Anything Like It," *New York Times*, April 25, 2018, https://www.nytimes.com/2018/04/25/us/lynching-memorial-alabama.html.

hired in 2014—in which I would bring together Americans from different backgrounds to try to understand one another. I wanted to do my small part to overcome the divisions that I felt were tearing our country apart. "We are not making an effort to understand one another," I wrote in a proposal to my bosses. "Americans often now cannot comprehend opposing points of view. They cannot conceive that there is anything to learn from understanding those who disagree with them. We are polarized, splintered, tribalized." I hoped to re-create my own experience of speaking face-to-face with those who thought differently, to break down barriers, and then to share the stories of those encounters with the millions of readers at Yahoo! News.

"What does a 47-year-old welder in Ohio not understand about the 32-year-old lesbian cofounder of Black Lives Matter? And vice versa?" I wrote. "What has a 26-year-old gay activist in St. Louis not considered about the life and point of view of a suburban evangelical homeschool mother? And vice versa? What do the political establishment and the nation's elites fail to understand about the anger from the grassroots? And are those same grassroots considering the role that Mitch McConnell no doubt sees himself as playing, as a check against the passions of the moment?"[8]

I wanted to ask questions that would direct people toward really trying to see others as uniquely human and noble rather than as "the other." This was rooted in my belief that each person has a divine spark and is made in the image of God. "The questions will be the same: What are your core beliefs and principles? What is your role, your purpose?" I wrote. "What experiences, books, ideas, art, and people made you who you are? Why do you believe and think what you do? What do your opponents or critics not understand about what you do and why you do it? What do you not understand about your critics or those whom you view as hostile to you?"[9]

8. Memo, September 11, 2015.
9. Memo, September 11, 2015.

My aim was to get at the crucial idea that Russian novelist Alexander Solzhenitsyn expressed: "Gradually it was disclosed to me that the line separating good and evil passes not through states, nor between classes, nor between political parties either—but right through every human heart—and through all human hearts. This line shifts. Inside us, it oscillates with the years. And even within hearts overwhelmed by evil, one small bridgehead of good is retained. And even in the best of all hearts, there remains . . . an unuprooted small corner of evil."[10]

One pairing I wanted to propose was between Dixon, the liberal Black pundit from Boston, and a Tea Party leader in New Hampshire named Jerry DeLemus. I'd met DeLemus while covering the Tea Party in 2011 and 2012. He helped start the Rochester 9/12 Project during the Obama presidency, which complained about how the government was too big and intrusive. In June of 2011, on a trip to New Hampshire, I attended a meeting of his group in a local church, where he gave a speech, and then I went out to dinner with him and his wife, Sue, who had just been elected to the New Hampshire state legislature. We ate at a Friendly's and talked for close to two hours. Jerry was a former marine, and I'd met plenty of decent people like him. I saw his view of politics was somewhat naive, but I thought he had a good heart.

In the spring of 2016, I called Jerry to feel out whether he'd want to be part of this project and speak with people from the other side of the political divide. His wife answered and told me Jerry had been arrested.[11] Federal agents arrested DeLemus because in 2014 he had driven to the Bundy Ranch in Nevada, where a rancher was in a standoff with federal agents over a land dispute. DeLemus went to stand up against what he saw as the federal government's unlawful seizure of Bundy's land. He ended up becoming a leader

---

10. Alexander I. Solzhenitsyn, *The Gulag Archipelago*, vol. 2, *An Experiment In Literary Investigation* (New York: Harper Perennial Modern Classics, 2007), 746.

11. Sara Jerde, "Trump Campaign Official Arrested on Federal Charges Linked to Bundy Ranch," *Talking Points Memo*, March 3, 2016, https://talkingpoints memo.com/livewire/jerry-delemus-arrested-bundy-ranch.

of the armed resistance against the government, which nearly resulted in a shoot-out. He was sentenced to eighty-seven months in prison and did not get a pardon from then-president Donald Trump, despite the fact that he had been a leader of Trump's New Hampshire campaign. He was released in November 2021.[12]

My project, which I called "Tribes," never came to fruition the way I wanted it to. We did interviews with Trump supporters to tell their stories in their own words. But my bigger vision of facilitating real dialogue between members of different tribes fell by the wayside.

Overall, however, my move to Yahoo! News was an incredible piece of good fortune. I pinched myself to be working alongside incredible journalists and to be supporting our growing family. I did work I found meaningful but also had flexibility to prioritize time with my wife and kids. I was now writing for a national audience that included many people from communities like the deeply religious and conservative one I'd grown up in.

———

As I was identifying tribalism as a problem, others saw it as an opportunity. In November 2013, a who's who of conservative Christians gathered to celebrate the ninety-fifth birthday of evangelist Billy Graham. The party was a star-studded affair with eight hundred guests. Kathie Lee Gifford, Ricky Skaggs, and Michael W. Smith were among the entertainers. And titans of business and right-wing media showed up as well. Rupert Murdoch, the owner of the NewsCorp empire, took a photo with Graham, as did Bill Marriott Jr. The party was organized by the evangelist's son Franklin Graham, whose politics were very conservative. Jerusha Duford, one of Billy Graham's grandchildren, later told me that the famous evangelist would have preferred a much smaller birthday party but intimated that Franklin Graham used the event as a springboard to gather the rich and powerful in one place. "At ninety-five, my

12. Jennifer Crompton, "Rochester Man Imprisoned for Role in Nevada Standoff Returns Home," *WMUR*, November 9, 2021, https://www.wmur.com/article/rochester-man-imprisoned-for-role-in-nevada-standoff-returns-home/38203183.

grandfather was making very few decisions by himself," Duford told me. "He was not enamored by fame and fortune. If he had his choice, he would have been surrounded by his grandchildren."[13]

Instead, he was surrounded by right-wing politicians. When the hundreds of people in the room sang "Happy Birthday" to Graham, Sarah Palin and her husband, Todd, were seated at the table right next to him. And next to them, directly across from Graham, was another figure who seemed quite out of place at that point: Donald Trump.[14] Two years before he announced his run for president, Trump had clearly identified White evangelical Christians as a group worth getting to know better. Trump had been toying with a run for president for over a decade, and he seemed to sense that in a world that was increasingly splintered and polarized, conservative evangelicals could be won over, manipulated, and used as a powerful political weapon. He understood the deep distrust of mainstream media and culture in evangelical culture, their fear of racial change and of liberal control of government. He seemed to believe he could capture their fearful hearts. And he was likely coming to understand ways in which he could use the hypocrisy and corruption of some evangelical leaders to help himself.

At the party, Trump was photographed talking to Jerry Falwell Jr., who had taken over as head of Liberty University six years earlier. A year and a half before the Graham party, Falwell and his wife, Becki, had begun a relationship with a young man named Giancarlo Granda in Miami that, according to Granda, involved him having sex with Becki while Jerry Jr. watched.[15] In a few years, the Falwells would need help keeping salacious photos of Becki from hitting the web, and Trump would need a boost from someone with a big evangelical name.

13. Interview with Jerusha Duford, October 15, 2020.

14. "Billy Graham's 95th Birthday Celebrated with Party in NC," *Associated Press*, December 1, 2015, https://www.foxnews.com/us/billy-grahams-95th-birth day-celebrated-with-party-in-nc.

15. Aram Roston, "Business Partner of Falwells Says Affair with Evangelical Power Couple Spanned Seven Years," *Reuters*, August 24, 2020, https://www .reuters.com/investigates/special-report/usa-falwell-relationship/.

15

Disintegration

In the fall of 2015, I was coasting along on the very last jet fumes of the old traditional media reality. Of course, I didn't know this at the time. Sure, the internet had fractured reality into a million pieces. But reality was still reality, right? I flew to Iowa, rented a car, drove to the empty parking lot of a local radio station in Des Moines on a brisk and sunny Friday morning. I got out of the rental, and I hopped into the back seat of a black SUV. Already seated there was Ben Carson, the well-known surgeon turned conservative pundit turned candidate for president. For twenty minutes, as we drove past cornfields drenched in a bright midmorning sun, Carson and I talked. He sat in the rear passenger side seat, with his legs bunched together to the left, toward me. He spoke so quietly I had to hold my recording device up near his face to make sure it picked up his voice.

It was early October, and Carson was rocketing to the front of the pack in the Republican Party's primary, the contest that would determine its nominee. Carson and his advisers, with whom I'd arranged my time with the doctor, knew what I was there to do. I was not there to write down everything he said and repeat it exactly as he had, in the same order, with the same emphasis,

156

with no analysis or critique. They knew I was there to examine him, test him, question him, probe for weaknesses and hypocrisy, and evaluate him in a million other ways.

What gave me the right? It's a good question. One answer is that this is the way it had been done for a long time. People got their news and information about the world from journalists, because only media companies owned the means of production: the printing presses for newspapers, the satellites for TV and radio, and the money to pay all the people needed to collect the information and compile it into some sort of coherent package. The internet, however, had radically lowered the barriers to entry into this world of content creation. Anyone could publish anything they wanted, and it could potentially reach everyone in the world. Social media took this to another level by designing algorithms that took control of which content was seen by the most people. This change in who controlled amplification was happening as I sat in that SUV, and politics had been changing for years already as a result. But in 2015, we hadn't fully comprehended the implications. The rules of the game were still somewhat intact. Almost all politicians would have preferred to avoid the scrutiny of journalists, but they submitted themselves to it nonetheless.

All this was about to drastically change. Donald Trump was changing it right then. He had risen to the top of the polls over the summer. Although Carson had passed him and was in the lead during my interview with him in Iowa, Trump recaptured the top spot soon after. Trump blew up the rules, ditched the media, and millions of Americans loved it. And I get it. How could I not? I had grown up deep inside the world that said the media was out to get us.

I understand that most journalists lean left and that media bias is a real problem. But, fifteen years into a career in journalism, I knew that the stories I had been told about the media were wildly exaggerated. The press deserves plenty of criticism. Yet I also knew firsthand that journalism is a professional trade with norms and a code of honor that remain any nation's best hope of staying tethered to reality and of keeping tyranny at bay. I knew that the answer to the problems in the media was not to burn down the entire guard house that exists to keep marauders from entering the city.

I was alarmed by Trump's rise in the latter half of 2015, as he transformed from a joke to someone taken seriously. It was clear as day from the beginning that a Trump presidency represented a grave threat to American democracy. "He would throw the Constitution and the rule of law to the winds in pursuit of an aggressive promise of unilateral change," Ben Domenech, cofounder of the right-wing site *The Federalist*, wrote in August 2015.[1] At that point, Domenech said, it was "a remote possibility" that Trump could win the Republican nomination, but the idea that he would somehow beat Hillary Clinton and become president was laughable to most, including Domenech. Yet the possibility was alarming to most conservatives.

In fact, one of Domenech's senior colleagues at *The Federalist* emailed me unprompted in the fall of 2016—after Trump was the nominee—to express outrage at Christian conservative leaders who were endorsing Trump. This person, who said they did not want to be identified when I asked to do so years later, said this: "I'm so appalled by the behavior of so-called Christian leaders in this country that I can barely see straight. . . . The Religious Right—and by that I mean the men who sought to make the Christian church a subsidiary of the GOP—has done more to corrupt and destroy the Christian church in this country than any single person or group on the left. More than government, more than progressives, more than Democrats, more than atheists. They are the single most corroding agent in Christianity today." A few short years later, this person, like Domenech, would become a fierce defender and supporter of Trump. But before people started rearranging their views, even the most hardcore conservatives were ringing the alarm about Trump.

1. Ben Domenech, "Are Republicans for Freedom or White Identity Politics?," *The Federalist*, August 21, 2015, https://thefederalist.com/2015/08/21/are-republicans-for-freedom-or-white-identity-politics/.

Peter Wehner, a former aide to President George W. Bush, has been one of the few conservative elites who did not put his finger to the wind and reorder his convictions for convenience. Wehner warned in 2015 that Trump represented "what the Founders feared." Trump was a classic demagogue, "a political leader who appeals to emotions rather than reason and to people's fears and prejudices." Wehner added, "For the demagogue, the problems we face are simple to solve, if the right leader is given the reins of power. All this creates a powerful bond with his followers, who prize 'authenticity' over careful arguments and view the leader in nearly mystical terms. . . . The demagogue, the embodiment of anti-reason, is what the American founders feared. Indeed, the founders designed a system of government—checks and balances, separation of powers—that was meant to prevent the rise of demagogues."[2]

I had spent the previous few years studying and thinking about the ways in which our constitutional system of government was the model for our elections. So I understood that the checks and balances that had blocked demagogues from gaining power in the past had eroded or disappeared. Specifically, political parties had way less power to choose their nominees. "For a very long time, only the elites of the political parties came to select their candidates at their quadrennial conventions, with the vote largely restricted to party officials from the various states (and often decided in, yes, smoke-filled rooms in large hotel suites)," Andrew Sullivan wrote in the spring of 2016. "Beginning in the early 1900s, however, the parties began experimenting with primaries, and after the chaos of the 1968 Democratic convention, today's far more democratic system became the norm. Direct democracy didn't just elect Congress and the president anymore; it expanded the notion of who might be qualified for public office."[3] Once upon a time, Sullivan

2. Peter Wehner, "Donald Trump: What the Founders Feared," *Commentary*, September 9, 2015, https://www.commentary.org/peter-wehner/donald-trump -what-the-founders-feared/.

3. Andrew Sullivan, "Democracies End When They Are Too Democratic," *New York Magazine*, May 1, 2016, https://nymag.com/intelligencer/2016/04 /america-tyranny-donald-trump.html.

noted, "candidates built a career through experience in elected or Cabinet positions or as military commanders; they were effectively selected by peer review. That elitist sorting mechanism has slowly imploded."[4]

The irony of all this is that while the masses in the country hated the establishment, between 1970 and 2010 elites lost most of their influence over who could get elected president. Much of American politics—especially presidential elections—has become much more anti-elite. But nobody understood that, other than those who studied political history and the mechanics of power, which is a small number of people. I was learning a lot of this history in real time as I worked on my book about the 1980 election and the changes in primaries leading up to that in the 1960s and 1970s.

At the same time, the internet had destroyed the power of the press to serve as an independent check on those in power. Increasingly, politicians could go around the media and create their own reality for supporters, without accountability and the annoying requirement to tell the truth. Parties and the press were the old gatekeepers now. The new gatekeepers were big tech and social media.

In the age of newspapers, information moved through the gates if it was "newsworthy." This was an imperfect term with an imperfect implementation, but the idea was that information that would serve the public was amplified. In the age of social media and Big Tech, however, content was amplified if it was "sticky" and increased audience "engagement." Fact-checking and careful vetting for accuracy were out the window, because Big Tech companies didn't think of themselves (for a long time at least) as gatekeepers but as neutral platforms. And what kept people engaged was not accurate or newsworthy information but rather whatever made users most emotional. Usually, the most effective emotion for engagement was anger.[5]

4. Sullivan, "Democracies End When They Are Too Democratic."
5. Jay David Bolter, "Social Media Are Ruining Political Discourse," *The Atlantic*, May 19, 2019, https://www.theatlantic.com/technology/archive/2019/05 /why-social-media-ruining-political-discourse/589108/.

Trump was good at outrage. He also was intent on discrediting the media and destroying the idea that truth could be known. Trump set himself up as the only source of reality. This was scary enough. But he also encouraged violence.[6] As we entered 2016 and he gained steam, I began to warn my family and friends, especially those I thought would be wise enough to see through his deceptions.

At the end of July, my brother and I engaged in a long back-and-forth over email with my parents and siblings. "Starting in December, I have sent you and the rest of our family just over forty emails giving specific arguments and pieces of evidences for why I think Trump is a dangerous threat to the foundations of our Democratic Republic that have for 240 years guaranteed all Americans freedoms of speech, thought, religion, commerce, and the press," I told them. "I have made clear that I do not agree with Hillary Clinton on very many issues and that I have soberly assessed the potential consequences of allowing a Democratic president to nominate the next few Supreme Court justices. And I have explained through the course of these many emails why I believe Trump is a far greater threat to our liberty than is Hillary." I sent my family an article by a conservative scholar who concluded that Trump's candidacy "is how fascism comes to America."[7]

I was one of many voices ringing the alarm. "In terms of our liberal democracy and constitutional order, Trump is an extinction-level event. It's long past time we started treating him as such," Sullivan concluded in his March 2016 piece.[8] I made the same case over and over to family and close friends as well. In an email to family friends who are evangelical charismatics—who would

6. Fabiola Cineas, "Donald Trump Is the Accelerant: A Comprehensive Timeline of Trump Encouraging Hate Groups and Political Violence," *Vox*, January 9, 2021, https://www.vox.com/21506029/trump-violence-tweets-racist-hate-speech.

7. Robert Kagan, "This Is How Fascism Comes to America," *Washington Post*, May 28, 2016, https://www.washingtonpost.com/opinions/this-is-how-fascism-comes-to-america/2016/05/17/c4e32c58-1c47-11e6-8c7b-6931e66333e7_story.html.

8. Sullivan, "Democracies End When They Are Too Democratic."

become some of the most fanatical Trump supporters we knew—I said this a month before the election:

> From the first time I emailed all [of] you about my concerns over Donald Trump, my core objection to him has always been that I believe he is an unprecedented threat to our constitutional system, and that if he does what he has promised throughout the last year, he would shred whatever is left in our country's political system and our culture regarding a deep respect for the rule of law. By 'rule of law' I mean that justice is meted out based on law, not on the whims of whoever is in charge.
>
> While I share some of your concerns over targeting of conservatives by the IRS, over intolerance of religious institutions on the marriage issue, and I also share concerns over Hillary Clinton's private email server and her handling of classified material, we still in my opinion do have a country governed in most cases by a deep respect for the rule of law. . . . Donald Trump has repeatedly made clear he does not share these values in any way, which are at the core of what makes America unique in human history, and of what makes America great.

But most of my own family members and other evangelicals I knew were unfazed by warnings about threats to democracy and continued to view Trump through a traditional political lens in which voting almost entirely on the basis of their stance on abortion made sense. Abortion was the crucial issue that kept them in the fold of the Republican Party candidate. One sibling offered their assessment to me with typical Ward subtlety. "In my opinion, if you vote for Hillary, you are contributing to the murder of babies and you will have blood on your hands," they wrote in an email in June 2016.

I told this sibling that while I admired their passion and respected their view, I thought that Trump "could be the kind of president who destroys our constitutional order and all the liberties our forebearers have fought and died to create and preserve for over 200 years." I said I did not like the Democrats' positions on many things but that any issue could be engaged within our current functioning system and did not require or justify resorting to an authoritarian candidate.

I spent several hours in December 2015 going to Trump rallies and speaking to those who attended. Plenty of people there fit the stereotype of a Trump supporter held by many Democrats. For example, one guy told me that Obama was a Muslim and gay people were "the devil." But what made Trump a viable candidate was that there were many other people like my own family who did not fit that stereotype and who were also flocking to him. I wrote for Yahoo! News that many people I talked to "were not necessarily older, or all that conservative, or even White. What's needed, they feel, is someone larger-than-life, someone who they hope can bring about change and fix what's broken in the country through sheer force of personality."[9]

But there was something darker too. Some in my family also exhibited a desire to blow up everything in our government and politics out of some nebulous mix of fear and rage. The fear came from a sense that "the left" wanted to police their beliefs, their language, even their thoughts. Usually this related to their belief that it was wrong to be gay or that there was something off about transgender people. They were also outraged by the sense that discussing systemic racism was a way to label all White people as racist. This combination of factors produced a nihilism that shocked me. One sibling told me he wanted to burn it all down and see what emerged from the ruins. Another relative told me that if Trump turned out to be an authoritarian, Americans could turn him out of office with a coup. I looked at his face closely to see if he was joking. He was serious.

I understood their fears about censorship, though I thought the threat was exaggerated by politicians and talk radio hosts who built their fortunes and reputations by scaring people into supporting them and giving them money. But my deepest disagreement

9. Jon Ward, "These Are the People Who Wait Hours to See Trump," Yahoo! News, December 11, 2015, https://www.yahoo.com/news/in-line-to-see-trump-1318469047787574.html.

revolved around how to respond to any such threat. Faith gave us courage to stick to our principles even if there was a cost. Courage gave us the strength to engage lovingly and constructively with others who thought or believed differently from us. Fear, on the other hand, drove us to withdraw and retreat from dialogue and cooperation with others who were not like-minded. Fear would drive us to abandon our principles, to seek safety and protection at almost any cost, no matter who it hurt or how it reflected on our faith. As I looked around me in 2016, I saw conservative White Christians demonstrating much more fear than faith.

My concerns about Trump's fitness for the presidency never had anything to do with party or ideology. They certainly weren't about him being too conservative. In fact, much of what alarmed me about Trump was about how he was not conservative and could destabilize the entire country. To *conserve* the country's strengths would be to unite it, and it was clear that part of Trump's strategy—even his psychology—was to pit Americans against other Americans. He would seek to divide the country for his own political benefit, in a way no other politician had even come close to. And so for me, criticism of Trump was never about Democrat or Republican, liberal or conservative. From the moment Trump's candidacy began to be taken seriously, I was focused on the ways that a national leader like him would almost certainly have bad consequences for all Americans: White and Black, liberal and conservative, urban and rural, rich and poor.

Those who deeply understood how American government worked comprehended the grave threat Trump posed to democracy and the freedoms it preserves. Trump, who liked to talk about law and order, actually stood for lawlessness, as I told my family in a long email in March 2016. "He is summoning and encouraging hate and anger against anyone that he and his supporters think of as an 'other.' This is a mob mentality. You cannot control mobs. They hurt and maim and destroy and—yes, kill—indiscriminately and randomly," I wrote. "This is the Trump effect: the lawless in spirit are being encouraged to become lawless in practice. And in response to this mob mentality, liberals who are lawless in spirit will respond with their own lawlessness. And the cycle will go further and further toward greater chaos and discord."

I hoped, so very deeply, that I would be proven wrong.

Trump's unique and historic assault on truth was central to his malignance. I was in New Hampshire early in 2016 when I realized how blatantly Trump was going around lying about obvious things. New Hampshire is unique in that you can attend two or three or even four events in one day if you hustle. You can see one candidate early, another midmorning, a third candidate in the afternoon, and then you can top it off with a big rally in the evening for a fourth candidate. It's one of the great experiences of American politics, but I was not enjoying the sense of dread that pulsed through me as I witnessed up close what was happening with Trump and the Republican Party.

One day before New Hampshire Republicans voted in their primary, I was sitting in a low-rent coffee shop in the suburbs outside Manchester reading up on what different candidates had said on TV that morning. It was snowing hard, and I was between events. As I scanned the transcripts of Trump's interviews that morning, I couldn't believe what I was seeing. "I never called John McCain a loser," Trump said on *CBS This Morning*. "I didn't call him a loser."[10] Moments later he repeated his claim two more times: "I never called John McCain a loser."[11]

But a year earlier, he had, in fact, called McCain a loser.[12] It wasn't hard to figure this out because it was on video.[13] During an

10. Donald Trump, interview by Charlie Rose, Norah O'Donnell, and Gayle King, *CBS This Morning*, CBS, February 8, 2016.

11. Donald Trump, interview with Joe Scarborough, Mika Brzezinski, Chris Matthews, Willie Geist, Mark Halperin, and John Heilemann, *Morning Joe*, MSNBC, February 8, 2016.

12. Louis Jacobson, "I Never Called [John McCain] a Loser," *Politifact*, September 4, 2020, https://api.politifact.com/factchecks/2020/sep/04/donald-trump/yes-donald-trump-did-call-john-mccain-loser/.

13. "Donald Trump 2015 Family Leadership Summit FULL," YouTube video, 25:50, posted by Les Grossman, July 18, 2015, https://www.youtube.com/watch?v=eI_Y8l3U8mo.

appearance in Iowa, Trump had complained that McCain criticized him. Trump then said that McCain "let us down" when he lost the 2008 election. "He lost. So I never liked him much after that, because I don't like losers," Trump said of McCain. It was clear as day he'd said it. But months later, he was willing to repeat, again and again, a lie that was so clearly a lie that he was basically throwing down a gauntlet. He was challenging the legitimacy not just of the press but of an objective reality.

And he did this all the time. It wasn't one lie. It was dozens every day, about every issue under the sun. If he could lie so blatantly and still get people to support him, the lies could get bigger and bigger, and as he brought new supporters into his camp, he could convince them that what they heard from the press was the lie and that what he said was the truth. If this was possible— if reality was what one person said—then that was a weapon that could be wielded that could be stronger than democracy itself.

To Trump, "being right was a question of power, not evidence," wrote Russian American writer Masha Gessen in the 2020 book *Surviving Autocracy*. "He was asserting control over reality itself. . . . Trump was splitting the country into those who agreed to live in his reality and those who resisted and became his enemies by insisting on facts," Gessen wrote. "Unmoored from lived reality, the autocrat has no need to be consistent. In fact, the ability to change his story at will is a demonstration of power."[14] Novelist Iris Murdoch put it this way in 1972: "The quality of a civilization depends upon its ability to discern and reveal truth, and this depends upon the scope and purity of its language. Any dictator attempts to degrade the language because this is a way to mystify," she wrote. "Tyrants want to mystify."[15]

14. Masha Gessen, *Surviving Autocracy* (New York: Riverhead Books, 2020), 105–6, 108.

15. Quoted in Maria Popova, "Salvation by Words," *Pocket*, February 12, 2019, https://getpocket.com/explore/item/salvation-by-words-iris-murdoch-on -language-as-a-vehicle-of-truth-and-art-as-a-force-of-resistance?utm_source= pocket-newtab.

As I sat in that coffee shop looking out at the snowflakes, I absorbed Trump's contempt for truth. It violated the most fundamental principles of what I had been taught as a young boy, as a young Christian. "Behold, you delight in truth in the inward being," King David says in Psalm 51 as a prayer to God (v. 6 ESV). "Send out your light and your truth; let them lead me; let them bring me to your holy hill," Psalm 43:3 (ESV) says. Jesus said, "The truth will set you free" (John 8:32). Sure, Jesus was talking about deeper truths, but the everyday truths are no less important. The two go together. One leads to another. "Whoever is dishonest with very little will also be dishonest with much," Christ said (Luke 16:10). People always told me that every politician lies. Not like this, I said. Trump's lies were blatant and constant. He wanted people to know that he held only contempt for the idea of objective truth. This was not normal. I had spent years studying politics, day in and day out, and I knew the difference.

And then there was Trump's upside-down vision of what it meant to be strong. On that day in New Hampshire, I watched a father get out of his pickup truck in a parking garage in downtown Manchester. Two little boys, maybe eight and ten, got out with him. I watched them walk across the street and into the arena where Trump was holding a massive rally the night before the New Hampshire primary. My heart sank as I realized that this man considered Trump a role model for his sons. This man and many others were chasing an idea of strength that was actually weakness.

The strength I was taught came in part from my grandfather, the All-American football player who couldn't stomach the idea of showboating, who made one ferocious play after another and never drew attention to himself. After each play, he got up and went back to the line of scrimmage to get ready for the next. Real men didn't need to tell you how great they were. They showed you. And they "let someone else praise you, and not your own mouth" (Prov. 27:2).

Real strength, courage, and greatness came from self-sacrifice, not from stepping on others with insults and ridicule to elevate one's self. It certainly took no courage to demonize minority groups in the name of God and country. This was not greatness. This was smallness and cowardice. Jesus taught us to look out for our neighbor, and even to love our enemy.

But Christ's message was nowhere in evidence when Trump talked about Christianity. Trump spoke about faith as something one claimed for self-promotion and self-protection, not as a way of life that called on its followers to engage in self-sacrifice. This was crystallized for me when I watched Trump's speech at Liberty University early in 2021. "We're going to protect Christianity," he said. "Bad things are happening. . . . Other religions, frankly, they're banding together. . . . The power we have, somehow we have to unify, we have to band together."[16] He thought of Christianity as a tribe in which the goal was to war against other groups for power, not as a set of beliefs its followers held to be actually true, which then shaped their thoughts and actions. Domination, self-gratification, and personal glory: these things were his true religion. Trump worshiped himself, and he was teaching other Christians to do the same.

I had carried a vision of Christianity that had been crystallized in that sermon by John Piper from 2005. The path of the cross was the path of victory and the path to life. But it was narrow, and hard, and "only a few find it," Jesus says in Matthew 7:14. He wasn't talking about some ephemeral stairway to heaven when he said this. Matthew the disciple recorded him as saying, just before this, that each of us should treat others the way we would like to be treated. Trump thought that this was a sucker's game. It was weak to do unto others as you would have them do unto you. Rather, you should do unto others as you feared they were going to do unto you. Better to preemptively strike than to let "them" get you first. As Trump's son Don Jr. put it a few years later, "We've turned the other cheek, and I understand sort of the biblical reference—I understand the mentality—but it's gotten

16. Jon Ward, "At Liberty University, Donald Trump Again Stumbles When Discussing Religion," Yahoo! News, January 18, 2016, https://www.yahoo.com/news/at-liberty-university-donald-trump-again-stumbles-211607104.html.

us nothing. OK?"[17] Only a few find the way to life, not so much because the path is hard to find. It's just hard.

Later that night in New Hampshire, I went out to dinner with two colleagues at a steakhouse in Manchester. The snow was still coming down like crazy, as it had all day. As we ate, Trump walked into the restaurant with a large entourage, having concluded his rally down the street in which he called Ted Cruz a pu—y.[18] This was just the latest attack on decency and civility from Trump, one in a long string of them. Trump made a circuit around the restaurant, shaking hands with folks at each table. As he approached our table, I wanted so badly to stand and demand why he thought he could lie so brazenly about what he'd said about John McCain, as if the truth mattered so little. Instead, when he came to our table, I stood and—with my face twisted in a grimace—quickly put my hand into his and sat back down.

17. Tyler Huckabee, "Biblical Scholar Donald Trump Jr. Tells Young Conservatives That Following the Bible Has 'Gotten Us Nothing,'" *Relevant*, December 21, 2021, https://relevantmagazine.com/current/nation/biblical-scholar-donald-trump-jr-tells-young-conservatives-that-following-the-bible-has-gotten-us-nothing/.

18. "Donald Trump Calls Ted Cruz A Pu—y," YouTube video posted February 8, 2016, https://www.youtube.com/watch?v=UHcD5-TGHvY.

16

Collapse

D onald Trump held the same position on abortion in 2016
that Mitt Romney had held in 2012.[1] Actually, it was more
liberal than Romney's. Trump said he would change the
Republican Party platform—the party's official position—to support the right to an abortion in cases of rape and incest or if the
life of the mother was at risk.[2] Romney had never tried to make
that the official position of the GOP.

Romney's support for abortion, in cases of rape and incest or
if the life of the mother was at risk, had driven Lou Engle into
internal conflict in 2012 over whether to vote for Romney. Engle
finally resolved this conflict after getting guidance from a friend's
dream. But in 2016, Engle approached Trump's identical stance
on abortion with no such reservations. In late September, about
five weeks before the election between Trump and Hillary Clinton, Engle wrote for the website *Elijah's List* that "America is in

1. "Donald Trump Presidential Campaign, 2016/Abortion," *Ballotpedia*,
https://ballotpedia.org/Donald_Trump_presidential_campaign,_2016/Abortion.

2. David Wright, "Trump: I Would Change GOP Platform on Abortion,"
CNN, April 21, 2016, https://www.cnn.com/2016/04/21/politics/donald-trump
-republican-platform-abortion/index.

a defining moment. We believe that right now Heaven is looking for those who will shift our nation into a new day of mercy."[3] He called for Christians to fast for forty days, without specifying what to abstain from. (Often such "fasts" are recommended in general terms, and each person who wants to do the fast decides what to give up.)

Engle was careful not to explicitly endorse a candidate, seeking to preserve his claim that he was not "political" or "partisan." But he related another dream, this one "given to us" by "a young lady in Alaska" in which she saw both Trump and Clinton at the White House, in separate rooms. No details about Clinton were provided. But a vivid portrait was painted of Trump as a penitent believer. "Trump was kneeling down weeping and broken and she said that in the dream she knew that people didn't know the kind of man he really was. In the dream he had the Bible open and he was reading Ezekiel 22:30, 'I looked for a man to stand in the gap.'"[4]

Engle trusted a dream from "a young lady in Alaska" rather than real life. For example, a year earlier, Trump had said, "I'm not sure I have ever asked God's forgiveness."[5] But Engle related this vision of Trump praying to God as if it were more real than what everyone knew to be true. Engle was merely jumping on a train that had left the station many months before, as conservative evangelicals came to grips with the reality that they would have to rationalize voting for Trump.

The most creative justification came from a man named Lance Wallnau, the business consultant turned Pentecostal author who coauthored a book about the seven mountains strategy with Bill Johnson in 2013. In August 2016, Wallnau published a "prophecy" on *Charisma News*. It was fifty-two hundred words long and was

3. Lou Engle, "Lou Engle's Word about the Elections! A Call for a 40-Day Fast Starting Today!," *Elijah List*, September 30, 2016, https://www.elijahlist.com /words/display_word.html?ID=16718.

4. Engle, "Lou Engle's Word about the Elections!"

5. Ray Nothstine, "Donald Trump: 'I'm Not Sure If I Ever Asked God's Forgiveness,'" *Christian Post*, July 20, 2015, https://www.christianpost.com/news /donald-trump-im-not-sure-if-i-ever-asked-gods-forgiveness-141706/.

published over three days.[6] Wallnau began the first essay by saying he was not a "Trump apologist." But by the end of that essay he had concluded, "I for one will stand with him. . . . Everything is at stake."[7] How did he get there? Well, Wallnau was remarkably honest. He said quite plainly why he was backing Trump. It was about raw power and the will to dominate. He wanted the Christian point of view to reign in America and to be imposed on others.

What justified this kind of power-seeking by people who worshiped a poor carpenter from Nazareth who preached a message of service and self-sacrifice? Well, Wallnau believed that demons were causing America to fall into "cultural collapse." He wrote that "there is a spirit assigned to destroy America." Clinton, Wallnau wrote, would be a partner with or a tool of the devil in this enterprise. "Under Hillary, America will undergo the final phase of Obama's radical socialist cultural transformation with astonishing speed. Just one man stands in its path."[8]

Wallnau's most honest comments came when he said that "we"—meaning conservative, mostly White Christians—have "been losing the culture war decisively for the last decade." He admitted that he no longer believed that Christian values could be promoted through persuasion. Instead, he believed that Christian values needed to be forced on the country. "We assumed that culture is a reflection of the values of the majority of the people. If you can turn the majority, you can tip the culture. Or so we thought," Wallnau wrote. "The truth is that culture is shaped by

6. Lance Wallnau, "Prophecy: God Sent Donald Trump to Wage War against Destructive Spirits," *Charisma News*, August 16, 2016, https://www.charisma news.com/opinion/59276-prophecy-god-sent-donald-trump-to-wage-war-against -destructive-spirits; Lance Wallnau, "Donald Trump Key to Isaiah 45 Prophecy?," *Charisma News*, August 17, 2016, https://www.charismanews.com/opinion/59304 -donald-trump-key-to-isaiah-45-prophecy; and Lance Wallnau, "Is Trump Himself a Prophet? This Businessman Says Yes!," *Charisma News*, August 18, 2016, https://www.charismanews.com/opinion/59307-is-trump-himself-a-prophet-this -businessman-says-yes.

7. Wallnau, "Prophecy."

8. Wallnau, "Prophecy."

relatively few people, a remnant of elites in proximity to power. This is why you can't evangelize a nation into transformation."[9]

This view was at odds with the belief, so popular among many charismatic evangelicals, that the spirit world dictated what happened in the physical world and that you could pray and sing angels into battle to defeat the demons. Wallnau did say that "spiritual warfare is all about whose version of reality becomes manifest on the Earth," but most of his focus was on actual political battle in real life. And then he said this: because the next president would appoint three or four Supreme Court justices, "the winner has power to protect our constitutional freedoms or alter the meaning of the Constitution and punish, prosecute and persecute the opposition for the next 40 years."[10]

Wallnau's "prophecy" became famous because he justified all this by saying that Trump was like King Cyrus, who ruled over Persia from 559 to 530 BC. Wallnau described Cyrus as a "heathen king who was indispensable to the protection of the Jews but was frankly confused as to what God was saying." Fundamentalist evangelicals see themselves as God's chosen people, like the Jews are described in the Bible, so Trump could play a similar role for them in modern times. Trump was their "unlikely deliverer." Wallnau saw confirmation of this in the fact that he read about Cyrus in the forty-fifth chapter of the book of Isaiah, and Trump would be the forty-fifth president. Numerology is big among figures like Wallnau and the New Apostolic Reformation. He said he believed that "the Cyrus anointing" that lay on Trump would make him a leader who would "build and restore."[11]

C. J. Mahaney did not have time to worry about the 2016 election. He was fighting to preserve his church, reputation, and influence. In 2014, after moving his church to Louisville, he had voluntarily backed out of speaking at the Together for the Gospel conference.

9. Wallnau, "Prophecy."
10. Wallnau, "Donald Trump Key to Isaiah 45 Prophecy?"
11. Wallnau, "Donald Trump Key to Isaiah 45 Prophecy?"

He cited the civil lawsuit, which at that point had been dismissed because of the statute of limitations and was on appeal, as "a distraction from the purpose of this important conference." He added, "My withdrawal is not intended to communicate anything about the merits of the suit."[12]

Life went on for C. J. as he attempted to build alliances with Al Mohler and the various institutions Mohler was a part of or connected with, especially Southern Baptist Theological Seminary. But on the internet, a community had sprung up to discuss the lawsuit and the culture of Covenant Life Church and Sovereign Grace Ministries. Much of the conversation took place at a website called *SGM Survivors*. C. J. and other leaders in his movement told their followers not to even look at the website and certainly not to discuss it. That would be "gossip," they said.

Then in early 2016, a major investigation into the sex abuse allegations and how C. J. and other leaders handled them was published in *Washingtonian* magazine. Journalist Tiffany Stanley told the origin story of C. J. and Larry Tomczak's church, describing those days in the 1970s and 1980s as a heady time of dynamic growth and intense spiritual experience. She detailed how C. J. had consolidated control of the church and the church-planting umbrella organization and was "ensconced among the country's evangelical elite." C. J. was "a college dropout with no formal training" who "became an in-demand public speaker and author and befriended influential New Calvinist leaders."[13]

Stanley wrote about *SGM Survivors* and how it was a source of sunlight into what had become "a society unto itself, one that functioned parallel to mainstream culture and that distrusted that wider, secular world." She unpacked key components of the cul-

12. Nicola Menzie, "CJ Mahaney Drops Out of 2014 Together for the Gospel Conference Due to Sovereign Grace Lawsuit," *Christian Post*, July 2, 2013, https://www.christianpost.com/news/cj-mahaney-drops-out-of-2014-together-for-the-gospel-conference-due-to-sovereign-grace-lawsuit.html.

13. Tiffany Stanley, "The Sex-Abuse Scandal That Devastated a Suburban Megachurch," *Washingtonian*, February 14, 2016, https://www.washingtonian.com/2016/02/14/the-sex-abuse-scandal-that-devastated-a-suburban-megachurch-sovereign-grace-ministries/.

ture that had led to the mishandling of the abuse cases and possibly perpetuated the abuse. She contacted sixteen former and current pastors in the Sovereign Grace network, and none would answer questions on the record. A spokesman for Sovereign Grace said no leaders had ever "conspired to cover up abuse as alleged in this lawsuit."[14] But the terms *conspired* and *cover up* weren't the best description in real-world terms. The better critique was that Sovereign Grace's policies and practices had created an "environment conducive to and protective of physical and sexual abuse of children," as one writer put it.[15]

Stanley's article painted a clear picture of this environment—this insular culture created and controlled by the pastors—through the stories of victims she interviewed and their families. "We were told and strung along for quite some time that the church was taking care of it, that they would handle all of this," Jeremy Cook, who was one of three teenage boys abused by Nate Morales, told Stanley. Stanley wrote that "an investigation commissioned by CLC [Covenant Life Church] revealed that between 1990 and 2007 at least five members of the church's staff were told of Morales's abuse. None notified the police."[16] Morales moved to Nevada and married a woman who was a mother to five boys. Two of these boys later told their mom that Morales had abused them too.

There were multiple stories of young children abused by teenagers whose parents were discouraged from going to the police. They were instead pressured to meet face-to-face with the abusers, to pursue "reconciliation." Families told stories of being shamed and reprimanded for having a "carnal desire" to see the abusers suffer. The emphasis of the pastors was on rehabilitating the abusers rather than seeking justice for the abused and comforting them. When Stanley visited C. J.'s new church in 2015, she found him preaching a sermon on the biblical character of Job. According to

14. Stanley, "Sex-Abuse Scandal."
15. Kristin Kobes du Mez, "Far-Right Evangelicals Excused Sexual Abuse Long before Donald Trump," *Flux*, June 5, 2021, https://flux.community/kristin-kobes -du-mez/2021/06/evangelical-sexual-abuse-russell-moore-trump.
16. Stanley, "Sex-Abuse Scandal."

Stanley, in a near whisper, with tears in his eyes, C. J. lamented that Job's friends "turn on him and they attack him and it's relentless." Stanley noted the irony in C. J.'s next words: "This is a church where those suffering will be truly comforted."[17] He seemed to consider himself the victim in all this.

Stanley's article relayed that Sovereign Grace had suffered a decline, with churches leaving and pastors resigning, but that C. J. was "remarkably unscathed."[18] And, in fact, C. J. was invited to speak again at Together for the Gospel in 2016, despite the negative publicity and the presence of protesters outside the conference.[19] When Mohler introduced C. J. to speak at one of the main sessions, he seemed to describe C. J. as he wished to be seen: as a martyr. "He has modeled endurance," Mohler said. "We know he has demonstrated endurance in the face of an incredible trial." Mohler said that C. J. "continues to exert massive influence" and called him an example of "steadfastness." "The Christian man should be immoveable in the faith, in the truth, in Christ," Mohler said.[20]

Mohler closed his introduction by making jokes about the criticisms leveled by victims of sexual abuse, calling them nothing more than internet rumors. "I told C. J. that in getting ready to introduce him I would Google to see if there was anything on the internet about him," Mohler said. A low rumble of knowing laughter rippled through the audience and then grew louder. "And that's when I discovered, having discovered this on the internet, that C. J. cheers for the Washington Redskins and the Washington Nationals, and against the Dallas Cowboys, the New York Yankees and Duke Basketball. . . . I now know it to be true because I read it about C. J."

17. Stanley, "Sex-Abuse Scandal."

18. Stanley, "Sex-Abuse Scandal."

19. Bob Allen, "Pastor in Alleged Sex Abuse Cover-up Returns to Preaching Conference Roster," *Baptist News Global*, April 13, 2016, https://baptistnews.com/article/pastor-in-alleged-sex-abuse-cover-up-returns-to-preaching-conference-roster/.

20. "Albert Mohler and CJ Mahaney," Soundcloud, https://soundcloud.com/watchkeep/albert-mohler-and-cj-mahaney.

"I know that in this room that C. J. . . . has 10,000 friends," Mohler said.[21]

While Mohler was defending C. J. in this intramural dispute, he was also calling fellow Christians to resist Trump, unlike Engle, Wallnau, and others in the charismatic camp.[22] "When it comes to Donald Trump, evangelicals are going to have to ask the huge question, 'Is it worth destroying our moral credibility to support someone who is beneath the baseline level of human decency for anyone who should deserve our vote?'" he said on CNN. "I am afraid people are going to remember evangelicals in this election for supporting the unsupportable and defending the absolute indefensible."[23]

In the *Washington Post*, Mohler quoted from the Bible. "Jesus famously asked, 'What will it profit a man if he gains the whole world and forfeits his soul? Or what shall a man give in return for his soul?' (Matthew 16:26). . . . Perhaps the best we can hope for in this sad election cycle with these two unsupportable candidates is that we do not allow a national disgrace to become the Great Evangelical Embarrassment."[24]

It wasn't enough. Evangelical leaders would have needed to argue forcefully that Christians should vote for Clinton, despite their many objections to her. The threat to democracy from Trump was central, but all too often evangelical leaders focused only on personal morality. That was a concern, yes. But character was a

21. Brandon Withrow, "Pastor Accused of Covering Up Abuse Returns to Spotlight," *Daily Beast*, April 17, 2016, https://www.thedailybeast.com/pastor-accused-of-covering-up-abuse-returns-to-spotlight.

22. Jonathan Merritt, "Mohler's Turn to Trump Is the Crowning Flip-Flop of His Career," *Religion News Service*, April 17, 2020, https://religionnews.com/2020/04/17/mohlers-turn-to-trump-is-the-crowning-flip-flop-of-his-career/.

23. S. Craig Sanders, "Evangelical Support of Trump Destroys 'Moral Credibility,'" Mohler Says on 'CNN Tonight,'" *Southern Baptist Theological Seminary*, October 12, 2016, https://news.sbts.edu/2016/10/12/evangelical-support-trump-destroys-moral-credibility-mohler-says-cnn-tonight/.

24. R. Albert Mohler Jr., "Donald Trump Has Created an Excruciating Moment for Evangelicals," *Washington Post*, October 9, 2016, https://www.washingtonpost.com/news/acts-of-faith/wp/2016/10/09/donald-trump-has-created-an-excruciating-moment-for-evangelicals/.

concern primarily because it was part of the reason why Trump was a threat to the republic. One of the few well-known evangelical pastors who dared to endorse Clinton was a Black pastor from Washington, DC, named Thabiti Anyabwile, who had spoken at the Together for the Gospel conference that year alongside Mohler.

"To seek a quiet conscience by not voting seems to me an abdication of moral responsibility," Anyabwile wrote. "I regard a President Trump the worse of the two evils before us—and worse in a way that I cannot predict and on issues that there's been so much blood shed over already (i.e., the rights of minorities, women, and the religious). I'd vote for the incrementalist over the revolutionary. For revolutions almost never lead to progress."[25]

I was in New York at the Yahoo! News headquarters the night Trump won the presidency. We were doing a live show broadcast online. My two oldest kids, then nine and seven, had come with me. They were hanging out somewhere with a few other kids, eating pizza and candy. I went on set once or twice to update Katie Couric, who was hosting the show, on the latest numbers. It was closer than we had expected. And as it became clear that the unthinkable had happened, I went to sit next to my boss. Couric, during a break, walked over and whispered to us, "Can you believe this?" There was, indeed, plenty of hand-wringing. But some of my family members—who had been sending out doleful messages early in the night when Clinton took an early lead—were ecstatic, blowing up our family text chain with celebratory messages.

I was stunned by the capitulation of so many evangelical Christians to Trump. They had rejected Bill Clinton in the 1990s for sexual predation—the same kind of behavior that Trump was credibly accused of by many women. Many had rejected Trump before he was the nominee. But when they had to choose between a Democrat and a Republican, their political identity took over.

25. Thabiti Anyabwile, "A Vote to Check Unpredictable Evil with the Predictable," Gospel Coalition, May 10, 2016, https://www.thegospelcoalition.org/blogs/thabiti-anyabwile/a-vote-to-check-unpredictable-evil-with-the-predictable/.

They then spent the next few months or years convincing themselves that Trump was actually God's man. My own kin had gone from disgust for Trump, to supporting him with a sense of resignation, to eventually a full and enthusiastic embrace. From there, it would only deepen into cultic devotion.

I saw it as a surrender to fear of being a cultural and racial minority and an abandonment of faith. I understood that many conservative Christians—taught for decades to always sense a persecution around the corner—were alarmed by the Supreme Court's legalization of same-sex marriage in the summer of 2015. I did not comprehend the degree to which so many Christians would be so thoroughly ignorant of what Trump represented: a war on truth and on democracy. Some of their ignorance was willful, and some of it was the product of their disengagement from society.

In my view, Christians who claimed to prize discernment had demonstrated little of it. A church that talked about faith in the face of challenges had rejected the call to live out a prophetic witness to timeless truths and instead had embraced an authoritarian demagogue who promised to protect them and punish their enemies. Many Christians breezed past Trump's sexual promiscuousness and his vulgar attacks on women. These attitudes were connected to the way that churches like Covenant Life and the Sovereign Grace network trampled on women and children when they encountered sex abuse cases. And the fact that so many White Christians dismissed and disregarded the fears about Trump among Black and Brown Americans—or were not even aware of them—was an indictment of the insulated privilege in which so many White conservatives lived.

A few days after the election, I sent my family an email with Andrew Sullivan's prescient post-election analysis. "A country designed to resist tyranny has now embraced it," Sullivan wrote.[26]

"Have you considered moving to Canada?" one sibling wrote me back in a gloating reply.

26. Andrew Sullivan, "The Republic Repeals Itself," *New York Magazine*, November 9, 2016, https://nymag.com/intelligencer/2016/11/andrew-sullivan-president-trump-and-the-end-of-the-republic.html.

17

Choosing Not to See

One of my least favorite journalistic assignments every year was going to the Conservative Political Action Conference (CPAC). When Tucker Carlson spoke there in 2009 about journalism, the event was held at an older hotel in downtown DC. By 2017, one month into Trump's presidency, the gathering had moved to a brand-new complex adjoining a massive casino just outside the city in Maryland. But little else had changed. CPAC was still a depressing place to be, a revival meeting for political fanatics. Only, instead of selling hope, the speakers were preaching anger and resentment.

But editors always wanted me to go because I knew how to talk to conservatives. So every year I'd listen to the same speeches by the same people. And this year I was struggling to figure out how to do my job at all. The fact that Trump was president was not normal. I couldn't write about American politics as if it were normal. So I was looking for ways to do work that was solutions-oriented and focused on what mattered to everyday American people. Trump's circus of outrage and word salad was a distraction, a sideshow of no benefit to hardworking Americans. We didn't need an entertainer in chief. But cable TV news couldn't get enough of it because their ratings were through the roof.

On the day Trump spoke at CPAC, I was standing in the back of the room getting ready to go live on camera after his speech ended. My colleague Mike Isikoff, a legendary reporter who had made his name breaking stories of scandal about President Bill Clinton, was standing next to me. As I waited there, one line from Trump in particular caught my ear: "A few days ago, I called the fake news the enemy of the people, and they are. They are the enemy of the people."[1]

A chill went down my spine. Trump tried to minimize the rhetoric he was using by saying that he considered only "fake" journalists to be the enemy of the people, but that didn't matter. To use the phrase at all was dangerous and horrifying. It was a phrase with a bloody and evil history,[2] used by the Nazis to dehumanize Jews and then picked up by Soviet dictator Joseph Stalin to mark those he considered worthy of death or prison.[3]

About a week later, I was standing in the shower when I had a horrible vision of being in prison, naked, standing under a shower and undergoing a cavity check by guards. For the first time in my life, a person with control over government power was behaving and talking in such a way that—if taken to its logical conclusion—could result in people from my own profession being jailed for simply doing their job. And in that moment, I understood for the first time why Ta-Nehesi Coates often uses the term *Black bodies* in his writing. He is describing the feeling of knowing that

1. Media Matters Staff, "Trump at CPAC Calls Media Outlets 'Enemy of the People,' Demands They Stop Using Unnamed Sources," *Media Matters*, February 24, 2017, https://www.mediamatters.org/donald-trump/trump-cpac-calls-media-outlets-enemy-people-demands-they-stop-using-unnamed-sources.

2. Will Englund, "Why Trump's 'Enemy of the People' Bluster Can't Be Compared to Stalin's Savage Rule," *Washington Post*, January 17, 2018, https://www.washingtonpost.com/news/retropolis/wp/2018/01/16/why-trumps-enemy-of-the-people-bluster-cant-be-compared-to-stalins-rule/.

3. Steve LeVine, "When You Become the Enemy," *Axios*, August 1, 2018, https://www.axios.com/trump-reminder-stalin-enemy-of-people-f1e22406-5626-4747-ac61-28afde1b38f4.html.

your very flesh is vulnerable to attack, to seizure, by forces too powerful for you to resist. The threat was not imminent but it was real, and it gave me a window into the way that marginalized people felt about their own physical safety under government regimes that threatened them in far, far more immediate and violent ways.

I made a plea to my parents and siblings. "Can I ask you to spend 30–60 seconds thinking about how it would make you feel if the president said that about you?" I wrote. "This is not an attempt to start a debate or an argument. I'm not trying to comment on anyone's vote last fall. I am simply asking for one minute out of your day to be spent not thinking about the president's statement politically, or defensively, but with empathy for those it affects." My father wrote back. He allowed that the phrasing was unfortunate but defended Trump's arguments about media bias. And he said complaints about Trump's language were "just another hissy fit from the Left in their attempt to delegitimize the present administration."

I felt abandoned by my own father. But it helped me understand how good people could stand by and make excuses for bad people in power: they could not see past their own resentments and bias, even when people they loved were hurting or scared.

I wrote back to my father: "When my fears are greeted with argument or rationalization, it tells me I am alone in this, that you do not have the capacity to put down your self-defenses long enough to see the person who is talking to you, your own son and his heart. All you see is an argument, an opponent to fight. I have carried around this fear, and the hurt and frustration that I feel because I feel almost abandoned by own flesh and blood, for the last few days."

He responded: "You are my son and I will always support you and love you and stand with you! But I do not believe that loving you and standing with you means that we will always agree on things." He added, "I love you and am proud of you more than you can possibly imagine . . . even if I do not do a good job of expressing it!"

I couldn't hear or see any of those words, because all I saw was that my dad was siding with a politician who was using violent rhetoric against me.

Our family managed to stay connected, though. A few weeks after CPAC, I went to Florida with my dad and our oldest child to watch Washington's pro baseball team play a few spring training games. And when I turned forty that year, all my siblings showed up for a party at my parents' house. Frank was married with two kids, lived near my parents, and had a successful job selling computer software to the federal government. Lucas flew in from California with his new wife. My sister Liz, a convert to Catholicism, was a mother of five and also lived close to my mom and dad. Karen was a writer and a mom of three and had married a professional soccer player whose job took them around the country. Andrew was out of the marines after several years and in college studying engineering. Mark, the youngest, was on his way to becoming a nurse. None of us were as intensely into church as our parents had been while we were growing up, except for maybe Liz. But none of us had walked away from the faith either. We were all physically healthy and relatively happy. There was a lot to be grateful for.

We all posed together, smiling and laughing. I wore a red T-shirt they'd given me that said, "Making America Great Since 1977."

I was at a farmers' market on a Saturday afternoon in August 2017, browsing stalls of fresh garlic, goat cheese, and handmade pottery. I opened Twitter on my phone, aware that there was potential for trouble in Charlottesville, Virginia, on a day of protests against a White supremacist rally there that day. As I scrolled through a series of tweets, I saw that neo-Nazis and White supremacists were already clashing violently with counterprotesters in the streets. The footage was increasingly intense and violent. I felt ill.

I took my phone over to a friend, Keith, who was at the farmers' market and showed it to him. Keith came from the same part of Christianity as Lou Engle, and we had gone back and forth about politics the last few years, especially as I expressed alarm at the various things Trump had done. But on this day, Keith looked at my phone and shot me an annoyed look. "Why are you show-ing this to me?" he said. He made clear he didn't want to see it. I walked away, stunned.

I couldn't understand how fellow Christians could be so com-mitted to remaining inside a spiritual bubble that they wouldn't squarely look at the conflict and division engulfing our nation. All of it was being stoked and encouraged and inflamed by the sit-ting president. And Keith would continue to argue with me about politics and defend Trump, even though he refused to actually take time to understand what was going on in the country.

I worked hard to ground my point of view in history, based on years of reading and studying it. Keith strenuously objected when conversations about Nazi Germany came up and Trump was com-pared to Hitler. (Trump's own top military general, Mark Milley, eventually made this comparison.)[4] But Keith's denials were based not so much on real knowledge about history as on his own as-sumptions that he knew better than the critics making these claims.

Keith could not answer even basic questions about how our government functions. Yet despite this, he continued to express political conclusions and judgments with absolute certainty. For him and many others, detailed knowledge and expertise about this world were less important than knowing how to map conservative Christian readings of the Bible onto present circumstances.

Years later, Keith was outraged when I noted that White su-premacist and neo-Nazi activity was rising and that these groups were some of Trump's most extreme supporters. It was as if Char-lottesville had never happened. But I guess for him in a way it never had, since he had ignored it at the time. This willful ignorance was the norm among many evangelical Christians from these more insular and conservative settings. They spent most of their time and energy doing church things, and they no doubt did do good for others in those settings. But the church seemed to be an end

4. Susan B. Glasser, "'You're Gonna Have a F—ing War': Mark Milley's Fight to Stop Trump from Striking Iran," New Yorker, July 15, 2021, https://www.new yorker.com/news/letter-from-bidens-washington/youre-gonna-have-a-fucking -war-mark-milleys-fight-to-stop-trump-from-striking-iran.

unto itself in so many cases. So much time and effort was expended on meetings, and planning, and church services devoted to singing and talking about the Bible. But there was little vision of the common good that carried these believers outside the four walls of the church.

_____

After the Charlottesville clashes and attack, I was upset, grieving, and enraged. I was freshly angry with White evangelical churches' fear-driven blindness to the threat Trump posed to so many vulnerable Americans. Addictions to ease, comfort, materialism, and privilege had fueled the flight to Trump. Lack of empathy for racial minorities, and a self-centered apathy, had created an environment in which outright racists felt bold enough to march in public, carrying Nazi flags and KKK hoods.

The morning after the Charlottesville mayhem—which ended with the murder of thirty-two-year-old Heather Heyer by a White supremacist who drove his car into a crowd at high speed[5]—I went to church. I was out of town on vacation, so I found myself in a low-slung building labeled "Church of the Nazarene." It was across the street from a trailer park. I expected the church to be full of Trump supporters who either would not mention Charlottesville or would utter some variation of Trump's false equivalency, eager to downplay the culpability of White supremacists. I contemplated whether if given the opportunity to stand up and introduce myself—as sometimes happens with visitors in churches—I might say something about Charlottesville. I wanted to push back against the darkness in my own small way.

When I walked in a few minutes late, there were about thirty people in a room that had a capacity of probably two hundred or so. I sat in the back row on the right side. Five people at the front were leading congregational singing. There was no band, no one playing an instrument. The congregation sang along to music that

5. Denise Lavoie, "Man Sentenced to 2nd Life Term in Charlottesville Car Attack," *Associated Press*, July 15, 2019, https://news.yahoo.com/man-faces-second-sentence-charlottesville-050323204.html.

was being piped over the loudspeakers from a stereo. The sincerity of the people in the room moved me.

After a song or two, two middle-aged White men walked to the pulpit and made some announcements, and then the floor was basically opened to anyone in the room who wanted to say something. One woman talked about her struggles to quit smoking and about the way she interpreted seeing birds flying in the sky as a sign from God to keep fighting. One man—whose daughter was singing on stage—came to the front to talk into the microphone about his recent heart attack. Another man asked for prayers for his father, whose dog had just died. The dog was his father's closest friend and a reminder of his wife, who had died seven years ago.

My anger began to subside. I had been invited into these people's struggles and hopes simply by walking in the door. After thirty minutes of this, they began to wrap up, and I raised my hand from the back. I felt it would be rude to sit and listen to them share their stories and to say nothing about who I was or where I was from. I stood, introduced myself, and told them I needed to pray and worship with other Christians that morning because I was upset and grieving over Charlottesville. To my embarrassment, I choked up. I sat down quickly without doing or saying anything remotely confrontational or even mentioning racism. I left soon after.

On my way out, the wife of the man who'd just had the heart attack walked over to thank me for coming. A man about my age, who I'd seen sitting with a handful of young children, shook my hand and also thanked me for coming. Another woman walked out and caught me going out the back door also to thank me. "Thank you for coming to our church this morning, and I've been praying for them also down there, and for our country, and for God to fall on everybody," she said.

I was reminded that retribution does not break cycles of violence and injustice, but grace might. I resolved not to prejudge others based on appearance or background. I remembered that everyone is searching for God and for meaning. That is our universal common ground.

18

Rebuilding

A few experiences in 2017 deeply impacted my own search for God and meaning. As I struggled to make sense of what was happening in the country and my own shifting understanding of faith, someone gave me a book called *You Are What You Love: The Spiritual Power of Habit* by James K. A. Smith. In the book, Smith—a professor of philosophy at Calvin University, an evangelical college in Michigan—imparted to me a different way of understanding how the Christian faith could and should permeate my life, a way that was directly counter to the overly spiritualized, Gnostic approach I was raised with. Smith understood that when the Jesus Movement in the 1970s discarded tradition and historical practices in the church, it was severing a vital connection to a type of faith that could thrive in the real world.

In addition, the charismatic and Pentecostal traditions—in which emotional and spiritual experience was elevated to such a high level—had also, ironically, cut a cord between faith and one's physical body. Faith could not survive on ritual alone, that was true, and it had been a valuable impulse of the Jesus Movement to seek a greater sense of passion for God and truthful, ethical living. But faith was not transmitted from the theoretical to the physical by earnest singing or by how hard we prayed or by how high we jumped or raised our hands. Instead, faith was brought into the world by repetition and habit. And as Christians, we had many resources, many of them quite old and even ancient, to help us connect to these practices. There was the church calendar with its rhythms, and the Book of Common Prayer to help us implement prayer into our daily lives. Liturgical services gave us a way to enter into a trusted and tested format for expressing our souls and hearts to God in a manner that did not depend on our effort. And Smith understood how wonderful this was for anyone raised in a church in which people were expected to be outwardly expressive during church singing.

His chapter on youth group culture was a direct rebuke to the ways that so many churches sought to transmit the faith to the next generation. "We have effectively communicated to young people that sincerely following Jesus is synonymous with being 'fired up' for Jesus, with being *excited* for Jesus, as if discipleship were synonymous with fostering an exuberant, perky, cheerful, hurray-for-Jesus disposition like what we might find in the glee club or at a pep rally," Smith wrote. "For those young people who are either scared or suspicious of happy-clappy versions of youth group Christianity, ancient Christian disciplines and historic Christian worship can be received as a life-giving gift. When you have only seen forms of piety that value spontaneous expression and clichéd sincerity, to be given the cadences and rhythms of the Book of Common Prayer can be like receiving the gift of tongues."[1]

That was how I felt. My years of trying to be "fired up for Jesus" had left me depleted and exhausted. The more I learned about the historical practices of Christianity, the more it felt like I had been walking through a parched desert dying of thirst and I had found a spring of fresh water. These traditions and practices were, as Smith wrote, "gifts that channel [the Christian's] devotion and

1. James K. A. Smith, *You Are What You Love: The Spiritual Power of Habit* (Grand Rapids: Brazos, 2016), 146–47.

shape their faith. Instead of relying on their own internal piety and willpower . . . young people experience historic practices of prayer and devotion as gifts of grace themselves, a way that the Spirit meets them where they are."[2]

Liturgies, creeds, and prayers from the Daily Examen had been formed over time by many people, groups, and institutions. They had been through a rigorous testing process that I trusted, and this gave me confidence to participate more fully. By contrast, in a low-church charismatic setting, much of the crucial action in the church service came at the whims of the lead pastor or a worship leader, who could instruct the congregation to do this or that depending on how they were feeling that day. It was often spontaneous. There was little to no vetting. This created a situation in which people were either blindly following one leader or, like me, sitting there second-guessing every other thing because there were no guardrails on what could happen next.

Charismatics believe that spontaneous church services are crucial conduits for the work of the Holy Spirit. I've come to see this as an isolating and diminished vision of the Spirit's work. Holy Spirit guidance and strength are vital for the Christian life, but that sense of dependence on God is needed—maybe more than anything—to think through and live out Christian principles in the many gray areas of life where there is no obvious right answer or road map. The Holy Spirit is needed to help us step into the way of the cross in real life, because walking into vulnerable service is a high-wire act that can easily go wrong and harm others or ourselves. The Spirit of God can and does minister to our hearts too, for sure. But I don't think dynamic church services and emotional highs are on the top of God's agenda.

In the summer of 2017, I took two trips to write about a pair of Christian figures who represented different tensions inside evangelical Christianity. In Arkansas, near the Mississippi Delta, I visited Jemar Tisby, who I'd discovered through his podcast *Pass the Mic*.

2. Smith, *You Are What You Love*, 147.

Tisby had come up in his formative Christian years in a strain of Christianity similar to mine, rising through the ranks of conservative Christianity.

Like me, he had dreamed of relying on the Christian faith to forge healing between Black and White citizens. But also like me—and so many others over the previous few years—he had been learning a lot about America's racial history that he did not know, sparked by the growing number of police shootings of Black men that were recorded on video. His podcast combined a grounded, historical, Christian point of view with an increasingly outspoken stance on race. He had become a guide of sorts to helping me understand the interior life of a Black man in America.

As I listened to his podcast over the course of 2016 and into 2017, I heard him coming to grips with his own growing awareness that White Christians who had welcomed him into their churches had no interest in hearing his perspective on race. The election of Trump had been a slap in the face to him. He told me, "We said, like, 'This man is dangerous to us. . . . I go to the same churches with you. You've held my child in your arms. And none of that has impacted you to the point where you would change anything really. What has it really cost you, White evangelical, to have me in your presence? Versus, what does it cost me to be in your presence?"[3]

I could imagine the response to Tisby's question. Many White Christians would do what my father had done when I had expressed fear to him and asked for support. A request for support, friendship, and solidarity would be met with answers first, and maybe a little empathy second.

Tisby helped me see the ways in which White Christians had so much to learn about Christ from Black Christians. Many White Christians believe they are destined for persecution and in fact are already experiencing it. They feel increasingly like an isolated minority in the culture, with steadily decreasing political power. They

3. Jon Ward, "In the Age of Trump, Tired Are the Peacemakers," Yahoo! News, September 16, 2017, https://news.yahoo.com/age-trump-tired-peacemakers -090023694.html.

feel threatened and scared. Well, the Black church knows a little something about relying on faith in God to get them through times of oppression. Tisby pointed out that many White Christians did not even consider "how Christian community might be formed in the midst of a culture wherein Christians never had power."[4]

"This was, and in some senses continues to be, the reality for people of African descent in the United States. For centuries black people couldn't build their own institutions—not schools, not banks, not businesses," Tisby wrote. "The only option they had was the church. The church in the African American community became a powerful symbol of perseverance amidst persecution. The Black church represents the triumph of faith over fear."[5]

My second trip was to northwest Pennsylvania to interview a college professor named Warren Throckmorton. Back when I had written about a sex education fight in the Maryland suburbs in 2004, Throckmorton had been one of the most prominent voices arguing that gays could change their sexual orientation through something called reparative therapy. He taught psychology at Grove City College, a conservative Christian university. Over time, I'd noticed he'd shifted in his views, but I wasn't sure how or how much. When I spent two days with him, sharing a meal at a cheap Mexican restaurant and sitting in on one of his classes, what stuck with me was his surrender to unresolved tension: between competing ideas, between different views of reality, and between faith and reason.

"If someone said, gun to my head, 'Here's what you believe. Jesus is God,' yeah, I believe that. I've staked my life on it. I've kind of staked all my career on that whole thing," he told me. "I teach at a place that promotes that. I teach that." He then switched into an interrogation of himself. "But do you understand that there is actually decent evidence that may not be true?" Throckmorton said, posing the question to himself. "Yeah, I know that. And so,

---

4. Jemar Tisby, "Benedict Option Leaves Out Black Church," Reformed African-American Network, https://www.raanetwork.org/benedict-option-leaves-out-black-church/.
5. Tisby, "Benedict Option."

I think I'm more comfortable at this point in my life living with the tension that I believe something about which there is evidence to the contrary."[6]

Throckmorton had gone through an extensive reexamination of his advocacy for reparative therapy. People he had worked with, who said they wanted to become ex-gays, had abandoned the effort and said their orientation was not something that could be changed. "I went back and reread the criticisms of my work that I had mostly kind of shunted aside and decided that I really needed—you know, this was serious—I needed to figure this out. And so, no matter what my wish was about how things were, I needed to do more what I'm doing now, which is accepting reality as it is," he said. He began to argue against reparative therapy.

When I sat in Throckmorton's class, one remark in particular got my attention. "I want to just say there are two sources of truth. Some call it two books, two books you could read. One is revelation and one is experience of the world," he told his students. I had never heard it put in those terms. I had been taught growing up that there was only one book, the Bible, the book of God's revelation to us. But the idea of two books—two sources of revelation: the Bible and the external world—is not some novel concept, even though it was to me. It has been expressed in at least one historic Christian document: the Belgic Confession that came from the Dutch Reformed Church in 1559.

Throckmorton told his students that he did not think revelation and reality were hostile to each other or at odds but that there was still tension between the two. "For sure the Bible wasn't meant to be a textbook on human nature. The Bible may have authoritative things to say. However, the Bible doesn't comment on everything," he said. "There's a lot about human nature and human functioning that we just can't really know from reading the Scripture, so that's a problem."

6. Jon Ward, "The Evangelical Professor Who Turned against 'Reparative Therapy' for Gays," Yahoo! News, December 2, 2017, https://www.yahoo.com /news/evangelical-professor-turned-reparative-therapy-gays-174326663.html.

The greatest thing I learned on that trip is that, as Throckmorton said, "we just don't know everything we need to know," and it's okay to accept that. This, I realized, is the essence of faith. If we say we know something to be true 100 percent with no doubts, then we don't need faith. It's only when we realize we could be wrong, and we can't know for sure, that we must rely on belief. Easier said than done.

The soft-spoken professor ended the class with the closest thing to a recommendation he would give the students: "If something is real right in front of your face, if it's true, don't let a worldview tell you it's not. Let the evidence tell you it's not," he said.

Over the past decade or so, Throckmorton has become a high-impact blogger, often writing posts from a booth in the local McDonald's near the school campus. He exposed corruption at a megachurch in Seattle, unearthed inaccuracies in the work of a pseudo-historian named David Barton, and traced connections between American evangelicals and efforts to punish gay people with criminal sanctions in Uganda.[7] One version of the legislation there even prescribed the death penalty for "aggravated homosexuality," which included "homosexual actions with a minor or while knowingly carrying HIV."[8]

Among the prominent American evangelicals who were associated with the arch-conservatives in Uganda pushing this anti-gay legislation, one in particular drew attention for a visit to Kampala in 2010 to rally with the lawmakers behind the effort. It was Lou Engle.[9]

C. J. Mahaney was scheduled to speak once again in 2018 at the Together for the Gospel (T4G) conference alongside Al Mohler,

7. Sarah Posner, "Lou Engle Attempts to Backpedal on Uganda Anti-Gay Bill," *Religion Dispatches*, June 16, 2010, https://religiondispatches.org/lou-engle-attempts-to-backpedal-on-uganda-anti-gay-bill/.

8. Michael Wilkerson, "American Supports Ugandan Anti-Gay Bill," *Religion Dispatches*, May 13, 2010, https://religiondispatches.org/american-supports-ugandan-anti-gay-bill/.

9. Wilkerson, "American Supports Ugandan Anti-Gay Bill."

John Piper, and others. But in the spring of that year, C. J. and his followers acquired an unfortunate foe, which caused him to once again step aside from speaking at the big conference.

In 2016, Rachael Denhollander was the first athlete to publicly accuse USA Gymnastics doctor Larry Nassar of sexual abuse. She was the last witness to testify against Nasser at his sentencing at the beginning of 2018 and gained widespread praise for her poise and the power of her presentation. Nassar was convicted for crimes against a handful of the more than two hundred victims he abused and sentenced to what amounted to multiple life sentences.

As the Nassar case moved toward resolution, Denhollander began to speak out against C. J. and Sovereign Grace in early 2018. She had been tracking allegations against them for several years and had compiled an exhaustive record of the ways in which they had refused to engage in an honest accounting of how they had responded to sexual abuse cases, including rejecting an independent outside investigation.[10] C. J. and Sovereign Grace rejected her criticisms, and C. J. offered to step aside and not speak at the TG4 conference in 2018. However, other Sovereign Grace leaders spoke, and C. J. was still welcome.

But a year later—after Mohler met with Denhollander in person, which he said "fundamentally changed my understanding of the issue"—Mohler issued a profuse public apology for supporting C. J. and Sovereign Grace and for making light of the allegations of sexual abuse.[11] Mohler said that he had told C. J. he should step down from the pastorate until a truly independent probe was conducted. "This resulted in a severing of all personal and ministry ties, and I have had no relationship with C. J. or SGC since that time," he said.[12]

10. Rachel Denhollander, "Response to Sovereign Grace Churches," Facebook, last edited May 5, 2021, https://www.facebook.com/notes/1625049014354463/.

11. Bob Allen, "Al Mohler Says He Was Wrong about C.J. Mahaney," *Baptist News Global*, February 18, 2019, https://baptistnews.com/article/al-mohler-says-he-was-wrong-about-c-j-mahaney/.

12. R. Albert Mohler Jr., "Statement from R. Albert Mohler Jr. on Sovereign Grace Churches," Southern Baptist Theological Seminary, February 15, 2019, https://news.sbts.edu/2019/02/15/statement-r-albert-mohler-jr-sovereign-grace

The timing of Mohler's comments was noteworthy. His account came out after the *Houston Chronicle* contacted him[13] to talk about the findings of its report that found more than seven hundred victims of sexual abuse inside Southern Baptist congregations since 1998, some of which were never reported to law enforcement.[14] He revealed that he had actually talked to Denhollander nearly a year previously and that was when he had last spoken with C. J.

Mohler said he had not talked about any of this publicly before because he "was concerned it would appear self-serving and a political effort to save face."[15] Nonetheless, Sovereign Grace was part of a broader tableau that connected it to the Southern Baptist scandal. C. J.'s empire had been a canary in a coal mine, an early indicator of a male-dominated culture that suppressed the suffering of victims and denied accountability for abusers.

In April 2019, C. J. and Sovereign Grace officially rejected an independent third-party investigation of their handling of sex abuse cases. Even as Mohler—alongside congregations from within their body of churches—called for them to submit to such an accounting, they audaciously claimed that doing so would "dishonor Christ."[16]

Mohler's shift on C. J. and Sovereign Grace came as he positioned himself to run for president of the Southern Baptist Convention. Later that year, he was nominated for the position by H. B. Charles,

---

-churches/. Sovereign Grace Ministries (SGM) underwent a name change to Sovereign Grace Churches (SGC) in 2014.

13. Robert Downen, "Leading Southern Baptist Apologizes for Supporting Leader, Church at Center of Sex Abuse Scandal," *Houston Chronicle*, February 14, 2019, https://www.chron.com/houston/article/Leading-Southern-Baptist-apologizes-for-13618120.php.

14. Robert Downen, Lise Olsen, and John Tedesco, "20 years, 700 victims: Southern Baptist Sexual Abuse Spreads as Leaders Resist Reforms," *Houston Chronicle*, February 10, 2019, https://www.houstonchronicle.com/news/investigations/article/Southern-Baptist-sexual-abuse-spreads-as-leaders-13588038.php.

15. Mohler, "Statement from R. Albert Mohler Jr."

16. Kate Shellnut, "Sovereign Grace Calls Outside Investigation 'Impossible,'" *Christianity Today*, April 18, 2019, https://www.christianitytoday.com/news/2019/april/sovereign-grace-churches-sgc-sgm-independent-investigation-.html.

the pastor of a predominantly Black Baptist megachurch in Jacksonville, Florida.[17] As Mohler pursued his ambition, he evolved in other ways as well. In 2020, he reversed his previous criticism of Trump and endorsed him for reelection. A "militant right flank in the SBC" convinced Mohler that "the winds are blowing" in Trump's direction, and "this is not his fight anymore," said Heath Carter, professor of American Christianity at Princeton Theological Seminary.[18]

The leader of the self-styled intellectual wing of conservative evangelicalism seemed to have capitulated to the Pentecostals, prosperity gospel preachers, and faith healers.

In the summer of 2019, I took my daughter out for breakfast on her birthday. Then we walked along the beach, exploring the coastline, picking up rocks, and taking photos. It was a beautiful day. At one point, I looked out at the ocean, wondering what I still believed in. The previous few years had called so much into question. So many people I'd trusted and looked up to had fallen short. So many assumptions I'd held had been shown to be faulty. Everything was up for reexamination. I did not want to mislead my children. What could I tell them that I knew was true, and what could I tell them that I hoped was true? Where did knowledge end and where did faith begin?

I looked at the sky, the water, the trees. I believed that a Creator was behind all of this. That was something. Beyond that, however, I wasn't in much of a mood to make many declarative statements. There was so much to wonder about after the past few years, so much unsettled and so much exposed. We had friends who thought my wife and I were questioning parts of our faith because of things

17. Michael Gryboski," Al Mohler Accepts Nomination for Southern Baptist Convention President," *Christian Post*, November 7, 2019, https://www.christian post.com/news/al-mohler-accepts-nomination-southern-baptist-convention-presi dent.html.

18. As quoted in Jonathan Merritt, "Mohler's Turn to Trump Is the Crowning Flip-Flop of His Career," *Religion News Service*, April 17, 2020, https:// religionnews.com/2020/04/17/mohlers-turn-to-trump-is-the-crowning-flip-flop -of-his-career/.

that had happened in our churches growing up. They seemed to have no clue that it was their triumphalist use of faith mixed with materialism and support for politicians who demonized poor and minority people that was part of the reason that the Christian faith had become questionable to us. Increasingly, we saw that they and so many other American Christians who talked and sang loudly about their love for Jesus seemed to be living lives that did not share Jesus's concerns.

Privately, they were ethical and caring people. But beyond that came the problem. Jesus did care very much about personal ethics and character and integrity, but he was not primarily concerned with religious practice or experience, or with emotional reverie, or with obtaining political power to procure and expand rights. Jesus was about giving away power and lifting up the oppressed. And integrity was not merely a personal matter. Integrity included the ability to discern and tell the truth about reality.

I saw no reason to throw out my Christian faith. But I could also hold it with an open hand, since I was open to the idea that I might be wrong about just about anything. Embracing an openness to being wrong was incredibly freeing and weirdly encouraging of my faith. I resonated very much in the summer of 2019 with David Brooks's description of faith: "The way I experience faith is not a block of concrete. Faith is change. Faith is here one moment gone the next, a stream that evaporates." He quoted Frederick Buechner, who talked about waking up each day and asking, "Can I believe it all again today?" The answer: "At least five times out of ten the answer should be No because the No is as important as the Yes, maybe more so. The No is what proves you're human in case you should ever doubt it. And then if some morning the answer happens to be really Yes, it should be a Yes that's choked with confession and tears and . . . great laughter."[19]

---

19. David Brooks, *The Second Mountain: The Quest for a Moral Life* (New York: Random House, 2019), 246. The quotation from Frederick Buechner originally appeared in his novel *The Return of Ansel Gibbs*.

The third evangelical figure I wrote about in 2017 was a good example of how many conservative Christians were discrediting themselves. Eric Metaxas had been a popular figure for years after publishing a bestselling biography of Dietrich Bonhoeffer. But after he publicly backed Trump in 2016 and declared that Christians "must vote for Trump," he morphed into someone who was increasingly unrecognizable, even to many of his friends. I set out to write a profile of him and sent him a set of questions that were clearly based in a critical view of Trump. He responded with fifty-five hundred words that contained so many contradictions and intellectual cul-de-sacs that there was little coherence to his arguments. In my profile, I wrote that reading his email "was like entering a house of mirrors."[20]

It was not Trump, he said, who had aroused and played upon xenophobia as a candidate by his endless talk of a wall between the US and Mexico and by his slur of Mexican immigrants as "rapists" and by his talk of banning all Muslims from entering the country. Rather, "Beltway and Manhattan elites" were engaged in a "new and accepted tribalism and xenophobia" against "White European 'Christian' varieties" and in favor of Islam. In his arguments, he painted opponents with a broad brush, using the most extreme or negative examples. And he avoided the most substantive critiques of his support for Trump by launching personal attacks on his critics. He called them "vile," "obscene," "childish," and "impotent." This was after beginning his email with the complaint that "graciousness and empathy and trying to see the other side's point of view has fallen by the wayside."[21]

The disjointedness of his positions was stunning, and depressing. Of course, I had also discovered in my research that Metaxas's Bonhoeffer book had been criticized by serious scholars, who said

20. Jon Ward, "Author Eric Metaxas, Evangelical Intellectual, Chose Trump, and He's Sticking with Him," Yahoo! News, February 23, 2018, https://news.yahoo.com/author-eric-metaxas-evangelical-intellectual-chose-trump-hes-sticking-100012875.html.

21. Eric Metaxas, "My Email Exchange with Yahoo! News," March 7, 2018, https://ericmetaxas.com/blog/email-exchange-jon-ward-yahoo-news/.

he'd distorted history to serve ideological arguments.[22] Nonetheless, Metaxas's decline was a reflection of the Christian right's demise. And he was just getting started going down a bizarre road of increasingly strange behavior, driven by a need to justify his support for a president who forced his supporters to defend the indefensible.

He seemed to be having some kind of psychic rupture. It was only a prelude to a bigger and broader disaster.

22. Victoria J. Barnett, "Review of Eric Metaxas, *Bonhoeffer: Pastor, Martyr, Prophet, Spy: A Righteous Gentile vs. the Third Reich*," *Contemporary Church History Quarterly* 16, no. 3 (September 2010), https://contemporarychurchhistory .org/2010/09/review-of-eric-metaxas-bonhoeffer-pastor-martyr-prophet-spy-a -righteous-gentile-vs-the-third-reich/.

19

Losing Reality

When the world shut down in the spring of 2020, I was a bundle of nerves for a few weeks. I searched frantically for house rentals in remote locations and almost threw thousands of dollars down the drain. Ali helped talk me down from that terrible idea. Like everyone else, our family entered a cocoon of isolation. In those first few weeks, when life itself had been paused and the world was quiet with uncertainty, I would wake up around 5 a.m. Instantly, my stomach would fill with butterflies and my feet would begin to sweat. My mind raced. I couldn't get back to sleep.

Ali saw my pain. She got up each day in that 5 a.m. hour and came downstairs to sit at the kitchen table with me. We slowly made espresso, and then she and I played gin rummy. Some mornings when I came downstairs, I could barely move. I just wanted to melt into the floor. But Ali got me through it, as did our extended time together with the kids. We had moved a few years earlier to a bigger house with a yard, and as the weeks slid into months, we spent a lot of time working in the garden, taking on bigger and bigger projects, getting our hands dirty, grounding ourselves in the soil.

One morning in April, I wrote that I was "sitting in our house, wondering, waiting to see what the new world will be like."

Months later, we emerged into the summer of 2020. The pandemic was still raging, killing thousands, but we knew more about it, and the strange twilight of uncertainty from the spring had passed. We knew what we had to do to beat it, as long as we all worked together, and it seemed like life was sort of getting back to normal. But then I was sitting on the beach one day in August and alarm bells went off in my head.

I was talking with a family friend, a sensible and good-hearted man. As we chatted, he expressed exasperation at how difficult it was to know what was true and false in the modern information environment. I agreed with him wholeheartedly. He said he read the *New York Times* and listened to National Public Radio. But then he asked if I had heard that Anthony Bourdain's death might have happened under suspicious circumstances. He said Bourdain had been working on a documentary that was going to expose something. I sat up a little. I was a big fan of Bourdain, and I knew this sounded wrong. But I didn't dismiss it out of hand.

A quick search on my phone turned up only one link. It was something posted on a website called *Neon Nettle*, which I'd never heard of. The website made up a story out of thin air, based on assertions with no evidence, and used two tweets from Bourdain that were twisted completely out of context. It implied that Bourdain had been working on a documentary that would "expose an elite pedophile ring just before he died" and that because Bourdain had publicly criticized Hillary Clinton in the past, maybe his suicide wasn't actually a suicide.[1]

1. David Mikkelson, "Was Anthony Bourdain about to Expose an Elite Pedophile Ring?," *Snopes*, June 9, 2018, https://www.snopes.com/fact-check/anthony-bourdain-expose-elite-ring/; and Jay Greenberg, "Anthony Bourdain Was about to Expose an Elite Pedophile Ring Before He Died," *Neon Nettle*, June 9, 2018, http://www.neonnettle.com/news/4269-anthony-bourdain-was-about-to-expose-an-elite-pedophile-ring-before-he-died.

I realized that I was looking at a website spreading QAnon conspiracy theories.[2] But I'm not sure my friend even knew what QAnon was. He certainly never talked about the sprawling world of baseless fantasies in which Democrats were part of a child sex-trafficking cabal that was going to be defeated by Donald Trump. He did tell me he often looked at an Instagram account run by a pastor at Bethel Church in California, the same church overseen by Bill Johnson, the author of the book on the seven mountains mandate. The Instagram account belonged to a Bethel leader named Danny Silk.

Silk had until that summer been known as the author of several books about family and relational health. But in mid-July, he abruptly started posting on his account about child sex trafficking. I went back through his feed and saw no mention of the topic until July 20, when he used #savethechildren for what appeared to be the first time. By early August, he was posting explicitly QAnon content that drew completely baseless links between Democrats and the Clintons and pedophile rings. This sudden spike in an obsessive focus on child sex trafficking was not sparked by a rise in cases. It did, however, come soon after the murder of George Floyd.

Many conservative evangelicals had been openly supportive of protests against systemic racism and police abuse in the weeks after Floyd's killing in Minneapolis on May 31. But Silk's Instagram account was part of a larger change in emphasis among conservative White evangelicals in the weeks after Floyd's killing.

I called Silk out publicly, that he was using spiritual language to hide an agenda of dishonesty and politically motivated lies behind a veneer of false righteousness. "This is a radical lowering of standards for how we know what is true and false," I wrote. "It's noteworthy that Christian leaders are contributing to this erosion of knowing, since truth is at the heart of the Christian

2. Caroline Mimbs Nyce, "QAnon Is a New American Religion," *The Atlantic*, May 14, 2020, https://www.theatlantic.com/newsletters/archive/2020/05/qanon -q-pro-trump-conspiracy/611722/.

faith. They might claim to be liberating people from a 'controlled narrative' in the mainstream media, but that is a distraction from the factual, substantive standards for information that I'm talking about here. Accusations of wrongdoing must be supported by evidence. If there isn't credible evidence, you shouldn't share information online and on social media that hints that there might be wrongdoing."[3]

"The biggest reason that this is a dangerous and even poisonous standard for believing something, or sharing information based on it, is that it makes all of us vulnerable to abuse," I added. "If anyone can be smeared in the public square—on social media or elsewhere—simply on the basis of circumstantial evidence or even claims that don't have a shred of evidence behind them, then you, or people you love, or figures you support who are doing important work in the world can be attacked with nothing but lies, and there won't be much you can do about it."[4]

When I checked the *Neon Nettle* page months later, the site had posted a correction that was almost as ridiculous as the original post. "An earlier version of this article suggested Anthony Bourdain may have been killed or that his death may not have been a suicide. Bourdain's death was officially ruled a suicide. The previous version also suggested that he may have had knowledge of an 'elite pedophile ring' that may have led to his death. No evidence has ever been produced to suggest that he was killed due to knowledge he may or may not have had," the correction stated.[5] The site changed the headline from "Anthony Bourdain Was about to Expose an Elite Pedophile Ring Before He Died" to "Anthony Bourdain Found Dead, Death Ruled Suicide."

3. Jon Ward, "A Survival Guide for Normal People: Part 2," *Medium*, August 19, 2020, https://medium.com/jon-ward/a-survival-guide-for-normal-people -part-2-e873bbcbb6fc.

4. Ward, "Survival Guide."

5. Jay Greenberg, "Anthony Bourdain Found Dead, Death Ruled Suicide," *Neon Nettle*, June 9, 2018, https://neonnettle.com/news/4269-anthony-bourdain -found-dead-death-ruled-suicide.

That was obviously too little too late. The damage had been done, by this web page and thousands like it that preyed on people who were trying to navigate the Wild West of an internet increasingly being choked by bad faith disinformation and lies. It was a window into how far we had drifted as a society from a set of shared facts. Anything could be true, and now nothing was. It applied to everything: masks and social distancing, the pandemic itself, the thousands of lies that poured forth from the president's mouth. My industry often made things worse with breathless, instinctively negative, and hyperactive coverage. But for Christians from the charismatic world, like my friend, like Lou Engle, and like my own family members, everything had seemingly boiled down to whether Trump was for it or against it.

To differing degrees, many people I know had handed over control of what was real and true to one man rather than to a system of knowledge production. No system is perfect, but author Jonathan Rauch describes a "constitution of knowledge" that had until recently served humanity well for a few hundred years. Because we have abandoned that system of verification, we are now living through an age of information chaos. Most people don't know what to believe or how to figure out what's true and false. If we can't fix this, the vacuum of authority and consensus is likely to be filled by violence, by demagogues and totalitarian leaders. The way to avoid that is to rebuild a system of rules for knowledge that ended the bloody religious wars of the fifteenth and sixteenth centuries in Europe. It was a set of "social rules for turning disagreement into knowledge," Rauch writes,[6] so that we could "kill our hypotheses rather than each other."[7]

This set of rules prioritizes "facts over feelings, evidence over emotion, observations over opinion." It "needs supremacy in the realm of public knowledge, but not in the realm of private belief."[8]

6. Jonathan Rauch, *The Constitution of Knowledge: A Defense of Truth* (Washington, DC: Brookings Institution Press, 2021), 15.

7. Rauch, *Constitution of Knowledge*, 59.

8. Rauch, *Constitution of Knowledge*, 115.

In other words, we preserve freedom of religion by preserving a society in which we can argue and reach consensus on matters of politics and public life that affect everyone. Rauch concludes, "If we care about knowledge, freedom and peace, then we need to stake a strong claim: anyone can believe anything, but liberal science—open-ended, depersonalized checking by an error-seeking social network—is the only legitimate validator of knowledge, at least in the reality-based community."[9]

Trump knew that many Americans were jaded about institutions in general and distrusted the media in particular. My profession, the media, contributed plenty to this dynamic. Mainstream media outlets often caricatured religious conservatives as backward rubes or treated them with disdain and portrayed their views with contempt. Opportunists and tricksters had successfully stoked panic among evangelicals for a long time, precisely because the concerns and fears of religious conservatives had systematically been dismissed, mocked, and punished rather than being listened to and engaged with. So the relationship between Republican voters and the media had been damaged and unhealthy for a long time. It was hanging by a thread when Trump came along. It was like a thin branch barely attached to a tree. Trump came along, ripped the branch off the trunk, and snapped it in half. Once his followers lost their connection to reality, Trump took them into an alternative universe. He seemed to sense that if he could be the one person who determined what was true and false, that would give him incredible power.

But Masha Gessen made a crucial distinction about how someone like Trump would seek to control reality, and it was very unlike authoritarians from decades ago. "Where totalitarian regimes of the past sought to control media, today's autocracies seek to dominate it," Gessen writes. "And where a totalitarian regime sought to suppress media rights, the autocrat seeks to neutralize them. . . . The end result is not a controlled communications sphere where reality is dictated from above, but a weak one, where

9. Rauch, *Constitution of Knowledge*, 87.

nothing can be known, no reality is tangible."[10] According to Gessen, "The path to peace of mind lies in giving one's mind over to the regime."[11]

Trump was the regime that so many gave their minds over to. And his assault on truth—which had been clear in 2016 when I sat in that New Hampshire coffee shop—had continued unabated for four years by this point. In fact, it had increased and accelerated. In his first year as president, he averaged six false claims every day. In his second year, that number went up to sixteen false claims a day. In year three, it was twenty-two. And then in his final year, his false claims vaulted up to a staggering average of thirty-nine per day. In all, he uttered more than thirty thousand lies, deceptions, and misleading statements during his four-year presidency.[12]

This wasn't run-of-the-mill political shading of the truth or claims that could be argued one way or another. These were falsehoods, statements that could be verifiably disproven. And in doing this, he was forcing his supporters to make a choice, not just about who they supported but about who they believed: him or the media.

Most people don't like to exist in a constant state of flux, of complexity. If things are more confusing than ever, people want to find a way to feel like they have some sense of certainty. It's human nature to seek binary reality, where good and bad are clear. Evangelicals love to have the "peace of mind" Gessen writes about. But this "peace of mind" may not be the kind that Jesus preached. To struggle toward truth, to refuse easy answers, and to remain in a place where uncertainty and complexity present ongoing challenges—that seems closer to what Jesus would want. It would require a more active reliance on God in everyday life for those who claim the name of Christian.

10. Masha Gessen, *Surviving Autocracy* (New York: Riverhead Books, 2020), 134.

11. Gessen, *Surviving Autocracy*, 110.

12. Glenn Kessler, "Trump Made 30,573 False or Misleading Claims as President. Nearly Half Came in His Final Year," *Washington Post*, January 23, 2021, https://www.washingtonpost.com/politics/how-fact-checker-tracked-trump-claims/2021/01/23/ad04b69a-5c1d-11eb-a976-bad6431e03e2_story.html.

By the summer of 2020, it seemed as if the events of a historic few months had pushed everyone to a breaking point. The Floyd protests at times turned violent and destructive. People had been cooped up at home for months under pandemic lockdowns. But for many Trump supporters, there was an added element of psychic stress, as it became more difficult to defend their leader.

Trump's response to the multiple crises of 2020 was indefensible. His handling of the pandemic was bumbling, shambolic, and shortsighted day in and day out, even though his administration should get credit for its role in developing an effective vaccine.

When it came to the nation's conversation about race, Trump was divisive and polarizing. It appeared to be intentional. He poured gasoline on the conflicts tearing our country apart rather than seeking to lead the country toward a better place. It was a dizzying and horrifying spectacle.

Many Christians who had rationalized their way into voting for Trump in 2016 had long before 2020 come to resent the incessant criticism and attacks on him. Many people took them personally. This was part of why they wanted to vote for him again. But how could you do so if you lived in reality? He had always been unqualified for the office. He had utterly failed the test of leadership amid multiple crises in 2020. And when confronted with a growing realization in the nation that America owed itself a reckoning on the legacy of systemic racism, he rejected this. He demonized those protesting for justice and tried to paint all of them as violent rioters. He actively sought to turn Americans against one another.

This was a lot of motivation to descend into epistemological hell, a place where there was no certainty about what was true, and so anything could be true, and anything could be false. So as he politicized a pandemic, many of his supporters denied basic scientific facts about the usefulness of masks and physical distancing and the threat of the virus overall. They dismissed the deaths of hundreds of thousands of Americans as trivial and lunged wildly to latch on to a fantasy that Trump was actually fighting a child-trafficking ring directed by Democrats.

I was so disturbed by my conversation with our friend who referenced the Bourdain conspiracy theory that I spent hours of my vacation writing down a guide on how to try to navigate the internet and tips for discerning what was credible and what was noncredible.[13] But I realized in the next few months that I was fighting against something decades in the making: a failure of discipleship by much of the American church. The church had failed to train its members in exercising discernment.

Over the rest of the summer, I tried to understand the links between how I was raised and how people still in that world were so lost while believing themselves found. I found it terrifying to watch many people I knew intensely and angrily support a prelude to fascism. The wisdom of Martin Luther King Jr. had been long forgotten. "The church must be reminded that it is not to be the master or the servant of the state, but rather the conscience of the state. It must be the guide and the critic of the state—never its tool," King said. "As long as the church is a tool of the state it will be unable to provide even a modicum of bread for men at midnight."[14]

My political convictions were driven more than ever by my Christian faith and the message of the gospel. But they were seen as nothing more than partisanship by my family. Some of my siblings rejected me entirely as I sought to counter Trump's many lies about the 2020 election. They dismissed me as corrupt and immoral. I gave them ammunition one day about six weeks before the election.

In late September, Alison and I took our kids to visit my parents. We hadn't seen them in over two months. And when we pulled up to their house in the Maryland suburbs, there was a blue sign in the middle of their yard, facing us. "Trump/Pence 2020," it said.

13. Ward, "Survival Guide."
14. Martin Luther King Jr., "Draft of Chapter VI, 'A Knock at Midnight,'" Martin Luther King Jr. Papers, 1954–1968, Howard Gotlieb Archival Research Center, Boston University, Boston, Massachusetts, https://kinginstitute.stanford.edu/king-papers/documents/draft-chapter-vi-knock-midnight.

I had been working for months, since the late spring of 2020, to research and investigate how Americans would be able to vote during the pandemic. I had tried to understand and explain the process and how it was changing as our understanding of the COVID-19 virus evolved and grew. As I did this, Trump spread lie after lie about it, seeking to undermine faith in the upcoming election.

In the weeks leading up to our visit to my parents, I'd been reporting almost every day on how three states that would likely decide the election—Michigan, Wisconsin, and Pennsylvania—had rules that would delay the counting of mail-in ballots. It was easy to fix. But the state legislatures in these three states were all controlled by Republicans, and they refused to solve the problem. It was becoming evident that Republicans planned to use delays in counting mail-in votes—a problem they'd created—to claim fraud.[15] It was a road map for a coup attempt. It foreshadowed exactly what would end up happening.

I understood my parents' instinct to vote for the Republican candidate. But to see them celebrate the name of the man who was attacking our free elections overwhelmed me. My response, however, showed my own shortcomings. The kids jumped out and went inside to say hello. I walked over to the sign, pulled it up out of the ground, and placed it in some bushes under a nearby tree. I didn't want the sign in the yard while I was there. But I didn't want to ask them to take it down. I wanted to avoid all discussion of politics. They knew how I felt. I didn't need to tell them again. They could put it back after I left. I should have just said something to them about the sign.

My even bigger mistake was that when I walked into the garage and saw a second sign, I took it and put it in my car. I was clearly not thinking straight. In the following days, my dad called me and asked where the signs were. He was calm, as ever. But when

15. Barton Gellman, "The Election That Could Break America," *The Atlantic*, November 2020, https://www.theatlantic.com/magazine/archive/2020/11/what-if -trump-refuses-concede/616424/.

I told him, my siblings then found out and took shots at me on a family text thread.

"It's a terrible thing that when someone disagrees with another's beliefs, that they feel the RIGHT to take something that's not theirs (theft), damage it (destruction of property), and not feel any remorse for it," one sibling wrote. "We should all have respect for one another's beliefs religious and political, and have enough common sense and consideration for others not to do something like this. The problem with the extreme left is that they think they are right in anything they do even when it's wrong. They will twist and distort and justify themselves so that they don't have to take responsibility for their actions. This is even more disgusting when someone does this to a family member.

"Jon, I think you need to take a good look at your morals at this point," this sibling continued. "You should feel ashamed. Someone needs to speak up to you at some point."

I was looking for a way to defuse the situation. "I love you," I wrote. "I'd be happy to have a conversation face-to-face sometime and talk through all of this."

"I love you too, Jon, and that's why I am speaking up to you," my sibling answered. "I don't want to have a conversation with you. Our views are so far apart and it wouldn't be a good use of my time." I sent a few texts to this sibling in the weeks afterward, asking to talk on the phone. There was no response. Those were the last words I'd hear from that sibling for almost two years.

A week after our text exchange, the same sibling sent a picture to the family text thread one night around 10 p.m. It was a shot of them waving a large American flag outside Walter Reed Hospital, where Trump had been admitted with a serious case of COVID-19.

Our family was tearing itself apart, just like so many others around the country.

About two weeks after the election, Trump lawyers Rudy Giuliani and Sidney Powell held a bizarre press conference at the Republican National Committee, where they speculated and gesticulated about wild conspiracy theories that had no proof.[16] I had been spending every day at work studying all the accusations made by Trump and his allies and painstakingly explaining to our readers why there was nothing to them.[17] As the press conference went on, another message came across our family text thread. It was my dad, telling everyone they should turn on *Fox News* and watch the press conference.

After Giuliani and Powell finished their display, I sent the family a tweet from Erick Erickson, a conservative talk radio host from Georgia who often criticized Trump but voted for him and donated to his campaign. "I feel very sorry for the people who believe the bulls—t we just heard," Erickson wrote in a tweet that he later deleted (but which I preserved). "There are a lot of broken people who are being lied to and many of them want to believe the lie because their religion has become politics and they cannot believe their god is abandoning them." Another conservative writer, Stephen L. Miller, pointed out that Trump's lawyers were not presenting any of the arguments in court that were being made by Giuliani and Powell in their public comments to the press. "Ask yourself why," Miller wrote in another text that has since been deleted. "If they have all this secret evidence of massive fraud, why not present it in court?" I texted that as well to my family.

Not all my siblings were on the Trump train, and they chimed in. One sister asked my family if they thought I was "out to sabotage not only us, but all Americans? Do you think he is intentionally trying to mislead us? That he's a liar? Or do you just think he's a sh—y journalist?" Ali spoke up too. "I don't often chime in on this thread. If ever. But I've been wondering the same thing," she wrote. "And honestly I've been pretty hurt for him by the seeming

16. "Rudy Giuliani Trump Campaign Press Conference Transcript November 19: Election Fraud Claims," *Rev*, November 19, 2020, https://www.rev.com/blog/tran scripts/rudy-giuliani-trump-campaign-press-conference-transcript-november -19-election-fraud-claims.

17. Jon Ward and Andrew Romano, "The 2020 Election Wasn't 'Stolen.' Here Are All the Facts That Prove It," Yahoo! News, November 12, 2020, https://news .yahoo.com/the-2020-election-wasnt-stolen-here-are-all-the-facts-that-prove -it-184623754.html.

dismissiveness and/or disrespect of what he spends the bulk of his day working on each and every day. He has spent countless days and hours investigating all of this. Reading affidavits. Talking to election officials. Tons of research. But if Fox News doesn't say it, [it] doesn't count."

The answers to these questions came in short order. One sibling berated me on the text thread over and over for hours, long after everyone else had stopped responding. By the end of the day, he had sent 130 separate texts. As the day wore on, his messages became increasingly personal and angry.

You should be ashamed of yourself.

Do you consider yourself a journalist?

You are enslaving yourself . . . pathetic.

I sat in a restaurant booth with my wife that evening as the text messages from this sibling continued to pour in, one after the other. I felt sadness, pain, and anger. I could not believe I was watching my own family, and many people I had known for years, doubling down. Their connection to reality had been severed, so they thought the election had been stolen or that there had been cheating. I was a physical manifestation of the stubbornness of facts. But our family connection was overwhelmed by their tribal identity. I was collateral damage. That didn't make it hurt any less.

My father seemed to shift a bit, however, in December, around the time my old pen pal Eric Metaxas seemed to increasingly lose touch with reality. "We need to fight to the death, to the last drop of blood," Metaxas said.[18] He said he knew Trump had won in a landslide, even though there was no evidence of meaningful fraud and despite the fact that he was—by his own admission—"ignorant of the details" regarding the legal disputes over the election.

Metaxas emceed a rally of Trump supporters in Washington, DC, on December 12. A day earlier, the US Supreme Court had unanimously rejected a lawsuit that sought to throw out the votes of millions of Americans in an attempt to overturn the presidential

18. Rod Dreher, "Eric Metaxas's American Apocalypse," *American Conservative*, December 10, 2020, https://www.theamericanconservative.com/dreher/eric-metaxas-trump-bloodshed-american-apocalypse-live-not-by-lies/.

election.[19] The rally with Metaxas was preceded by a group of Trump supporters marching around the Supreme Court building. They called it the Jericho March and walked around the court building seven times, seeking to reenact the biblical story told in the book of Joshua. The Israelites marched around a hostile city seven times, they blew their horns, and the walls collapsed. Then they "utterly destroyed all that was in the city, both man and woman, young and old . . . with the edge of the sword" (Josh. 6:21 KJV).

It was a cold December day, and I went over to the Supreme Court to watch for a few minutes. I posted video on Instagram of a man yelling while he marched around the building, surrounded by people draped in Trump flags. He pointed at the US Capitol a block away and screamed, "Spirit, get out of there! Be gone! Be gone! Be gone!" A family friend commented on my post: "So wanted to be there and join the march." I arrested my thumbs from tapping out a response.

During the rally that day, right-wing Catholics, Jews, and evangelicals dumped all their most cherished rhetoric and spiritual rituals into a proverbial pot, brewing a toxic stew of syncretic religious nationalism. Trump had been robbed. They didn't need proof. They believed it to be true. They felt it to be true. God had told them in their hearts it was true. Just like many of the testimonies I'd heard in church growing up, it was too good of a story to check for accuracy.

Conspiracy king Alex Jones showed that any form of madness could be sold to many people simply by sprinkling the name of Jesus throughout one's rantings and ravings. "Jesus Christ is King!" he roared from the stage. "This is the beginning of the Great Revival before the Antichrist comes! . . . Revelation is fulfilled! . . . GOD IS ON OUR SIDE!" he screamed. "We will never bow down to the Satanic pedophile New World Order!"[20]

19. Adam Liptak, "Supreme Court Rejects Texas Suit Seeking to Subvert Election," *New York Times*, December 11, 2020, https://www.nytimes.com/2020/12/11/us/politics/supreme-court-election-texas.html.

20. Rod Dreher, "What I Saw at the Jericho March," *American Conservative*, December 12, 2020, https://www.theamericanconservative.com/dreher/what-i-saw-at-the-jericho-march/.

My dad emailed me, aghast, after reading Rod Dreher's account of the day. But he also said it was similar to what people on the left did. An unequivocal condemnation was too much to ask.

———

Meanwhile, in Louisville, the sermons had barely changed. As 2020 shifted into 2021, my old pastor C. J. Mahaney was preaching week after week on the theme of "Holiness and Hope for a Harassed Church."[21] It was the same old victim story. Like much of conservative American Christianity, C. J. and his flock were largely keeping to themselves, neglecting anything outside their church, largely disengaged as other Christians sought to overthrow democracy in the name of Jesus.

Not everyone from that world of conservative Christianity was silent. John Piper was one of the few speakers who did speak out with some vigor against Trump. Piper said he remained deeply troubled by the abortion policies of Democrats but tried to make a biblical case for not voting for either Trump or Biden. "When a leader models self-absorbed, self-exalting boastfulness, he models the most deadly behavior in the world," Piper wrote of Trump. "He points his nation to destruction. Destruction of more kinds than we can imagine. It is naive to think that a man can be effectively pro-life and manifest consistently the character traits that lead to death—temporal and eternal."[22]

Lou Engle was outraged by this. He responded to Piper in writing. He quoted from the book of Daniel, which says that "the Most High rules in the kingdom of men and gives it to whomever he will, and sets over it the lowest of men" (4:17 NKJV). From this Old Testament passage, Engle drew a rather stunning lesson. "God is not always making character the foundation of his appointments of those

21. C. J. Mahaney, "Holiness and Hope for a Harassed Church," Sermon Series, Sovereign Grace Ministries, accessed April 6, 2022, https://www.sgclouisville.org /sovereign-grace-church-louisville-sermons/series/dear-thessalonians:-holiness -and-hope-for-a-harassed-church.

22. John Piper, "Policies, Persons, and Paths to Ruin: Pondering the Implications of the 2020 Election," *Desiring God*, October 22, 2020, https://www .desiringgod.org/articles/policies-persons-and-paths-to-ruin.

in authority," he said.[23] Engle often described Biden as someone who supported abortion all the way up until the moment of birth. That wasn't true. Biden had always said he opposed late-term abortions and supported a ban on such procedures.[24] And Engle talked about the election as if it would decide whether abortion would be legal or not. He did not mention, though he must have known, that even if *Roe v. Wade* were overturned, abortion would remain legal in the more liberal states comprising roughly half the country.

After the election, Engle released nearly two dozen videos on his YouTube channel[25] in which he ranted about the election and interpreted much of what was happening through dreams and visions. "I believe there are spiritual powers in heaven and on earth who are moving in corruption and in fraud," he said.[26] He called on Christians "to give themselves to fasting and praying, crying out for the exposure of voter fraud."[27] And he was angry. "Joe Biden is not my president," Engle said. "Until inauguration day my authority in this nation is President Trump."[28] He was particularly upset by Beth Moore, a nationally known Bible study teacher, when she tweeted that "Trumpism" was "seductive and dangerous to the saints of God." Moore also tweeted that Christians should not "sanctify idolatry by labeling a leader our Cyrus. We need no Cyrus. We have a king. His name is Jesus."[29]

23. Lou Engle, "John Piper Is Sadly Mistaken and Misguiding Others," *Charisma News*, October 29, 2020, https://www.charismanews.com/politics/opinion/83137-lou-engle-john-piper-is-sadly-mistaken-and-misguiding-others.

24. Jocelyn Grzeszczak, "Fact Check: Does Joe Biden Support Late-Term Abortion Up Until Birth Like Donald Trump Claimed?," *Newsweek*, October 6, 2020, https://www.newsweek.com/fact-check-does-joe-biden-support-late-term-abortion-until-birth-like-donald-trump-claimed-1536686.

25. Lou Engle YouTube Channel, https://www.youtube.com/c/LouEngleMinistries/videos.

26. "Expose, Expose," YouTube video, 4:08, posted by Lou Engle, November 4, 2020, https://www.youtube.com/watch?v=ipHnE2zGd-k.

27. Lou Engle, "Do Not Resign!" YouTube video, 7:05, posted by Lou Engle, November 9, 2020, https://www.youtube.com/watch?v=g7kQB_CBVAw.

28. Engle, "Do Not Resign!"

29. Tyler Huckabee, "Beth Moore's Condemnation of 'Trumpism' Is a Watershed Moment," *Relevant*, December 14, 2020, https://relevantmagazine.com/current/nation/beth-moores-condemnation-of-trumpism-is-a-watershed-moment/.

Engle responded to Moore with a bizarre complaint: "Witches rose up and removed President Trump by their hexes and their witchcraft. . . . It makes me angry when people like Beth Moore actually speak against this man . . . while witches worldwide are cursing him."[30] It would be easy to dismiss these ravings as irrelevant and harmless except for the fact that Engle remained a respected and influential leader to many evangelical Christians. For many, it was hard to comprehend that someone could be both a kind and gracious Christian in his personal life and yet also a false prophet.

In his response to Piper, Engle began by reading a quote from Abraham Kuyper, the Dutch theologian and journalist who rose to become prime minister of the Netherlands from 1901 to 1905. Kuyper was also a Calvinist. Kuyper's thinking had influenced those who believed in the seven mountains philosophy that was now driving the political activism of many in Engle's circle of influence. Engle quoted, "When principles that run against your deepest convictions begin to win the day, then battle is your calling and peace has become sin."[31] Battle is your calling. Peace has become sin. It was rhetoric like that, voiced in the face of clear evidence that there was no significant fraud in the election, that helped lead to one of the greatest crises in American democracy.

The irony of it all was that I had done what Engle and others had called for. Engle and Bill Johnson and other "seven mountains" adherents had called for Christians to ascend to the heights of cultural influence and live out their faith in that context. I had done that for years. I had started my ascent years before those around Engle were talking about "seven mountains." I had kept Christ and his teachings as my North Star. And I had been reporting back for years on how government and media worked and how Christians should think about them. I had been warning, along with many others, of the danger Trump posed, based on the knowledge and expertise I had acquired during my decades-long

30. "Daniel Fast Day 17 – Trumpism!?," YouTube video, 4:12, posted by Lou Engle, December 17, 2020, https://www.youtube.com/watch?v=3P3xHCTOsZI.

31. Engle, "John Piper Is Sadly Mistaken."

journey up this mountain. But the warnings fell again and again on deaf ears. Leaders like Engle were so committed to their point of view that they could not incorporate new information or evolve in any real way, because doing so would threaten their identities, their followings, and their livelihoods.

Engle's hope was that the election would be decided by the Supreme Court. "We need five judges. We need to secure the judges," he said.[32] In that moment, it was clear that the pursuit of the Supreme Court was as much about pure power as anything else. It showed the way that the pursuit of raw power can corrupt those who claim to speak for God.

The pursuit of seven mountain dominance had led Christians away from the way of Christ, wrote conservative author David French.

> And don't forget, the Son of God himself spent his entire life on earth far from the mountaintop. . . . He was persecuted and punished by a "mountain king" named Pilate and executed next to a thief. When he rose, he appeared not to Caesar but to a small band of ordinary men and women who would become martyrs, not rulers. Christ prevailed . . . not by fighting from the commanding power of the heights, but by fighting from "utterly different terrain." When scripture calls Christians to "take up your cross and follow me," it's declaring . . . that "our mountain is Golgotha"— the dusty Israeli hill where Christ was crucified.[33]

Or as Franciscan priest and author Richard Rohr put it, when Jesus was crucified, "the image of God was one of absolute vulnerability. How could we have missed the point?"[34]

32. "Pennsylvania," YouTube video, 9:26, posted by Lou Engle, November 18, 2020, https://www.youtube.com/watch?v=uFe2TctfnL4.

33. David French, "How a Rising Religious Movement Rationalizes the Christian Grasp for Power," *The Dispatch*, February 28, 2021, https://frenchpress.the dispatch.com/p/how-a-rising-religious-movement-rationalizes.

34. Richard Rohr, "The Story of the Cosmic Egg," *Another Name for Everything, with Richard Rohr*, February 27, 2021, https://podcasts.apple.com/us/pod cast/the-story-of-the-cosmic-egg/id1452609613?i=1000510864387.

20

A New Normal

As 2020 staggered to a close, there were fresh signs of mental collapse among Christians we knew. Christian leaders railed against the lockdowns in their states. One told his congregation that their governor should "take authority" over COVID-19 through praying in the name of Jesus. He defended meeting together without masks by citing the fact that Jesus visited leper colonies and wasn't afraid of getting infected. This made no sense. We wore masks to protect others in case we were infectious, not primarily because we were afraid for our own health. We avoided large gatherings and practiced social distancing to slow the spread of the virus so that our hospitals were not overloaded with cases. The analogy to Jesus was illogical. Jesus went into leper colonies and healed the disease. He didn't do things likely to spread the disease and then shrug it off by saying God was in control.

One friend vented his frustration about restrictions on large public gatherings and business closures. He also railed against masks and social distancing. Somehow he failed to see that masks and distancing were the most effective tools we had to do exactly what he was so frustrated about: allow society to open back up as quickly as possible. He considered masks to be instruments to foster fear and to manipulate the public. The weak were on their own. This friend felt that those at risk should bear the burden of responsibility for protecting themselves rather than imposing on others precautions against spreading the virus. This was the perfect crystallization of a hyper-individualistic Christianity. In his view, none of us are part of a whole. We are atomized souls who speak to Jesus one on one. "America's idolatry of individual rights over the common good has made fertile ground to see any inconvenience as persecution," wrote Shane Claiborne, a Christian author and activist.[1]

More than one person I know said that many of the deaths from COVID-19 were among older people or those with bad health. The clear implication was that, well, these people were going to die anyway. But this wasn't something they said in lament, sad that we had been unable to protect people by doing as much as we could to value life. No, they made these points to defend not wearing a mask or following basic distancing guidelines. I kept telling them, yes, let's reopen and get our businesses going, and let's make the basic small sacrifices to protect the vulnerable. "It's not a defensible position to say, 'These people were going to die soon anyway so I'm not going to do my very small part to protect them,'" I told a friend.

Mindy Belz, a journalist for the evangelical Christian *World* magazine, had spent years taking trips to Iraq and Syria, writing story after story and then a book about the suffering of Christians at the hands of the Islamic State in the Middle East. She had seen real religious persecution up close. "For 6 yrs I've reported on Christians chased from their homes & churches by ISIS, seen their testimony, steadiness, care for one another," she tweeted in May 2020. "How utterly disheartening to watch the American church come apart in a 10-wk shutdown. They shall be known by their demand for their rights."[2]

1. Shane Claiborne, Twitter, August 29, 2021, 12:14 p.m., "America's idolatry of individual rights over the common good has made fertile ground to see any inconvenience as persecution," https://twitter.com/ShaneClaiborne/status /1432013791131316236.

2. Mindy Belz, Twitter, May 22, 2020, 5:40 p.m., "For 6 yrs I've reported on Christians chased from their homes & churches by ISIS, seen their testimony,

I asked my friend, "Do you want to be known for your demands for your rights, even at the potential cost of other people's lives? Or do you want to be known as the type of Christian who is happy to be inconvenienced to serve the weak around us? That's what this is about." My friend responded with, essentially, a shrug. He felt that the threat was not as great as many "alarmists" purported and that there were plenty of other people who felt exactly the same way he did.

On a winter day near the end of 2020, I watched a recording of a church service in which the pastor invited a woman to the front of the congregation who told the story of John G. Lake, a Pentecostal faith healer and missionary. "He said, 'The blood of Jesus runs through my veins. No bacteria or virus can live.' And they said, 'Prove it,'" the woman said. "What did he do? He spit on a slide, a microscopic slide. They took some of his blood. Before they took the blood they could see the bacteria moving around, moving around in his spit. It was the bubonic plague. And the blood, when it fell on it, killed every germ. So I am going to walk in that kind of faith. And I ask you to join me." When the woman finished speaking, one of the musicians on stage said with a dreamy smile, "You can say that kind of stuff when you're living in another world."[3]

The musician was more profound than he realized. So many of the decisions and choices and opinions that made so little sense, and did so much damage in the real world, were caused by what that musician described: people living in another world. In this alternative reality, logic and reason were optional. Political views like anti-mask sentiment, which seemed to flow directly from the fact that Trump didn't like masks, were dressed up in spiritual language and sanctified as righteous.

This transformation of fantasies into beliefs blessed by God is what led to January 6. There was no significant or even semi-significant

steadiness, care for one another. How utterly disheartening to watch the American church come apart in a 10-wk shutdown. They shall be known by their demand for their rights," https://twitter.com/MindyBelz/status/1263947753756995584.

3. There is an audio recording of this service, but it is not available online.

voter fraud. The election was fair and just. Yet many of the insurrectionists that day believed God was on their side.[4] One man carried a giant wooden cross, and a group of others looked on as people violently assaulted police and entered the Capitol. They chanted, "The blood of Jesus covering this place."[5] Ché Ahn, the close friend of Lou Engle who was a leader of my childhood church with my dad and C. J. Mahaney, spoke to Trump supporters in DC on January 5 and told them, "We're gonna rule and reign through President Trump and under the lordship of Jesus Christ."[6]

What an irony it was, then, that in the Christian calendar, January 6 is the Feast of Epiphany, "when Christians celebrate how the light of Christ spreads to all nations," as Tish Harrison Warren wrote in *Christianity Today*.

> Epiphany calls us to light and truth. It reminds us that the promise of Isaiah is fulfilled in Christ: "Nations will come to your light, and kings to the brightness of your dawn" (60:3). Light is beautiful, and it is also revelatory. The season of Epiphany reminds us that we do not just *receive* the light of Christ. We are charged with sharing it with all the world. But if the nations were watching recent events in DC—as people destabilized democracy while carrying flags that read "Make America Godly Again"—would any onlooker want anything to do with this Christ? The violence wrought by Trump supporters storming the Capitol is anti-epiphany. It is dark and based in untruth. The symbols of faith—Jesus' name, cross, and message—have been co-opted to serve the cultish end of Trumpism.[7]

4. Kathryn Joyce, "How Christian Nationalism Drove the Insurrection: A Religious History of Jan. 6," *Salon*, January 6, 2022, https://www.salon.com /2022/01/06/how-christian-nationalism-drove-the-insurrection-a-religious-history -of-jan-6/.

5. "Peace in the Name of Jesus," *Uncivil Religion*, January 6, 2021, https:// uncivilreligion.org/home/media/the-blood-of-jesus.

6. Peter Montgomery, "Christian Nationalism and Threats of Violence at Pro-Trump Rally on Eve of Electoral College Certification," *Right Wing Watch*, January 6, 2021, https://www.rightwingwatch.org/post/christian-nationalism-and -threats-of-violence-at-pro-trump-rally-on-eve-of-electoral-college-certification/.

7. Tish Harrison Warren, "We Worship with the Magi, Not MAGA," *Christianity Today*, January 7, 2021, https://www.christianitytoday.com/ct/2021/january -web-only/trump-capitol-mob-election-politics-magi-not-maga.html.

As religious believers lost touch with reality, they lost faith in a free society, even as they yelled loudly about their love of freedom. In a free country—a democratic constitutional republic—problems are solved through legislative bodies and courts: deliberative bodies governed by a set of rules that are written down. There are checks and balances to keep power dispersed rather than concentrated. The rule of law is sacrosanct, because it preserves the ideal of fairness and the equality of every citizen. America has never perfectly lived this, of course, but it has never publicly turned its back on the goal.

January 6 made it clear that some in this country were turning away from democracy. If they didn't think they could be the dominant majority group in a pluralistic nation of many religions and racial identities, then they had decided that maybe freedom wasn't so great after all and could be discarded for security.

I texted my father the morning of January 7. I was raw from the trauma of watching the Capitol being attacked by a violent mob of people yelling about freedom and taking back America for God.

"Am I still hysterical? Am I still throwing a liberal hissy fit?!!!" I wrote. "I warned you and I warned you and I warned you. For years. It was clear this was where this was heading. You let your political identity blind you to love for country [and] of YOUR OWN SON!! This was never about party or ideology. It was about the good of our country. This is the culmination of five shameful years. What a disgrace. An utter disgrace."

Dad said he wanted to discuss it in person but noted that he condemned the violence and held Trump responsible for it. Finally, there was something unequivocal from him.

"I appreciate it," I wrote. "I'm just so angry. This is always what I feared. He told us he would do this. This absolutely did not have to happen. I am so. F—ing. Angry."

Surely, I thought, the horror of that day would be enough of a wake-up call that the nation could course correct.

I was wrong again. As 2021 wore on, it became clear that the old normal was not coming back. We thought the pandemic would be in the rearview mirror. The vaccines were released. Maybe misinformation would slow down, and those who had bought into conspiracy theories about COVID-19 would come back to reality when they had an opportunity to take a vaccine that had been developed during the Trump administration.

I thought that after January 6, the warnings about Trump's danger to democracy would be crystal clear. He had just demonstrated it. He was disgraced. His cult would disband. The fever would break.

Yet COVID-19 mutated, and one variant led to another. More people died in 2021 from the pandemic than in 2020.[8] We started the year with just under four hundred thousand dead and ended it with over eight hundred thousand Americans having been killed by the virus.[9] One out of every one hundred Americans over age sixty-five died from COVID-19.[10] Anti-mask and anti-lockdown attitudes hardened into anti-vaccine and anti-mandate defiance. The virus ripped through unvaccinated communities of people, killing mostly people who were not inoculated.[11] Misinformation continued to persist. Millions of Americans blinded themselves to reality, to obvious facts, and insisted the vaccines were either ineffective or harmful.

Trump went into hiding and licked his wounds for a brief time but reemerged to continue making claims that the 2020 election was stolen. Republican politicians, knowing this is a lie, shockingly came back to him and propped up a new architecture of misleading

8. Renuka Rayasam, "5 Pandemic Predictions for 2022," *Politico*, December 16, 2021, https://www.politico.com/newsletters/politico-nightly/2021/12/16/5 -pandemic-predictions-for-2022-495483.

9. Julie Bosman, Amy Harmon, Albert Sun, Chloe Reynolds, and Sarah Cahalan, "Covid Deaths in the United States Surpass 800,000," *New York Times*, December 15, 2021, https://www.nytimes.com/2021/12/15/us/covid-deaths-unit ed-states.html.

10. Julie Bosman, Amy Harmon, and Albert Sun, "As U.S. Nears 800,000 Virus Deaths, 1 of Every 100 Older Americans Has Perished," *New York Times*, December 13, 2021, https://www.nytimes.com/2021/12/13/us/covid-deaths-elderly -americans.html.

11. Damien McNamara, "Almost All U.S. COVID-19 Deaths Now in the Unvaccinated," *WebMd*, June 28, 2021, https://www.webmd.com/vaccines/covid-19 -vaccine/news/20210629/almost-all-us-covid-19-deaths-now-in-the-unvaccinated.

Reformation

and false assertions to justify Trump's deception. Tucker Carlson told his three million or so viewers a night on Fox News that President Biden wanted to imprison and torture them for their beliefs. Carlson was either lying or paranoid, but many believed him, and he planted new seeds of destruction. When I wrote an article pointing out the lack of evidence for his claims, he attacked me on his show and lied about what I'd written.[12]

As we neared the end of 2021, I felt like my job required me to gaze deeply into the soul of a country that was losing its sanity. I felt for a time like my work was physically poisoning my body. Rather than repair the damage done over the previous few years, many Christians were consumed with moral panic. Instead of seeking to rebuild democracy and find unity, they listened to politicians and activists who exaggerated the threats of things like child abduction and sex trafficking or demonized teaching about the history of racism in our country or the debate over transgender rights. Fear still dominated. And then on the left, I saw little desire to listen to the concerns of conservatives over these issues, which might have been the best way to deescalate the situation.

I saw that the task was to come to grips with a new reality and forge ahead with courage, fortitude, and love. "It is despair making if you insist on clinging to your previous vision," novelist George Saunders said. "But if you take this as a period when the universe is correcting your a—, at least it's more interesting or exciting maybe. . . . In the scale of the universe that's kind of all you've got: the little pod around you of things you can influence. And if in one's despair about the big pod you forget to be attentive in the little pod, then you threw away both games."[13]

I reflected at the end of 2021 on the previous weeks of spending time with my wife and children in my own little pod. I found myself repeatedly thinking, *I'm more grateful than I've ever been.*

12. Jon Ward, "Why Tucker Carlson Attacked Me on TV," *Medium*, January 5, 2022, https://jonward11.medium.com/why-tucker-carlson-attacked-me-on-tv-2b55490a468c.

13. "#469: George Saunders," *Longform Podcast*, December 2021, https://longform.org/player/longform-podcast-469-george-saunders.

Everything felt more tenuous and fragile, and so the good was that much more precious. But I also felt, perhaps, the physical and psychic impact of having really inhabited the season of Advent. For a few years, I'd been reading the sermons of Episcopal priest Fleming Rutledge during this season, but I sensed it would take years to really absorb the full meaning of Advent. Finally, it seemed that I was feeling, in my bones, the rhythms grounded in ancient traditions that led me to walk through much of December in lament over the brokenness of our world.

"The Advent season offers something remarkable to the church—the calling to live in two places at once," Rutledge said in a 2016 sermon. She went on to say,

> If the church is doing its job, the people of God are going about their December routines in a double sense. We are shopping, decorating, baking, wrapping, and creating as much magic for the children as possible. . . . But in our hearts and in the worship of the church, the Advent season begins in the darkness, in the depths of the night. In the world of darkness, refugees are homeless; families shopping at Christmas markets are run down; the people of Aleppo are hunted from house to house. In our own country, we are divided and wary of one another. It is the midnight of the year. . . . This is the right moment in the year for the announcement of the coming of the Lord.[14]

I found myself hoping that this story of Christmas might be true, needing faith to believe that it could be, and deeply grateful for the blessings I have here and now.

―――――――――

I was taught about the cross a lot growing up. It was an instrument of torture that the Roman Empire used to execute Jesus. It is the focal point of the Christian story. It was all we talked about after I began taking my faith seriously as a twenty-year-old. But I was not really shown how to take up my cross and actually follow Christ. The crisis of American Christianity basically boils down to this

14. Fleming Rutledge, *Advent: The Once and Future Coming of Jesus Christ* (Grand Rapids: Eerdmans, 2018), 370–71.

failure. I still don't claim to know how to walk the way of the cross or the path of resurrection very well. But I think that the quest to do so is still at the heart of a meaningful faith. What does it look like to live sacrificially but also incarnationally? Christ was God incarnate, made flesh. How do we walk through death to life, here, now?

Curtis Chang, a theologian at Fuller Seminary, described living in "incarnation mode" as being the kind of person whose first instinct is not to point fingers or complain but to "stretch out our arms" as Christ did on the cross.[15] There are many possible applications of this paradigm.

One way of spreading our arms open is to live in the middle of extremes, reaching out to those who are drawn to go too far in any one direction. When we know people whose views or actions we find repugnant or offensive or harmful, we might want to angrily confront them and condemn them. Or we may want to write them off and reject them and have nothing to do with them. Sometimes one of these approaches, within reason, may be called for. But more often, it's likely that Christians may be obligated to stay in relationship and stay in conflict, lovingly. (I would not apply this to a case of clear abuse or victimization.) That could mean we discuss our disagreement. It could mean we keep quiet. This is a dynamic and contextual approach. It is painful. It requires guidance from God and reliance on him. It may be one application of this incarnational living.

I have walked on the same ground in Jerusalem that Jesus is reputed to have staggered along on his way to crucifixion: the Via Dolorosa. But I often feel as if I am standing on the threshold of actually walking that path in my real life, always holding back and not fully entering. What has my faith actually cost me? What impact has it made on the world around me? On the other hand, am I trying too hard to be a martyr of some sort? Should I go easier on myself? We all have crosses to bear in life. But suffering is not a contest. Everyone experiences pain if they live long enough. Perhaps

15. Curtis Chang, "Should Christians Trust the Vaccine When the System Is Flawed?," Christians and the Vaccine, https://www.christiansandthevaccine.com/episodes/06.

the real goal is to embed my life and my family in the larger world so that our everyday decisions organically benefit others, not just in our immediate relational network but in the larger community in which we live.

I do feel good about how I've prioritized my wife and kids over my career. I made decisions over the last twenty years to push away from the world of television and punditry because I thought the incentives in TV were bad for truth-seeking and because I knew TV promised an exchange of more money for less time with family. I've done far less traveling as the kids have grown older, and I've made it a priority to be present in their lives. I still have a lot of work to do to be emotionally present, not just physically so. I've done more to share the work of domestic rhythms. I'm less interested in proving myself and more eager to help Ali flourish in the next phases of her life.

Most days I want to make the "pilgrimage toward the margins of society," as Makoto Fujimura puts it. This is a "moving away from [your] own secure borders of familial tribal culture."[16] Living in a neighborhood where we are a racial minority in Washington, DC, has helped us do this. I've seen that the pull of racial segregation by choice is very strong and cuts across political views. In the DC neighborhoods around the US Capitol building, known as Capitol Hill, almost everyone is wealthy, liberal, and White. Racial injustice and poverty are huge concerns for many who live there, but there is not much everyday proximity to the poor or to areas that are majority Black. And real change, it seems, comes only through regular contact and relationship.

Ali and I are trying to live lives and make choices that chip away at injustice, but I still feel like I don't know what I'm doing. We struggle with how to raise our kids. There's a lot we're probably doing wrong. There's a lot we're doing differently than the way we were raised. There's also a lot we owe our parents, who gave us so much good, who stayed together, who instilled many of the right lessons in us through their examples.

16. Makoto Fujimura, *Culture Care: Reconnecting with Beauty for Our Common Life* (Downers Grove, IL: InterVarsity, 2017), 70–71.

"Don't forget about your remarkable family who gave you The Book," Michael Olmert, my old Shakespeare professor from the University of Maryland, wrote me in 2017. "And then the very secular nudge you got from UMd. You embody the best of both worlds."[17]

_____

Oh, and I'm trying to understand how to read the Bible. I had been programmed to read the Bible as an instruction manual. It will take me years to be able to pick up the book and not try to "get it" right away. I had been taught that getting it meant knowing, right away, what action I should take as a result, which we called "application." And I was also supposed to have some ineffable emotion as I read. "Hearing from God" meant experiencing a sensation of emotional or spiritual ecstasy. At least, that's how it was in my early twenties, the period of my greatest spiritual intensity.

I have come to realize in recent years that most evangelicals don't know how to read the Bible the way it has been read for most of Christian history. Evangelicals love the Bible. They live their entire lives by it. But they have hugged the Bible so tightly that they have suffocated it.

"Millions of evangelicals" have been "thinking they are honoring the Scriptures, yet interpreting the Scriptures on questions of science and world affairs in ways that fundamentally contradict the deeper, broader, and historically well-established meanings of the Bible itself," evangelical scholar Mark A. Noll wrote in his 1994 book *The Scandal of the Evangelical Mind*. The fundamentalist reading of the Bible could be called "Bible-onlyism" or "versification." Critics often call this "literalism." I prefer "hyper-literalism." My objection to calling it literalism is that I don't think one needs to reject the idea that the Bible is inspired by God to reject the fundamentalist approach to the Bible. Noll describes it as "a weakness for treating the verses of the Bible as pieces in a jigsaw puzzle."[18]

17. Personal communication, December 12, 2017.
18. Mark A. Noll, *The Scandal of the Evangelical Mind* (Grand Rapids: Eerdmans, 1994), 126.

It was a revelation to me when I learned that the Bible was not broken up into separate verses until 1551, by French printer Robert Estienne. For most of Christian history, there was no concordance. There was no ability to look up a topic or word and find all the verses in which that topic or word is mentioned. The Bible had to be read more holistically. Religion was still used to control and subjugate and dominate in other ways. But this proof-texting approach, in which one could rip verses out of context and build whole theologies to fit one's preferences, was relatively new.

One of the most common tropes that evangelicals use to justify or excuse their lack of depth or thoughtfulness, or a lack of seriousness about thinking, or their lack of knowledge or expertise, is pointing to verses that talk about being a "fool for Christ." It may surprise some readers, but many people I personally know have actually defended simplistic thinking or cautioned against becoming too smart for one's own good. That phrase, "fool for Christ," appears in the fourth chapter of Paul's first letter to the church in Corinth, known as 1 Corinthians. The far more commonly cited passage, though, is in the first chapter of that book. "Where is the wise person? Where is the teacher of the law? Where is the philosopher of this age? Has not God made foolish the wisdom of the world?" Paul says. "God chose the foolish things of the world to shame the wise; God chose the weak things of the world to shame the strong" (1 Cor. 1:20, 27).

But the broader context of that same passage qualifies whether those statements are meant as some kind of literal set of rules for living or whether they are a way of describing and clarifying a larger point. Paul is getting at a dynamic about power here in this particular passage, as much as anything else. When he talks about a wisdom that those outside the faith don't get, he's talking specifically about how Christ introduced a new version of winning by losing, of finding life through death, of obtaining power by giving it up. "We preach Christ crucified: a stumbling block to Jews and foolishness to Gentiles," Paul writes. This—victory through self-sacrifice—is "the power of God and the wisdom of God" (1 Cor. 1:23–24).

John Calvin wrote, "By being fools we do not mean being stupid. . . . The profession of Christianity requires us to be immature, not in our thinking, but in malice."[19] There's nothing in the broader message of Jesus's teachings or in the rest of the Bible that encourages people of faith to neglect their minds. You would have to ignore part of Christ's first and greatest commandment—his instruction to love God with all your mind—to adhere to fundamentalism and hyper-literalism.

Another biblical passage often cited to attack intellectualism is from Proverbs 3: "Lean not on your own understanding, but in all your ways acknowledge him, and he will make your path straight" (vv. 5–6 NKJV). It's a passage I know well, because my father drilled Proverbs into me. But the passage doesn't say to throw out my understanding. It merely indicates that we should ask God for help as we seek to use our brains and not to overestimate our ability to comprehend truth or reality fully or perfectly. It is a call for epistemological humility. This is the opposite of what I see in Christians who claim to know that God speaks to them through their dreams, or that their view of politics or the Bible is the only possible answer.

Over the past few years, I have listened to a ten-minute devotional many mornings. I found I had to do a lot of unlearning mental exercises. When the narrator of the devotional said to "ponder the presence" of the Spirit of God, all my old inclinations of what that meant rushed back. It was a bodily instinct, going much further or deeper than just an idea in my brain. I had to remind myself to reset, to stay a blank slate, to make room for new experiences, for an honest experience of the divine.

My family and my work give me purpose and meaning. My friends ground me. When it comes to faith, some days I feel purpose. Other days I feel lost, or unsure. But I'm not in a hurry to figure it out. The point, it seems, is to be honest in the pursuit and true to the most basic teachings of the faith: to love God, to love those around you, and to lift up the downtrodden. It doesn't seem like it should have to be too much more complicated than that.

19. Noll, *Scandal of the Evangelical Mind*, 38.

Conclusion

Restoration

The Trump years were intensely disturbing. I often burned too hot. Even if it was justified, it wasn't effective. I realized anew that seeking truth alone is not enough. Truth must be accompanied by love.

"How do we tell the truth and make that truth bearable?" asked the author Kate DiCamillo.[1] She found an answer in the writer E. B. White, in his famous children's story *Charlotte's Web*. It's the story of a spider named Charlotte who befriends a lonely pig, Wilbur. Charlotte saves Wilbur from being slaughtered by his owner but dies soon after. Yet Wilbur takes her egg sac back to his barn to raise Charlotte's children. Even then, many of these children leave Wilbur. A few stay behind with Wilbur, and this process of life and friendship, and then death, repeats itself year after year. It is a story that does not hide the tragic nature of life from children. But it is also a story that vibrates with the glory of creation.

"E. B. White loved the world. And in loving the world, he told the truth about it—its sorrow, its heartbreak, its devastating beauty,"

---

1. Kate DiCamillo, "Why Kids Books Should Be a Little Sad," *Time*, January 12, 2018, https://time.com/5099463/kate-dicamillo-kids-books-sad/.

DiCamillo wrote. "He trusted his readers enough to tell them the truth, and with that truth came comfort and a feeling that we were not alone. I think our job is to trust our readers. I think our job is to see and to let ourselves be seen. I think our job is to love the world."[2]

I wrote this book out of love. I have spent my career learning to see as clearly as possible. I have let myself be seen in this book. I wrote this book because I was raised to believe that Christianity means something profound and that it offers something real to a world that badly needs it. But I've been brokenhearted to see many Christians abandon so much that the faith represents. I've seen that too much of American evangelical culture does not teach Christians to love this world like White did, much less like God so loved it and still does.

C. J. Mahaney and Lou Engle represent two streams of conservative evangelicalism that rose out of the Jesus Movement. They started out in the same place but quickly diverged. Now, five decades later, they represent elements of conservative evangelicalism that are quite different. But to understand the problems within evangelicalism, one has to grasp the role that each archetype plays.

The C. J. archetype inhabits a world of theology, precision, and control. He is intellectual to a point, but knowledge is often a tool for control rather than exploration and discovery. He is isolationist toward the world outside the four walls of the church building. He is quietist, most of the time, regarding politics. Because of his time spent in study, he sometimes has better instincts than the Engle archetype about application of his faith in public life. But he shrinks back from acting. That leaves a vacuum for the Engle archetype, who is less interested in head knowledge and much more passionate about life experience.

The Engle archetype is a man of action and of big visions. He wants to dream dreams, perform miracles, and experience revival. He delivers results, defeats the enemy, slays the dragon. He is a man's man. He does not let obstinate facts get in his way, and he does not suffer long the foolish questions of the doubters. He is more than a

2. DiCamillo, "Why Kids Books Should Be a Little Sad."

conqueror, claiming the power of God to carry out the tasks given to him and him alone. For him, thinking too long and too hard is a dangerous game, since it could lead to inaction, the ultimate sin.

———

Writing this book has forced me to ask: What would a more Christian witness look like?

It would look like a Christian community that lays down its love of dominance and getting its own way and embraces the idea of being a minority. A person in a minority group is aware that laws and customs must protect all minority groups. That kind of thinking would make conservative White evangelicals much better neighbors. In the interior life of the soul, as well, letting go of the need to always have one's way goes to the core of the Bible's teaching. Love "does not insist on its own way," the apostle Paul (an actual apostle) writes (1 Cor. 13:5 ESV).

Conservative White Christians have much to learn about faith from Black Christians. The Black church has truly relied on faith to face up to and get through unimaginable challenges and suffering in this country. That witness continues to this day. Yes, things are better now than they used to be when it comes to race, but there is, in fact, much work left to do. The ongoing legacies of White supremacy persist and continue to create systemic injustice. Will White Christians in America look the other way, or use scare words like "critical race theory" to avoid doing the hard work of repentance, because the status quo is pretty good for us? Or will we set aside comfort and ease, put our faith into action, and be good Samaritans ourselves?

I believe faithful Christians are a vital part of America's ongoing reckoning with its racial legacy. Without the faith community, those pressing for justice will underemphasize self-examination, forgiveness, humility, and grace.

A more Christian presence in America would value the mind. It would seek to love God with all of one's heart, soul, strength, and mind (Mark 12:29–31). The more American Christians dismiss the need to think deeply, to be intellectual, the more they make the error of the Roman soldiers who carried out the crucifixion of Christ. Jesus said of them, "They know not what they do" (Luke 23:34 ESV). They *knew* not. "Jesus was nailed to the cross not simply by sin but also by blindness," Martin Luther King Jr. wrote in his sermon "Love in Action." "Never must the church tire of reminding men that they have a moral responsibility to be intelligent," King said. "The heart can never be totally right if the head is totally wrong."[3]

Christians can and should become agents of nuance rather than of reductionism. This means embracing complexity and rejecting easy explanations. Writer Judy Wu Dominick contends that this is a Christian's duty. "Nuance is the loving pursuit of accurate understanding, accompanied by an awareness that 'we know in part and we prophesy in part' (1 Cor. 13:9) and that 'we see only a reflection as in a mirror' (1 Cor. 13:12). Such a pursuit demands levels of patience, humility, discernment, and self-control that black-and-white approaches to people and issues do not."[4]

According to Dominick, nuance is advanced in relationship. "Our capacity and skill for nuance is primarily forged in the fires of the relational suffering we endure as we attempt to live out Jesus' commands to 'love each other as I have loved you' (John 15:12), and 'forgive as the Lord forgave you' (Col. 3:13). It is a tall order in a broken world where people continually sin against us and us against them."[5] Writing this book has been a way for me to lick my wounds and to steady myself for more of this kind of work.

In short, Christians should be leading the way in building bridges and binding up the wounds of their communities, starting at the local level and expanding beyond that when appropriate. Unfortunately, I have watched as conservative Christians in America have largely done the opposite. Some have focused on building walls and cheered those who demonize the weak and powerless. Some are eager to travel to foreign countries as a benevolent savior

3. Martin Luther King Jr., *Strength to Love* (Minneapolis: Fortress, 2010), 35, 39.

4. Judy Wu Dominick, "The Christian Mandate to Subvert Tribalism," *Christianity Today*, October 24, 2017, https://www.christianitytoday.com/ct/2017/october-web-only/christian-mandate-nuance-subvert-tribalism.html.

5. Dominick, "Christian Mandate."

to poor Black and Brown people abroad. But as for poor people of color in America, who are still suffering the impacts of decades of systemic injustice perpetrated by our ancestors? They need to pull themselves up by their bootstraps.

An effective Christian presence would be active, out in the world and for our neighbors: all of them, not just those in our church. It would not be secluded in church services that deprive us of the richness of true community. It would be generative, aiming to be a positive creative force, bringing new life into the world for the good of all.

And a faithful Christian presence would take part in the building and repair of key institutions that make healthy culture possible. It's crucial that Americans reevaluate what institutions are and why they exist. We need to rediscover our need for them and reimagine what they can look like in this brave new world we live in. Christians should be clamoring to help rebuild the constitution of knowledge in society that Jonathan Rauch writes about, to repair the damage done by our widespread confusion over what is true and what is not. Faithful Christians should be less interested in promoting what they think is the right answer to this question or that and more invested in helping all people find a way to agree with one another on matters of public life.

Politically, a credible Christian presence would be prophetic. It would not be captive to any one political party. It would be free to praise both Democrats and Republicans, and free to critique them both as well. To the degree it would be a voting bloc, it would represent a group of voters who could not be won over with appeals to tribal identity or by fear-based appeals that demonize minority groups or the "other side." This voting bloc would support politicians who demonstrate a devotion to solid principles. These voters would reward politicians who put the good of the whole country—or state or county or town—ahead of their own careers, who risk losing their political post in order to preserve the stability of the political system for future generations. These voters would spurn politicians whose positions change with the wind, whose actions demonstrate that power is their priority, who are demonstrably dishonest in their pursuit of influence.

These voters would not be captive to one political issue. They would be sophisticated in their understanding. But to become "as shrewd as snakes and as innocent as doves" (Matt. 10:16)—as Jesus instructed his disciples to be—is not possible if people are unwilling to work hard to understand the times in which they live.

Evangelicals have incredible spiritual resources available to them: their heart connection to God gives them immense power for good. The country needs those resources because America's future looks grim. "The violence of January 6th was not the end of something but the beginning," Evan Osnos wrote.[6] Millions of evangelicals have helped set the nation on this dark path. And a small remnant will need to call them to repentance, through word and deed. I do not think most evangelicals will turn from their ways. It will have to start small, with a spark.

My own faith was dimmed because for years I was told or shown that following Jesus meant avoiding people who don't think like you, prioritizing emotion over critical thought and question asking, and trying to avoid difficulties in life through prayer and other "spiritual" tools. The difference between Christians and non-Christians was supposedly that we were a little weird and should be glad to be thought of that way, because we were old-fashioned on things like sex and drugs and drinking and cussing. But if we just held on, and stayed "pure," we'd get to heaven.

But the faith I was taught beckoned to something I still want: a fullness of life. I am puzzled and discouraged and heartbroken that something that promised so much good has contributed to so much destruction, damage, and hurt. My tribe has sought to escape reality through religion that deemphasizes this world, or by trying to control it and bend it to their wishes. This is not the way of sacrificial love, truthfulness, and weakness.

6. Evan Osnos, "Dan Bongino and the Big Business of Returning Trump to Power," *New Yorker*, December 27, 2021, https://www.newyorker.com/magazine/2022/01/03/dan-bongino-and-the-big-business-of-returning-trump-to-power.

My faith has been sparked by seeing that the real Jesus beckons me to follow him into a life of vulnerability that threatens the false gods of comfort and ease. Like many others, I'm trying to figure out how to walk that path. It's daunting and scary, and most days I feel like I'm not doing a very good job. But it does at least have the ring of truth.

Acknowledgments

No person has been more vital to seeing both my books into existence than Bridget Wagner Matzie. For roughly a decade now, she has partnered, prodded, encouraged, and guided me. She held my hand many times through the writing and editing process of this manuscript. I can't thank her enough or praise her too much. Thank you, Bridget.

Katelyn Beaty at Brazos Press sent me a message in the summer of 2019 asking if I'd thought about writing a book about my evangelical background. It came just as I was getting serious about such a project. Katelyn's interest was one of the reasons we felt good about working with Brazos, and her feedback along the way was hugely helpful in getting the final manuscript where it needed to go.

Julie Zahm at Brazos did an incredible job of helping me through the latter stages of the editing process, and I'm so grateful to her. Laura Powell's cover design is stunning and evocative. Erin Smith was a delight to work with, along with Jeremy Wells and the entire Brazos marketing team.

For almost a decade now, Dan Klaidman has been the best boss I can imagine working for and a good friend. I've been lucky enough to work the last few years with my partner in crime Will Rahn, hand in glove, day in and day out. The entire team at our fabulous

Yahoo! News team is worth mentioning, but in particular Colin Campbell, Lauren Johnston, Jerry Adler, and Sharon Weinberger have been fantastic leaders: caring, talented, and generous.

Thank you to the individuals who have been inspirational models and mentors to me: Makoto Fujimura, Yuval Levin, and Jonathan Rauch. Yuval and Jonathan have both also been trusted advisers and dear friends.

To Olmert, thank you for lighting a flame that has sustained me all these years. I'll keep sending those pineapple photos.

To Phil and Joe, thanks for waiting around for me to figure out how important friendship is. I love you guys.

Thank you to all my friends who have talked with me, laughed, argued, and laughed some more about this project and its themes, and especially to those who read the manuscript or cheered me on: Mark and Amy Fedeli, Karl Schickler, Phil and Jessica Gallo, Joe Walker, James and Megan Haughery, Rob and Mary Grange, Chris Mutimer, Josh and Robin Drobynk, Darren and Sonya Bearson, J. R. Weaver, Michael Wear, John Dickerson, Russell Moore, Paul Raushenbush, Eboo Patel, Amy Sullivan, Jonathan Davidson, Mindy Belz, Tim Keller, Maggie Haberman, Duke Kwon, Greg Thompson, Charlie Peacock, David French, Deana Bass Williams, Peter Wehner, Josh Good, Miranda Kennedy, Guy Cecil (thanks for the MLK sermons), Dustin Wahl, Michael Samway, Matt Maasdaam, and Tim Alberta.

Thank you to Jemar Tisby and Warren Throckmorton for the time I spent with you in 2019 and for modeling faithfulness and perseverance in the faith.

Neil King, Matt Bai, and Carolyn McCulley not only read the manuscript but they also gave extensive feedback and strategic advice as well as much-needed praise. You three are the unsung heroes of this project. Your feedback made this book much better, and your confidence in me and in this project was a vital boost. I can't thank you enough.

Cousin Patrick, thank you for giving me a deeper connection to my family, especially in years when that connection began to fray in some places.

Duke, it meant so much that you read a draft and that you said it helped you. You and Jenne are our partners forever and we love you.

Bill and Sue, we know what kind of grandparents we want to be, thanks to you. It's the greatest lesson you'll ever give me, and I hope I can live up to even a fraction of the standard you've set.

Dad, thank you for showing up for the conversation about this book. Thank you for giving me your honest opinion and listening to mine. I hope you see, in these pages, the eyes of a boy who will never stop wanting and needing his dad's love, acceptance, and approval, especially when we disagree. Your response to this book has shown how much character you have.

Mom, I'll always see what you did in your life, and we will keep telling our kids and our grandkids your story. The church may not have valued the stories of women like you, but we will. Thank you for your countless acts of selfless love, day after day after day.

Cat, you're a great sidekick, and you're on your way to playing the lead.

Joe, thanks for listening to me and understanding, and for just saying, "I'm sorry. That's hard." I needed that, and I will always appreciate that you did it.

No person in this world has my back more than Alison. I instinctively knew that would be the case when we met. I don't know where I would be without you. Thank you for reading multiple drafts and for being a partner in every sense of the word: in this project, in trying to live out what we say we believe, and in life. I love you.

Jet, I meant what I said that day in the car after a training session: you'll be a better man than I, which is what any decent father hopes for. Just know that you never have to earn my love or approval: it's all there for you all the time—no matter what. I love you.

Gwen, you are a fiercely independent thinker. I know you're going to channel that intensity in directions that will surprise, delight, and sometimes confound me, and I can't wait to watch and cheer you on and then talk about it. I love you.

Etta, you are one of the kindest people I know, and you don't do it to look good. It's who you are. You are both lovely to others and deeply creative and talented. Look out world. I love you.

Juniper, my one and only. You strut, you dance, you stomp, you prance, and then you look at me with those deep blue eyes. I wouldn't be complete without you in the world. I love you.

Susie, you embrace being the youngest, and it makes you stronger. You are a delight, a ray of sunshine on a cloudy day, a warm hug when it's cold and lonely. I love you.

Finally, my children, remember when you have your own kids and they start coming of age, it will be time for you to start learning from them even as you continue to be their teachers. Listen to Bobby Dylan's verse in "The Times They Are A-Changin'." He'll explain it to you.

Jon Ward is the chief national correspondent at Yahoo! News. He has covered American politics and culture for two decades, including as a White House correspondent traveling aboard Air Force One and as a national affairs correspondent writing about two presidential campaigns. He is the author of *Camelot's End: Kennedy vs. Carter and the Fight That Broke the Democratic Party* and hosts *The Long Game* podcast. His writing has appeared in the *Washington Post*, the *New Republic*, *Politico*, *Vanity Fair*, *HuffPost*, and *Christianity Today*.